6 January 2018

Smoke for Breakfast

To Herman Kuekler

A Vietnam Combat Pilot's Story

Peace, Health & Blessings

Brian H. Settles

Brian H. Settles

DEDICATED IN LOVING APPRECIATION TO
MAMA BERNICE LAVAUGHN SETTLES

ACKNOWLEDGMENTS

There is a distant place, just beyond the invisible mind's eye, where disbelief lives. It is the place where the memories of our most extraordinary encounters with life reside, encounters we can't revisit because time has moved on and our current minds cannot fathom we actually lived through our pasts. I experience the occasional flash of awareness that I actually survived twenty thousand hours piloting jet airplanes and being shot at in military combat in service to my country.

Indeed, what a strange ride it has been. Certain life events are unforgettable and change us forever. Our personal philosophy for living determines whether those experiences become positives or negatives. As former U.S. Senator Max Cleland of Georgia suggested in his title, **Strong at the Broken Places,** describing his body-shattering ordeal of surviving Vietnam, we must always seek to identify the blessings in our lives even when they may be draped in the trauma of crisis.

Being able to write this book has been a blessing for me. The manuscript was written over a five-year period on airline layovers in exotic destinations ranging from Shannon and Dublin, Ireland; Catania, Sicily; San Juan, Puerto Rico; to Los Angeles and San Francisco. Countless hours of writing and rewriting were spent while on American Trans Airline Reserve callout duty in apartments I shared with other pilots in Chicago. I am confident their prevailing memory of me is the image of my sitting on a couch with a laptop perched on my legs for days at a time.

I have pondered why it took me so long to tell my story. Now I understand that the Lord blessed me with a love for language and that my story would happen when and only when it was time. I have confessed to my closest family and friends that, had Mama Settles still been alive, I would not have been able to reveal it in such raw reality and rude language. I would not be who I am had it not been for her inspired motherly love and patience with me.

I thank my sons, Amiri and Rahsaan, and my family members for inspiring and urging me to get this story told. My fellow ATA Boeing 757 Captain, John Sullivan, is my soul brother of loving support. I was further helped by the encouragement of ATA Captain Bruce Jacobs after I read an excerpt to the crew on a layover in Catania, Sicily. This book would not have been possible without the long-term support, motivation, and honesty of my lifelong friend, Dr. Gregory Howard Williams, former president of the University of Cincinnati and author of an outstanding story about growing up on the streets of Muncie, Indiana, *Life on the Color Line*. Besides Greg, I render my deepest appreciation to my lately departed friend, Gilbert Marshall of Highland Park, New Jersey, for his two major edits to the manuscript; sadly, he did not win his battle against cancer to see the story in print.

Although the ordeal of sending query letters to agents, begging editors to take on my work, and waiting for responses was a maddening Catch-22, I thank successful authors like Clyde Edgerton, *The Float Plane Notebooks*, Sena Jeter Naslund, *Ahab's Wife*, and Virginia DeBerry, *Sleeping in the Bed You Made*, for sharing their experiences and sustaining my motivation.

I also thank former Doubleday Executive Editor Janet Hill for taking time to read my un-agented manuscript and validating my neophyte writing skills. Lastly, I express my sincere appreciation to former Oxford University Press editor, Rosemary Wellner, whose creative and philosophical connection to my work assisted immeasurably in carving **Smoke *for Breakfast*** into more edible proportions.

Unfortunately, still today, dedicated U.S. servicemen and women are dying and being maimed while embroiled in another controversial, meandering military strategy in Afghanistan. The setting for my story might be in a different time and place, but the ordeal of combat is universal and unchanging. Vietnam writer and historian Bernard Fall once titled it as "Hell in a very small place." I am hopeful that the raw honesty of my reflections will enable readers to identify with someone they know and reflect on whether their choices are truly representative of who and what they are standing for in life.

I request that my pilot brethren, fellow service members, their families, and other Americans who read my story will step outside the comfort zones of their worldviews and often hair-trigger conclusions to withhold judgment until they have experienced its last sentence. Life is not always as it seems. Each of us views it through the filters of our own experience. The memories of incidents, people, and feelings are as I perceived them; for any departures from reality, I beseech your understanding and forgiveness.

TABLE OF CONTENTS

CHAPTER 1: THE SECOND BEGINNING

The dark gray Philippine sky had thick clouds that hung over the land like a dirty blanket, convincing the drenched populace living below that the sun no longer shone. Lieutenant Bill Smoyer and I bounced along the rain-soaked streets in the blue U.S. Air Force bus that swerved from side to side, attempting to avoid the pothole-studded streets.

It was Monday morning, September 2, 1968, and we had just completed Air Force Jungle Survival School as well as F-4 fighter training six months earlier. Spiffy in our khaki summer uniforms with open collars and straight-cut trousers held up by navy blue belts, we sat across from each other, two young officers, both twenty-four years old, attempting to conceal our anxieties.

Three years earlier, in February 1965, Vietcong forces had attacked the Bien Hoa American airbase at Pleiku. By the fall of 1968, hundreds of fighter pilots had already been shot down. The war escalated rapidly. Our expanding involvement was abetted by the arrogant and misguided convictions of Secretary of Defense Robert S. McNamara, Secretary of State Melvin Laird, and other presidential advisors. They were our best and our brightest as the book title suggested: Ambassador Henry Cabot Lodge, General Maxwell Taylor, McGeorge Bundy, George Ball, General William Westmoreland, et al. Our leaders were convinced that a few more battalions, a few more fighter squadrons, and a few more of the latest gadgets of destruction would bring about a quick end to the National Liberation Front and the NVA (North Vietnamese Army) that were sustaining the war effort south of the 17th parallel, usually referred to as the demilitarized zone (DMZ).

Bouncing and swaying in the bus, we felt like two alien travelers in a foreign land. We wondered whether either of us would ever return to Clark Air Force Base.

Bill interrupted the quiet. "Let me bum one of your Salems, Dumbshit."

I deliberately hesitated in reaching two fingers into my shirt pocket to withdraw a cigarette. Rolling my eyes, I complained, "Jesus Christ, man, I buy 'em and you smoke 'em."

Extending his hand to retrieve the Salem, he responded, "Fuck you very much, Bee."

I laughed and took another gut-burning swig from the fifth of Smirnoff I held wedged between my legs. I passed the bottle to Bill. He gulped such a hit it made me wonder if he would be able to keep it down. I withdrew a Salem from my shirt pocket, lit it, and took a deep draw. During a pause in the otherwise incessant rain shower, I stared through the color prisms dotting the bus window and at the brownish-black-feathered hens and roosters strutting around the trash-littered yards of the shanty homes that lined our route. I felt remote and detached, as if I was viewing my existence rather than actually being part of it. My mind revisited the shock and dismay I experienced when I saw the impoverished humans existing on a thread of life in the refuse at the outskirts of Mexican cities like Nuevo Laredo and Tijuana, the people Franz Fanon had labeled "the wretched of the earth" in his book of the same title. They eked out meager subsistence, cloaked in numbness, holed up in cardboard homes, living off daily scroungings.

My mind seemed to be running its own picture shows, fast-forwarding to the future. I saw my copilot self sitting in the F-4 Phantom, whizzing earthward in a five-hundred-mile-an-hour dive, dropping napalm on the thatched huts of Vietnamese peasant farmers. I could visualize them taking their breakfast rice while the same scrawny-looking hens and roosters scurried for their lives in the front yards of their jungle abodes. I grimaced and snapped back into the reality of the bouncing bus, my temporary refuge from what lay ahead.

I had a foul mouth before becoming a fighter pilot, but Bill's language embarrassed me. The more we drank, the worse Bill got. There is a fog over the remembrance of what we talked about. Both of us had left new brides behind in the States. We were gripped in our private musings and could barely hear each other's quiet hysteria.

We overcompensated with loud and boisterous chatter; it seemed to help drown out the roar of our private thoughts.

Occasionally, the enlisted airmen seated in front of us cast furtive glances over their shoulders. Self-conscious over some notion that we were officers and should retain some semblance of military bearing, I admonished Bill, "Cool it, man. You're grossin' everybody out."

He snapped back indignantly, "What the fuck, over. They're gonna send us back in plastic body bags in six weeks anyway for Christ's sakes."

I was silenced.

Since my mind was now like a short-subject movie reel that kept rerunning episodes of my life, I recalled a scene played out two nights earlier around a campfire in the Philippine jungle. I was sitting beside a young, blond-haired, blue-eyed helicopter pilot listening to his horror story of Vietnam. The light from the blazing logs danced as it flickered and flashed, reflecting off his face. He looked like a mere teenager squatting next to me, his buttocks resting on his heels, as if taking a crap. In subtle condescension, I had spoken to him. "Hey, guy, you wanna trade those Salems in your C-ration box for these Winstons?"

He responded with equal distance and indifference. "Yeah, okay." That was the only exciting feature about C rations; besides containing canned food, they held mini-packs of five cigarettes. You never knew what brand you were going to get until you opened the thin cardboard box.

"Where you gonna be based in Nam?" I inquired casually.

"I'm on my tour now," he said. I discerned he was in the Army from the insignia on his fatigues.

"Well, didn't you finish survival school before going over?" I asked, knowing from experience it was not atypical of the military to screw up orders, often sending people on assignments out of sequence with training.

"Yeah," he replied, "this is my second time in jungle school."

"What the fuck? Why'd the Army send you back to go through this shit again?" I responded, thinking I had uncovered an administrative snafu.

He answered without looking at me, staring entranced into the flames shimmering off the crackling logs. His soft, low-key explanation left me numb.

"Well," he said, sighing, "ten days ago I was on a recovery mission of what was left of a company of grunts assigned to the American Division in I Corp. They were in heavy contact with some Cong when we went in for the rescue and got the shit hosed out of us. Two of the five we recovered were wounded badly. Our asses were shot down on the pull-off by .50-caliber machine-gun fire. One of the other choppers had to come back for us. The ground fire was so heavy we didn't have time to take the wounded off our bird; it torched as soon as we hit the ground. The copilot on the bird that rescued us took a round in his hip just as we lifted off."

The kid continued talking, never taking his eyes off the fire and never looking at me. "Then, last Thursday, I was on another rescue evac, fuckin' metal flying everywhere. On our third pickup we got hit bad and barely made it out. The pilot took one right in the side of his face, and the paramedic got his arm blown clean off. I grabbed control of the bird just before we hit the trees. I still don't know how we made it out. When I got back to the base, admin set me up to come back here on a lark R & R to jungle survival school. I guess they figured after gettin' shot down twice in one week a guy deserves a little break."

By the time he finished talking, I was staring trancelike into the fire myself, wondering how this handsome, baby faced dude was stooped there beside me acting so calm. I thought that if I had gone through what he had described, they would be sending me to the psycho ward, not jungle survival school.

Turning my thoughts away from the kid's campfire story, I took another healthy swig of Smirnoff and passed the bottle to Bill. We had to finish it before we arrived at the flight line to board the C-130 cargo plane that would propel us toward our destiny. My palms were sweaty with uneasiness.

Sadly, throughout the long stream of history, man still has not figured out how to resolve conflict without concluding that the only way out was to line up against the foe and shoot until there was only one person standing or someone surrendered. And now, like some ancient Spanish knight leaving his fair maiden for the Crusades or some GI about to storm the beachhead at Normandy, I was another insignificant human speck joining the legions of expendable warriors littering world history.

The dreary day following a wet week in the Philippine jungle, on the muddy bus ride leading us toward the Military Airlift Passenger Terminal, past the scrawny, rain-soaked chickens, was part of a series of ominous events moving me closer to an encounter like none I had ever experienced and for which my imagination was incapable of preparing me. My destination as a newly graduated F-4 Phantom copilot was Da Nang Air Base, Republic of Vietnam. There I would fulfill the orders for a yearlong tour waging aerial combat in a $2.5-million supersonic fighter-bomber.

The flight from Clark to Tan Son Nhut was a drunken blur, during which little time was spent in useful consciousness. The vibration and engine noise of the powerful turbo props made me feel fortunate that Bill and I were able to sleep through the trip. Before we knew it, we were on final approach for landing in Saigon. I was relieved we had a short ground time, discharging a few GIs and civilians before boarding more poor slobs whose assignments were bringing them with us to Da Nang.

In the wee hours of the morning, the hydraulically actuated cargo doors at the rear aircraft ramp began to close slowly, like giant whale jaws coming together before swallowing. The forward passenger boarding stairs were retracted by a short, burly potbellied master sergeant whose overly tight flight suit revealed that in nineteen years of Air Force service he had probably not missed chow call too often. The engine's propellers rotated in sequence as the eight-foot-long turboprop blades spun like a giant mix-master up to idle rpm. After the rumble and rattle of a short taxi-run, we took off from the dimly lit field into the night blackness destined for Da Nang.

With Bill next to me, uncharacteristically quiet and solemn, I peered through the window. There was no moon, no stars, only soup above. The shoreline, the rice paddies, and the Vietnam jungle were indistinguishable in the night landscape below us except for the recurring flares that spread, suspended like lights strung out in a Fourth of July backyard barbecue. There was nothing for the eyes to fix upon, only the darkness sprinkled with the light of flares descending earthward.

I turned my head away from the window, pondering the thought that people— Americans—were down there doing a job they were being paid to do. That job was to conduct war. Soon, I thought, I would arrive at the site from which I would wage my own war against the people of North and South Vietnam who had been declared enemies of the South Vietnamese government—an enemy that would be intent on shooting me out of the sky for attempting to deter them from carrying out their war of national liberation.

As our C-130 bored its way through the early morning darkness toward Da Nang, I actually believed the Vietcong and the North Vietnam Army (NVA) could not be victorious. A part of me loved the idea of being an F-4 copilot and my flight training had impressed me with the awesome firepower the U. S. Air Force was unleashing against the communist forces in Nam. There was no way, I reasoned, that we could lose. Coupled with this conviction, two gnawing apprehensions ate away at me; first, a lot of ass would get burned on both sides before the point was proved; and, second, the political/military history of Vietnam, dating back to the sixteenth century, raised serious reservations as to the prudence, propriety, and morality of the increasing level of U.S. involvement. Was it in fact a civil war, not unlike our own conflict over slavery and saving the Union, or was it their revolutionary war?

My disenchantment with participation in the Vietnam war continued to grow. With haunting misgivings, as I perceived more clearly later, I understood my only objective was to survive. I would piece it all together when I was safe back at home.

Having reached cruise altitude, the C-130 leveled off, rolled, and bounced, cutting its way through choppy air as the flight proceeded toward that once-in-a-lifetime rendezvous with the unknown. My thoughts once again escaped the reality of my destination. I missed my cat, Major, whom I had named after my sister Margerie, but then modified that after learning that Marge was a little male—the name didn't seem to work after that discovery. I longed for Celeste, my lonely bride. My concern for how she would hold up during my absence was rapidly becoming a preoccupation. She knew I had not wanted to go to Vietnam and that I had surrendered my convictions about the war. She realized more than any family members why my tour would be the greatest challenge of my entire life.

Throughout my combat tour, I wondered how my wife, family, and friends would handle the news that I had been shot down or killed, worse yet, taken as a prisoner of war. Perhaps it was my ego that distorted my sense of importance in the lives of all who knew me.

The C-130 abruptly lurched downward, raising us all off our seats before regaining stability. Bill, who sat silent and into himself most of the flight, turned to match my grin at the thought that the many motor drivers in the cockpit had gotten an unexpected nose pitch-down when they disconnected the autopilot for descent. Outside the windows the huge propellers sawed their way through the early-morning overcast. We bounced earthward in light turbulence, and reality came back into focus—the long trip to the combat zone from America the beautiful would soon be complete. The cloud cover on the approach to the runway at Da Nang reached to within a few hundred feet. Nothing could be seen outside the cargo compartment window until moments before touchdown. Then, with the abrupt screeching thud of rubber against concrete, we hit the runway. I was no longer going to Da Nang; I was there.

After taxi-in and engine shutdown, we were instructed by bullhorn to follow the passenger service co-coordinator from the aircraft, single file, to the Da Nang Air Base passenger terminal to await the arrival of our luggage and receive guidance on where the hell to proceed. The time was 0245, which most people know as 2:45 AM. GIs—Marines, Army, Navy, and Air Force—filled the passenger terminal. They were filthy and funky from hours in the morning heat and humidity, cramped like crawdads in a fishing bucket. I had little knowledge of what it would really be like at Da Nang, but I knew from what I saw that first night that I envied those leaving.

I was in Vietnam, suspicious and uncomfortable around every Vietnamese I encountered. I got the unjustified fear white folks often feel at being around inner-city Black youth with neck chains, baggy pants, and leather-laced hiking boots on a subway or dark street. At least half the crowd in the terminal was Vietnamese or Army Republic of Vietnam soldiers (ARVN) many of whom had their families with them. Babies wailed loudly, many clinging and clawing at mothers with big bellies, squatting down with buttocks resting on their heels. My old basketball knee injuries prevented me from bending my legs like that and I marveled at the exhibitions of contortion all around me.

Signs posted in the terminal were in English with the Vietnamese equivalent beneath. The air had a thick aroma of stale urine, garbage, and suffocating cigarette smoke. Everyone was greasy looking and sweaty. No one seemed happy, even though many of those people were going home. Laughter was sporadic and muffled. I thought about wanting to get the hell out of there before a bomb went off and killed us all. Numerous accounts of sabotage and Vietcong satchel charges detonating in public places fueled my anxiety in crowds. From that first day, I was perpetually leery of my surroundings whenever Vietnamese, military or civilian, were present. I realized then that uneasiness and foreboding would be constant companions.

The first stroke of good luck, I saw the 390th Tactical Fighter Squadron, my unit, directly across the street from the passenger terminal. Bill's baggage was delayed and I told him we'd hook up the next day. I headed out for the squadron. As I crossed the dimly lit street, I heard a deep but muffled rumble of distant heavy artillery bombardment and felt it beneath my feet. I wondered, *Are they really bombing enemy soldiers out there in the darkness and how far away are they?* It sounded too close. Suddenly, flares illuminated the sky over the departure end of the runway. It looked like Disneyland. But it was not Disneyland. The early-morning ambience echoed with the voice of war. The crack, crack, crack of small-arms fire ripped a sharp staccato through the night air. It seemed to be coming from the perimeter of the base. I thought, *Shit! Is this for real or what?*

I approached a concrete walkway between two stretches of barbed-wire fence surrounding three small rectangular structures. A small wooden guardhouse, beefed up with five-foot high stacks of Army-green sandbags, was situated at the opening in the fence. A helmeted Airman 1st Class security policeman instantly emerged from the guardhouse clad in green camouflage fatigues, wearing a full ammo belt with an M-16 slung over his shoulder. Rendering a crisp salute, he greeted me, "Good morning, sir. This is a restricted area. May I help you?"

"Yeah," I replied. "I see. I'm trying to find the 390th Tactical Fighter Squadron. They told me at the terminal it was over here."

"Yes, sir," he continued, pointing behind him "That's it right there. Do you have orders, sir?" Having been conditioned to the routine of presenting my orders to someone every five minutes wherever I traveled, I readily produced my papers.

"Okay, sir, proceed."

I couldn't resist an inquiry. "Is that artillery very close to the base?"

He replied, "Yes, sir, about five to ten clicks south. That's where the rocket attacks come from." Five clicks were equivalent to five thousand meters, a little more than a mile.

"Yeah," I responded, somewhat incredulously. "How often does the base get hit?"

"Regularly, sir," he said, obviously amused by my naiveté and the hesitancy in my voice. "This is fuckin' Rocket City. Welcome to Da Nang, sir."

"Right," I said, gathering my burden of bags, having heard all I wanted for the moment.

I trudged off into the humid morning darkness down the walkway leading to the squadron. Balancing a strange sense of pride with a palpable foreboding of what I was getting into, I couldn't help asking myself: *What happened to me? How have I taken this wrong turn?*

This is not who I am, but there is no escape. How did I get my life into this place?

CHAPTER 2: SLINGS AND ARROWS

Mama had a gnawing uneasiness in the pit of her stomach when in the fall of 1962 at age eighteen I naively signed up for Air Force ROTC at Ball State University. I simply wanted to be a member of the precision drill team and had been lured by the gung-hoism of James J. Winters, the student athletic equipment manager's assistant at Muncie Central High School where I played sports. I ran into JJ, as he was nicknamed, in the hallway outside the registrar's office during late registration after my basketball scholarship to the University of Colorado failed to materialize. Much of JJ's childhood was spent playing war games with his chums, wearing child-sized military fatigues and combat boots. His father, a lieutenant colonel in the Indiana National Guard, passed the baton of service to country and military adventure to him through his inspired example. JJ had always wanted to be a pilot and he directly influenced my decision to become one. After my graduation and commissioning from Ball State, Mama was numb with trepidation that her only son had selected pilot training in the U.S. Air Force.

Having flown but once in her life, Mama believed that flying should be limited to emergency travel only. Her intuition convinced her I had been overwhelmed by the lure of a capricious pursuit into the unorthodox, the unconventional, even the shocking. She was right.

I, Brian H. Settles, was setting sail on a voyage that was like signing up on Captain Ahab's whaling ship, the *Pequod*, to pursue my own personal Moby Dick. I thought I was choosing the voyage; I could never have known the voyage was choosing me.

Mama's angst prompted incessant questioning and she meticulously measured the rationality of my answers, many of which left me wondering why human beings were willing to enroll themselves in impossible-appearing missions. Why did they throw themselves into undertakings that defy logic, rational thinking, or prudent judgment—causes they might not even own, windmills that belong to someone else's dream?

Growing up on the streets of Muncie, Indiana, in a daily struggle for connection with my darker-skinned playmates, I hung out on the cruel playgrounds that at times seemed no less savage than the competition for survival among the creatures roaming the Serengeti. I had been conditioned by my own issues of race and skin color to feel that my biracial beginnings were an albatross that God had me carry through life. My entire existence was taken over by the need to be accepted as Black.

It all became clearer on that day Mama revealed to me, an innocent boy of five, the awful truth, that strange fairy tale of my beginnings. I can still see myself running up the steps leading to the wooden front porch and into the house, letting the screen door slam with a bang. I rushed into the kitchen of our five-room clapboard house across from the Munsyana Homes projects, looking for Mama. She was preparing supper at the stove. Daddy was still at work on the assembly line at Durham Manufacturing Company where he had a good job riveting metal card tables and chairs. The aroma of cube steaks, potatoes au gratin, and Brussels sprouts filled the air. I had something on my mind that day that a small boy needed to get an answer to. "Mama!" I announced, moving across the worn linoleum floor to reach her by the stove. "The kids on the playground are always sayin' Daddy ain't my daddy 'cause he's too black to have a son my color. And they say me and Margerie don't look alike either, Mama."

"Margerie and I," Mama corrected, realizing the inevitable day had come, but much sooner than expected. Mama sat me down at the wooden kitchen table Daddy had made from scratch and stained dark maple. Four metal card table chairs were placed around it. After turning down the heat under the saucepan, Mama returned to sit beside me. Bernice Settles then proceeded to tell me the awful truth. "My darling son, I loved you from the first day I ever saw you. I knew you would be a special child; you were so adorable with those big brown eyes and curly locks." Trying vainly to repel the flattery, my face surrendered a blush. She continued, "Howard and I wanted children after we got married, but couldn't have any. Our desire to have a family took us to the Social Services office downtown. After a year and a half wait we finally got a call from my friend Adelaide Turner who works in the welfare office telling me there was a little two-and-a-half-year-old boy in an orphanage out in Lincoln, Nebraska, who was available. Adelaide said the mother was white and had gotten pregnant at sixteen. The father was colored like us. They were too young to get married. That white mother gave birth to you. She loved you, but had to give you away because her people didn't want her to keep you.

"Howard and I took the first train to Nebraska. As soon as we saw you playing alone in the shade on the side of the building in your little striped shirt and bib overalls trying to dribble that basketball, we fell in love with you. We signed the adoption papers on the spot, and that day your name was changed from Brian Wesley Scheer to Brian Howard Settles. Howard wanted you to have his name since you were his only son. From that day you have been our son to love and give a home to forever. That's why you don't look like Howard; you're adopted, and we love you just as much as your real mother could. She just couldn't keep you."

I did not cry at hearing the awful truth from Mama, but my vision blurred with tears and my heart seemed suddenly loaded with an unshakeable burden. A subconscious detachment of not belonging came over me. Mama finished her story with an admission.

"I swore to myself, son, that when you were old enough, I would tell you the truth about your white mother. I didn't want you to find out someday when you were grown and have you hate your father and me for keeping it from you. I just didn't expect to have to tell you so soon. The color of your skin doesn't matter. What your parents look like doesn't matter. What matters is that you have a mother and a father who love you and will take care of you. So, now you know. I love you, son, and you can just tell those kids on the playground that you and your sister Margerie are both adopted and loved, and it's nobody's business."

The good news was that I knew the truth about my roots. The bad news was the impact being a light-skinned Black male had on growing and developing as a man in a society and culture consumed with issues of race and color by both Black and white Americans. My "whiteness" diminished me as a Black person, made me less than whole, unworthy of complete membership in the Black race, an imposter, a pretender. Diluted. From earliest youth I felt guilty about my yellow, olive-toned skin. I wanted to be darker. As a child I prayed to God at night, *"Dear God, if you were going to make me colored, why didn't you give me brown skin so my playmates wouldn't be jealous and want to fight me?"* As I grew up, floundering in imperfection and false bravado, I was a magnet for guilt about my appearance. In maturing wisdom, I came to know that white people found it easier to be around me than my darker skinned brothers and sisters. I was still a nigger, but a handsome, high-yellow one—a more acceptable one.

Adolescence and early adulthood were burdened by the emptiness I felt being half-white. I credit Jim Sullivan for saving me from the ravages of low self-esteem and my sense of inadequacy about being adopted. Jim was the only Black person in all of Muncie who was as light skinned as me—white looking just like his mother, who had one arm missing. He was a handsome sight with his freckles and reddish-brown wavy hair. He was adored by most people in Muncie, even the white people—a legitimate hero. At times when we walked down the street, he rested his muscular arm on my shoulder. Even Daddy never did that.

To conquer my self-consciousness at being taller than my classmates, I became obsessed with becoming the best basketball and football player. It was the quickest route to acceptance for a high-yellow Black like me to perfect skills that were important in Muncie's Black culture. Namely, have chicks crazy about me, learn to get over on chicks young and regularly, don't work too hard in school or risk being misunderstood as a showboater, or, heaven forbid, try to be like "Whitey" and jeopardize my acceptance.

The cunning sistas, who Mama termed "fast," threatened me, not physically, but with their flaunted sexual power. They were small-town goddesses sporting smooth brown chocolate bodies with tiny waists, round muscular butts, protruding nipples, and soft, wet lips.

At thirteen and fourteen they had already proven their powers to conquer the brothers in the hood and honed a spider sense that discerned my shyness and vulnerability. When I was thirteen, a playmate's cousin visiting from Cleveland captivated me with her seductive kisses beneath the catalpa tree along our backyard fence just before the gray evening light gave way to darkness. Warm bubblegum breath enticed me as she whispered temptations: "Oooh, Brian, you so sweet and fine; your lips are getting me fire hot. We could have a pretty baby. Why don't you come on in the bedroom upstairs with me so I can give you some?"

It seemed that my hip, dark-skinned sisters wanted to fill up with my biracial sperm. Cinnamon-complexioned babies were to be touted treasures, beautiful light brown babies with soft curly hair that was easy to comb and wouldn't need Royal Crown pomade or hot curling irons to keep it shiny and neat. We weren't choosing the standards of appearance for our lives; they were being imposed on us by our sociocultural circumstances.

But there was another deeper problem, more unwieldy than simply being pursued. From my young male playmates I received a distorted view of the importance of the almighty penis to a man's worth, especially a Black man's. My big-dicked childhood running buddies loved to pull it out for a piss anywhere they pleased—along the railroad tracks, walking through the coal cinder and broken-bottle-littered alleys, or during strolls in Heekin Park. Naively locked in the shyness of pre-adolescence, it took all the guts I had to practice being as bold as they were. I let myself fall prey to the teasing chuckles and giggling glances that suggested that I was shorter in the dick department. How could any child believe there was anything to be ashamed about with their body unless that notion was planted by the external world? The preoccupation with dicks and getting pussy in our neighborhood led me to buy into size as the only parameter for fulfillment in sex. Yes, I wanted a bigger one. I wanted a joint so big it would buckle any woman's knees to behold it.

The significance of dicks and dick myths in Black culture and American society in general added another weighty load onto the burdens of race, color, and inadequacy already bearing down on my psyche. I remember no conversations about it among family—too adult for discussion. Friends brought it up when it concerned how big or how small someone was. I courageously shared my complaint about the phenomenon of imposed inferiority and preoccupation of it all with my childhood buddy, Greg Williams. We had white blood commonality in our family histories but Greg looked stone white. That commonality was an Achilles' heel for me, and it provoked a fierce competition between us. Greg's father, "Buster" Williams, had grabbed eleven-year-old Greg (he called him Billy) by the arm one day and brought him down to our house. Buster wanted to help Greg reach out and make friends and I learned he had coaxed him, "Come on, Billy. I want you to meet this other half-breed boy named Brian Settles. Maybe you can be friends and he'll help you beat up these neighborhood kids who want to kick your ass 'cause you look white."

With all my other challenges, I was suddenly called on to take under my wing a white boy standing on my front porch who wanted to be my friend. We developed a close bond that was fraught with uneasiness on my part over something that never got discussed. Greg admired my natural athletic talent; I marveled at his machine-like discipline to excel in academics. Our ruthless competitiveness inspired Greg to delight in toying with me about my dick angst.

Another influential early friendship was with Brian "Chico" Conley, later Ameer Shabazz. Chico was hip and very bright. He set the curve in most classes we were in—math, English, and history. He had a dark brown complexion, small physical stature, and was bone skinny. To me, he was the coolest cat in the neighborhood. His older brother, Poochie, was real smooth and dressed impeccably. He paid to have his slacks pressed at the cleaners, wore crisp starched shirts and Stacey Adams shoes. He and his partners traveled frequently back and forth to Chicago and Detroit; they always talked the latest slang and listened to avant-garde jazz.

Greg was at the other end of the color pole, but it was not a case of opposites attracting. Chico, Greg, and I tried to run together, but my addiction to acceptance often caused me to sell out on Greg to retain good graces with Chico. We made a strange color sandwich walking down the streets of Muncie: me, yellow cornbread on one side, white biscuit Greg on the other, and Brother Chico, beluga caviar in the middle. I never realized that I struggled so deeply with conflicting needs in my friendship with Greg. He was white; I was high yellow.

How could I have understood that looking at his white face reminded me of what I hated about myself, my own whiteness. From the story of my white mother giving me to the orphanage, I developed a vulnerability to notions of being abandoned by a woman I cared about. Greg wrestled with a similar agony.

To compensate for my feelings of inadequacy, I chose to fly. My knees often became weak with the thought that flying was such an outrageous option for a young Black dude from Muncie, Indiana, in 1966. But just like that, JJ Winters had talked me into joining ROTC at Ball State University to be on the Marching Matadors drill team and then to Air Force Pilot Training.

Volunteering to fly fighters, a move that would require going to Vietnam, placed me in the dilemma of a lifetime. With my philosophical and sociological roots buried deeply in the Black cultural and civil rights struggle, how could I (as a sensitive, educated, politically liberal Black man) participate in what Black revolutionaries classified as a racist war to kill people of color in Southeast Asia? Even the arch hero of the civil rights movement in America, Dr. Martin Luther King, Jr., had begun to carry the antiwar flag.

Going to Vietnam put me out of touch with myself, out of sync with my beliefs and with my friends. I might have qualified as a conscientious objector, but I hadn't done enough homework to form a solid position. I was ignorant about whether the domino theory was real or just a logical extension of the Cold War hysteria.

Somewhere lost back in the dreamy childhood camouflage of a fine June day in Muncie at the colored branch YMCA, when the neglected empty concrete swimming pool was having the dried sledge and broken bottles shoveled up so black kids could swim again, my metamorphosis began. Somewhere in the innocence of early youth when the hot dogs were especially tasty on the vendor's carts in McCullough Park, a day when the robins were whistling an especially sweet song, my world shifted. The radio airwaves echoed the Chantelles' megahit, "Maybe" and one of the gang had grown weary from the agony of trying to belong and slipped silently off the precipice into the abyss. My life changed forever and no one noticed. For me, the defiant one, the rebel, whose mind was heaped in jagged struggle for belonging, fitting in, being accepted, being good enough, being Black enough, it was too much. Invisible forces I could neither understand nor measure took over and began manipulating what did matter. Mama's little boy was about to grow up real fast.

CHAPTER 3: SAYING GOOD-BYE

Mama kissed my cheek and hugged me in a tight good-bye as if for the last time. It was August 15, 1968. A mere twenty-four hours lay between me and departing her embrace. Celeste, my new bride of one year, was a master at being the strong wife and soothed the pain by holding back her farewell tears. Deep inside, she had an unspoken understanding of my eagerness to get on with being gone, to arrive at my war and begin serving the sentence of Vietnam. It was a sentence to which I had finally reconciled. Embroiled in the ambiguity of emotions over complying with my Vietnam orders, I had gained the requisite will during an encounter with my father-in-law, a former state senator and practicing attorney.

He was a brilliant civil rights lawyer in Indianapolis, a borderline genius who paid a great price in isolation and lifestyle for his intellectual gifts. He had a real affinity for the common working-class, blue-collar, or indigent Black man. He rarely earned his legal worth in fees. Unlike his peers, he rendered reams of legal representation pro bono to brothers and sisters of Indianapolis. At times he chose barter pay, getting his residence lawn mowed, accepting free dry cleaning at the One Hour Martinizing, or having a chef barbecue ribs at his lawn party political socials. I always admired his altruism and community-oriented professional life. My awe and respect made me want to be close to him as his son-in-law, but our interactions were generally stilted and superficial, involving such awkward canned inquiries as, "How was your trip?" "Do you like flying?" or "Where's Celeste?" I suppose it was all part of his way of self-protection, shielding himself from a sense of vulnerability with the façade of aloofness and condescension. On rare occasions, I summoned the courage to force exchanges, but they would often turn weird and contrived, like two people trying to have a dialogue but speaking different languages. It seemed very complex. In my own arrogance, I was confident I could carry on a chat with anyone, brilliant or not. Mostly, I felt my father-in-law was unwilling to bother himself with mundane small talk if it didn't serve his agenda.

I recall that night while Celeste and I were visiting her parents a week before my port call. I waited up late for him to get home from the office. Arriving as usual about eleven-thirty, he made his way through the den from the garage toward the kitchen where I sat on a barstool with my arms crossed and resting on the white Formica countertop. He greeted me with a nonchalant, "Hi, Brian. Where's Celeste?"

"Out with her girlfriend Mary Anne, talking girl stuff," I answered. He passed by me, dropping his briefcase against the wooden cabinet doors beneath the bar counter, stopping briefly to shuffle through the day's mail, routinely stacked beside the clear glass cake platter, seemingly disinterested in any envelopes not resembling a client's check. After hastily perusing the mail, he went to the refrigerator for a snack. He selected two slices of ham, cut a quarter-inch thick slice of onion easily three inches in diameter, placed them between two slices of Wonder bread, layered them with Kraft mayonnaise, and got a Schlitz. Placing the beer can on the plate with the sandwich, he did a balancing act, picking up his briefcase and waddling back toward the bedroom without so much as a peep directed at me. My father-in-law was a rotund man, five foot ten and rapidly sneaking up on 300 pounds. Waddling was the only accurate description of his walk. He proceeded down the short hallway past the master bathroom toward the main bedroom with me following like a puppy dog. I paused at the bathroom door to allow the attorney to settle into his bedroom. Then, waiting outside his door, I watched him set his plate and beer on the nightstand and step into the private bathroom.

Soon he emerged, brushing by me as I gently knocked at the door, more to let him know I was standing there than expecting him to say come in. I formally requested a moment of his time for a question. As if ahead of my thoughts, he inquired, "When are you leaving for Vietnam?"

Shocked that he even knew and more shocked that he raised the question, I confessed, "I received military orders to fly F-4 fighter-

20

bombers on a yearlong tour out of Da Nang." He listened while taking off his pants, blue dress shirt and tie, and crawled under the bedcovers wearing boxer shorts and a white T-shirt. There were books, maybe half a dozen or more, scattered about on the wrinkled covers revealing a bed that had remained unmade from the night before. He took a big bite out of his two-inch-thick sandwich and regarded me through his reading glasses, which magnified his eyes and made them appear small and beady. I continued, "I have come to the conclusion that my political disenchantment with the war and my sense of selling out on my convictions have led me to the decision to refuse my military orders and accept the consequences. It would mean a court-martial since I am a commissioned officer and a prison sentence to Fort Leavenworth where the military jails deserters and other servicemen convicted of crimes while on active duty."

I asked him for his perspective on the matter, always wanting to appear be up to his level conversationally and being careful to use my best grammar and vocabulary. As he was munching aggressively, the crisp crunch of the fresh onion dominated the silent pauses in the room. His response to my plea snatched my focus back from the sound of the munching. Without hesitation, he launched into a courtroom-like response with a question," Did you volunteer for fighters or were you assigned to fly those particular airplanes?"

It was a great question, I thought, the kind a sharp trial lawyer would ask. I answered honestly, "Well, fighter pilots are the pilot's pilot. I didn't want to fly transports or refueling tankers straight and level for hours and hours at a time. I chose the F-4 against Celeste's wishes, knowing it would force me to deal with going to Southeast Asia as part of the assignment."

After I finished my explanation, his response was brief. "Well, Brian, you volunteered for fighters and got official orders. The long-term impact of refusing to go to Vietnam and having a prison record for the rest of your life would have far greater consequences than the guilt you will experience from going against your conscience to Vietnam-if you live through it."

Wow, I thought. As simple as that, in that precise, isolated point in time, I was freed from my vacillation and clear that I would follow through with the F-4 assignment, shooting craps with my life for 365 days, praying that I'd make it. As he ominously implied in his closing remarks, "Go fly your fighter. I hope to hell you make it back, finish your time in the service, and get the hell out."

That was it. Leaving him reaching for a book he had picked up on the bed, I thanked him for his time and counsel, feeling resolved but forlorn and empty. As I stepped toward the bedroom door, I felt that I had glimpsed a brilliant, almost tragic figure of a man, alone in his home comforted by inhaling ham sandwiches and books before going off to sleep, only to start the routine all over again at six the next morning. What an incredible, bizarre life.

In surreal uneasiness, I had managed the quiet agony of good-byes with Celeste, dragging myself away from the comfort zone of Indianapolis and Muncie. I had deliberately arranged an early departure for Travis Air Force Base, California, to hang out for two or three days with one of my close friends. Perhaps it was a selfish act not spending every last minute with my wife and family, but in strained equanimity they surrendered their wishes to the preferences of one perceived as doomed, as if honoring a dying man's last requests. I needed communion with my dear friend, Ed Butler, Butt for short. Butt was among the few whose intellect I trusted to reveal my awful truths, to know my heartache and not despise or judge me for it. Our bond had been cemented back at Ball State as fraternity brothers. We both majored in languages, Butt in English and me in Spanish and shared mutual admiration for each other as jocks. Butt was a six-foot-six all-American prep star from South Bend, Indiana, who had matriculated on a full basketball scholarship, and he set all kinds of records in rebounding and scoring. I was the could-have-been star athlete whose career died young after back-to-back knee sprains to the left medial collateral halfway through my junior season and expulsion from the team in senior year for participating in the high school tradition of hazing underclassmen. The injuries and the expulsion sapped my will to pursue athletic scholarships.

True to form, living out his love for life and nature's beauty, Butt and his wife, Cynthia, resided in Berkeley in the hills overlooking San Francisco Bay--the perfect venue for the last place I would visit before leaving the United States. My closeness with Butt was special; we were bonded like brothers. We recognized each other as jocks with poets' souls. He was one of the first friends, other than Greg, whom I grew up with in Muncie, who could discuss any number of subjects we were studying at Ball State with fascination and honest intellectual engagement, as opposed to the routine conversations about who was buying the next pint, or when the next Kappa gig was going to take place, or who was giving up some leg on campus. In those days, most of us hung out behind a façade of being cool and having it together.

Despite the raw honesty in our relationship, Butt did not know I smoked reefer. I recall his awkwardness when he first discovered it during that visit to Berkeley.

Butt had a joyous life with Cynthia that required the usual coordination of chores and trips to the market. On the second afternoon of my visit, Butt told me he wanted to introduce me to a good buddy of his named Larry whom he was sure I would dig. Memory remains warm of that afternoon when Butt dropped me off at Larry's, also in the Berkeley hills but closer to campus. As we parked his VW Beetle and approached the wonderful little cottage lined with student cars easily identified by their Berkeley stickers, I caught another great view of the Bay Bridge through the opening between the gigantic oak trees in front of Larry's place. His house seemed to be vibrating with the sounds of "Dance to the Music," the megahit recording of Sly and the Family Stone. We knocked on the door and rang the doorbell. After no response, I boldly suggested that maybe we try the doorknob. Reluctantly, Butt slowly twisted the knob and the door eased open, exposing us to the blasting music and the shocked expressions of Larry and his two female guests. There was a sudden blur of scrambling, shuffling hands and wrists, newspapers and shoeboxes being placed aside and under the coffee table, as we slowly walked in, both of us suspecting we had interrupted something a little different. Larry, a light-skinned brother sporting a big Afro and wearing tinted sunglasses, got up, with a half-busted look on his face, and said, "Hey, man. What's happening, fellows? Hey, man, Butt, what's happening?" not seeming to realize he had asked us what was happening twice.

Butt joked, "Yeah, brother, we were out there knocking for five minutes."

"Wow, man, we didn't even hear you cats." I laughed out loud, my nose having detected the aroma of burning cannabis. Butt eased closer to Larry and immediately engaged in the formality of The Handshake, which in those early days of Black Is Beautiful was a ritual that required a checklist until you had it down properly. Butt quickly introduced me to Larry, announcing I was his homeboy from Muncie, Indiana, and out there for two or three days before going to Vietnam. Larry's eyes got big, peering at me from behind his rose-colored shades; his eyebrows rose at Butt's announcement. He stared at me incredulously, tilting his head forward to fix his beady hazel eyes on me, saying, "Wow, man, what a bummer," presuming that I had been drafted and was being forced out of the country against my will.

Butt asked Larry if it was okay if I hung out for a bit while he ran some errands with Cynthia. Larry responded, "no problem." He shifted his voice intonation and politely introduced me to the two exotic-looking sisters. One was wearing bright strawberry-red lipstick and popping bubble gum like Flo, the red-haired waitress on TV's *Alice,* and the other sported a roundly shaped Afro as big as a basketball with large gold hoop-styled African earrings. She looked real sexy. Erect nipples bespoke her braless state and made it challenging to remember to look her in the face when she spoke. They sat there like Bobbsey twins, music still blaring behind them. Butt looked back over his shoulder at me with a mischievous grin and said in a loud voice, "I'll join the party later."

I sat down shyly at the open end of the couch. There was no mistake that Larry and his lady friends were having a ball that sunny Saturday afternoon. The smell of marijuana was thick, and the smoke hung in an amazingly horizontal layer over the living room. I knew that we were getting ready to have a good time after Butt left. The door had barely slammed shut when Larry held out a big fat, badly rolled joint, tilted his head down, and, peeking at me over the top of his shades, asked, in full deliberate elocution, "Do you indulge, my brother?" Feeling another flush of embarrassment at the question, mostly drowned out by the next cut on the Sly Stone album, I responded, "Hey, right on."

As Larry invited me to get high with them, I was imagining a miniature figure of Butt sitting on my shoulder gasping at my surrender to the temptation, wondering if he knew that Larry partook of the weed and if he was astute enough to discern a stoned person. There was the typical anxiety rush of paranoia at being a rule breaker, occasionally unable to resist pushing the envelope of societal norms, even lightly breaking the law. The first little puff of Larry's Acapulco Gold quickly assisted in flipping the diminutive conscience of Butt backward off my shoulder and I gleefully leaped into the unknown with these new-made acquaintances on my last lost Saturday afternoon in the United States. Half an hour later, another tiparillo-sized joint was rolled. I shrunk back, hesitating. Not yet knowing the potency of what Larry and his gal pals had laid on me, I thought, *What is wrong with these people? How high do they want to get?*

Reefer smoking experiences were as varied as candy-bar selections in a movie theater. There were lightweight dopes, medium-weight dopes, and international dopes that later became known as rope-a-dope. Their potency could easily foreclose on one's ability to socialize, inducing severe impediments to coherent communication, often dumping one's vocabulary from the mind or paralyzing one with a three-second memory retention in which any pause or delay in conversation rendered one incapable of retrieving a lost point without assistance. A request for help in subject retrieval, "Where was I going with that?" or "What was I talking about?," rarely secured any response if one's audience was equally bombed. The challenge of recalling the subject often produced instant abandonment of the search with hysterical laughter and a final "wow," "far out," or "I heard that." The tingly mind groove was a numbing delight but produced a helpless dopiness when one struggled to achieve conversational objectives; it was as if one were in mental overload, juggling too many thoughts to be manageable. Maybe that's why they called it dope.

An hour later, Butt returned and I wrestled with a new paranoia over the challenge to simply speak in coherent sentences. I was gripped by fear that Butt would find out, bust me, and realize that his dear brother Brian, his athletic soulmate, was a narcotic-using degenerate. Miraculously, having switched the music genre to Ahmad Jamal, we heard his knock at the door. Butt stepped inside the door and asked simply, "You ready to go home?" I was actually glad to see him, to get rescued from that marathon session with the Berkeley freaks. As we said adios to Larry and the ladies, I thanked them for their great hospitality. One of the women wished me good luck in Vietnam; I never really knew if she was serious. Butt and I walked out and crammed ourselves back into the yellow Beetle. He had a smile on his face and the twinkle in his eye told me I had his blessing for enjoying myself, high or not.

I was known for being a chatty Cathy. Butt repeatedly laughed out loud as I spewed a bountiful supply of humor on the way back to his house. History had proved that such sessions of absurd indulgence were always followed by a snack and a serious nap. I recall an agonizing eagerness to return to Butt's and lie down for a few hours before round two. We were scheduled to go out for the last supper with another of Butt's friends from Indianapolis, a b-ball player named Bigso who had attended the all-Black Crispus Attacks High School a few years after the Hall of Fame NBA player Oscar Robinson.

During that last night at dinner, neither my dear frat brother Butt or his wife Cynthia gave me any grief about my decision to go to Nam. Even though they had reservations about the war, they lovingly accommodated my choice and saw it as the lesser of two evils, going to jail being the alternative. But their eyes bespoke pity and their voices were softened by a quiet apprehension that I might not make it back. I sensed their concealed sorrow, the shadows of a sadness that I might die in a war I didn't believe in. The occasional awkward silences bespoke their foreboding; their furtive eye contact seemed to be witnessing the last partying with a friend they might never see again.

CHAPTER 4: MEETING THE BROTHERS

I departed the M P guardhouse with my bags in tow and walked the short distance down the curving concrete sidewalk that led to the front door of the 390th Tactical Fighter Squadron. It was close to 0300, about 3 AM, as I set my briefcase down to free a hand to open the squadron door. Twisting the knob slowly, I eased the door open and held it with my right foot as I grabbed my items. My delay in entering had given the bleary-eyed duty officer a second to regain consciousness from his snoozing behind the desk. His eyes were bloodshot; it wasn't immediately clear if the redness was from sleep or boozing it up earlier. "Hey, guy, Brian Settles, new recruit for the 390th," I announced.

"Glad to meet you. Wes Darrell. I'm stuck with permanent Duty Officer until I get back on flight status," he stated in sleepy bluntness. All junior officers had to serve as Duty Officer to perform gofer chores every hour of every day of the week. The insignia on his uniform was my rank, first lieutenant. Feeling invited to inquire further, I asked him why he was off flying status. I listened amazed as he told me the brief story of a happy hour at the officers' club that deteriorated into a drunken fun and games mêlée that led to his being thrown over the bar counter by a fellow back-seater. He had temporarily lost consciousness from the blow to his head when he landed upside down. Among pilots, even temporary loss of conscious was a serious medical concern and always resulted in immediate grounding for testing and observation.

I shared my sympathies and asked where I might crash until I could get "in-processed" the next day. He scanned the crew roster on the clipboard and said, "Oh yeah, McKnight is on temporary duty to Clark; his roommate, John Reilly, is up flying on Black Jack flight. You can bunk there until billeting assigns you a place in the bachelor officers' quarters. I'll get the van key and run you over."

Wes retrieved the key from a nail on the wall next to the Plexiglas scheduling board, then, grabbing one of my bags, he said, "Brian, right?," as if testing his memory.

I responded, "Yeah, but I go by Bee."

Wes came back, "Dee?"

"No, Bee, as in bumblebee."

"Okay, got it," he said.

As we moved down the walkway, the muffled sounds of distant mortar rounds again intruded on the early-morning tranquility. The steady flickering of flares being dropped from helicopters cast a glow in the spaces of darkness off the end of the runway like bright lanterns dangling from a black sky. We climbed into the van. Wes slid into the driver's seat, and I took my place on one of two long padded benchlike cushions that ran the length of the van on each side. After three attempts, the rundown van's engine finally caught and kept running. In less than two minutes, Wes brought the vehicle to a gentle stop and announced, "This is it." We were stopped in front of a wood-framed open-air barracks with screen walls. It looked spooky; there were no lights in any of the cubicles and only a dim center hallway bulb provided a glow at the entry. Seven-foot-tall clothes lockers and sheets of plywood formed the hallway between the cubicles. Wes led me down the hallway a short distance and turned into a cubicle that had a door-like entry covered by a green Army blanket. Inside a small, low-watt lamp offered dim illumination, but I could make out two beds parallel to each other.

Wes, seeing the shock on my face at these humble living conditions, explained that arrangements were being made to get all the fighter squadron people moved to the concrete bachelor officers' quarters across the street, but, for the moment, we had to put up with this. He warned me, "Make sure you pull that mosquito net around the bed when you hit the sack. Reilly will tell you where to go in the morning when you get up. I gotta get back to the squadron. Welcome to Da Nang, Bee," he said, extending his hand once again.

"Thanks, man. I appreciate your help."

"No sweat, Bee. Good night."

Talk about feeling alone in the world. There I sat in the sweltering humidity of the wee morning hour in an open-air barracks with dozens of snoring strangers stashed away in dark cubicles up and down the makeshift hallway. Exhausted, staring down at the concrete floor beneath my boots, I said to myself, "You gotta be shittin' me." Wanting to surrender to my desperate need for sleep, I pulled off my uniform and laid it across the one chair in the tiny room. Casting off the mild repulsion of sleeping on a stranger's sheets, I closed the mosquito net and rolled over, facing away from the dim light. At that moment, the low hissing whine of taxiing jet aircraft suddenly built into a crescendo of roaring that shattered the night silence with a rumbling that was the closest thing to an earthquake I had ever experienced. During my F-4 training I had heard many fighter takeoffs, but these F-4s had a more ominous sound. The room vibrated. It was as if the night air amplified the blast, making me feel I was laying on a cot beside the runway. After the flight of fighters took off, the early-morning peace returned and I thought I would get to sleep. I was soon awakened by the familiar hiss and whine of another set of fighters taxiing for their takeoff. Once again, goose pimples rose on my skin as I was blasted by the horrifying tremors of the fighters taking off into the night. I could only sleep in spurts, but I was too exhausted to be annoyed.

The next day I was in-processed and assigned my own cubicle, a vacant space across from Reilly and McKnight. I spent two more nights there until we were all assigned more comfortable quarters across the street in an old concrete building with air conditioning and, most important, no need for mosquito nets. It was truly a time to thank God for small miracles. I was soon assigned my first in-country combat missions and was ready to start finding some surrogate buddies.

The Da Nang Officers' Open Mess, the DOOM Club, had its daily happy hour. It was heavily attended by the quiet agonists, the ground-pounders, people who didn't fly but were voluntarily confined to makeshift offices with walls of corrugated fiberglass creating a plastic world of mouse-in-a-maze cubicles. They also serve who only sit and suffer. The war survived on the paper-shuffling administrative army that fought a war of documentation. Office work centers littered the base up and down the flight line, like micro cities, just as those stateside. The worker bee admin types' daily routine assured that the timeliness of the drinking ritual of happy hour remained predictable and punctual. The fighter pilots, the many motor drivers, the "bullshit bombers," the rescue chopper pilots, and all the related support staff on the base converged on the DOOM Club at five o'clock to down a few drinks and get a bite to eat. Out of habit, when the schedule permitted, we rolled into the club around sixish, not wanting to appear too anxious to start drinking or perhaps be mistakenly labeled alkies, derelicts, or something like that.

On my return to flight status after an early bout with the flu, I was finally feeling reunited with my ego. I had completed my third mission. The only other brother in my squadron beside Bill Cobb, who was about to rotate, was Lieutenant Lorenzo Pugh. Lo, as he was nicknamed, was another pilot back-seater, guy in the back (GIB) like me. He was a graduate of Tennessee State in Nashville; he had gone through its ROTC program and into Air Force pilot training. At our first meeting, I held instant respect for Lo, not simply due to his being in the F-4, but because I knew what it had taken in skill, intelligence, and perseverance for him to get to the backseat of the Phantom.

In observing Lo's smooth brown-skinned face, I flashed back to the Air Training Command instructor pilot at Laredo Air Force Base, Texas, who had tried to wash me out after personality clashes developed. My intuition whispered to me that he held a preconceived notion that Blacks were not really suited to fly airplanes. My instructor, like a few other white pilots I met later, seemed to feel disappointed there were Black people who could do a job as well as he—that Black men could fly a jet, and get through pilot training. White perceptions about Blacks being backward, superstitious, and afraid to fly had many Black folks believing they were too out of touch and dumb to become pilots, astronauts, doctors, or any highly specialized profession.

31

I had glimpsed racism myself; I knew what it took for Lorenzo Pugh to be there in Nam as an Air Force fighter pilot. Lo had quintessential Negroid features: dark brown skin, large beady brown eyes, and a richly African nose with broad nostrils. He had the physical build of a football running back, five foot eleven with muscular and broad shoulders that tapered down his rippling back, forming a tight thirty-one-inch waist. He had a soft, high-pitched raspy voice that reminded me of Harry Belafonte. When I looked at Lo, I could see the past in his gaze, somewhere far back among the muffled screams of the wee hours, long before morning dew's evaporation, the oppressive scene of an antebellum Mississippi plantation. It was the gaze of a Mandingo warrior whose blood and genes coursed with the possibility of fighter pilot within him.

We first met on my third day at Da Nang. After bleeding through a lifelong ritual of revealing my credentials and establishing my ethnicity as a brother, Lo welcomed me warmly to the squadron. All things aren't what they seem; I had spoken that lesson most of my life. People saw me, whether they were white, Latino, Black, Chinese, or Vietnamese, and would often wonder, not knowing what I was. There was an inescapable reality of racial burden in America. You had to be something—you had to belong to some ethnic group, be called something, labeled more definitively than just homo sapiens.

There had always been a folkloric notion among Black folks that no matter how light the skin, another person of color could be spotted in a crowd of Caucasians. From way back in my childhood, people of color saw me and wondered. But curly hair and voice inflection had served me well over the years to reassure puzzled brothers and sisters that I was one of them. It was a strange, dehumanizing ordeal to wade repeatedly through the race association process before warmth and welcome were rendered. That was the by-product of racism for all of us, white and Black. Light-skinned brothers and sisters who looked white were viewed with puzzled glances from whites and curious suspicion from Blacks who wondered if they were "goin' for Black" or "passing" for white. My light skin and background roots had driven me to seek the acceptance of everyone in the neighborhood, especially the lowest socioeconomic group, the group from which Mama was running. I wanted to relate to them and for them to admire and accept me. Slang proficiency was a tool I employed to gain winning advantage and get me over with brothers and sisters all my life.

Once I had passed the social screening, Lo enthusiastically invited me to rendezvous at the DOOM Club for happy hour to meet some of the other brothers stationed at Da Nang. Brotherly acceptance by Lo left me with a giddy delight to have "connected" so quickly, and I agreed to come to the club.

That afternoon, after tidying up my room, I walked down the hallway wearing only a towel around my waist to the open-bay shower that separated one end of the quarters from the other to take a good wash. I ran into another brother unexpectedly, Captain Bill Cobb, also in the 390th. His blue satin neck scarf bespoke his affiliation. I couldn't believe it. I was impressed—two other brothers in my quarters and, as it turned out, in my squadron as well.

I assumed Bill, who wanted to be called Cobb, was a navigator since many navigators were higher-ranking officers. Black pilots were such a rare breed, I was convinced he could not be one but flight suit wings indicated otherwise; Cobb was indeed a pilot. *Wow,* I thought, *this is far out.* Cobb didn't know who I was or what I was until I spoke. I could discern from his lack of eye contact and body language that he had no desire to meet me. He thought I was just another white dude, an officer or somebody nondescript, trying to be friendly, until I spoke. "Hey. What's happenin'?"

I had often felt that Mama was driven to seek approval from white people. She perpetually fought off the phobia of being perceived as an uneducated, common Black. She seemed threatened by "street people," Black folks who were uneducated, fornicated, drank a lot, took dope, cursed and fought, and occasionally disrupted public meetings with real and subterfuge militancy. Intuitively, I sensed that lumpen Black folks embarrassed her and she didn't want to be mistaken for one. That was a point of conflict for us. Running the streets of Muncie with my friends, Greg and Chico, I had perfected my dialogue to "sound" Black. It wasn't Ebonics. Mama

33

was college educated, and we spoke Standard English at home. She hated it when I went off into Black slang or "hip talk" as she would disapprovingly describe it. The Bill Cobb–type brother was exactly who Mama didn't relate to. Naturally, it made me want to be his friend.

Cobb had the look and gait of a hip brother. He kind of "macked" when he walked, tipping by with his right foot sort of pushing his body up against gravity as he passed along, which made his head bob up when that right foot hit the ground. He also tilted his head to the right, creating the visual illusion he might fall over from leaning too far. He was wearing shades inside the quarters, not standard Air Force issue, but custom sunglasses, dark with black frames that looked as if they were purchased from a sidewalk vendor at Amsterdam and 125th Street in New York. Puzzled and unsure of the contrast between my appearance and the Black inflection in my greeting, he made contact. "You got it, man. You just get in-country?"

"Yeah, two weeks now," I answered hesitantly, unsure of my informality with him, given his rank and his much older appearance.

Cobb responded, "Are you the new cat in the 390th?" It was an indication the grapevine was operating. There were so few minorities flying airplanes that brothers always spread news and enthusiastically welcomed others into the fold instantly.

"Yeah, brother. I just flew my fifth mission," I offered.

Cobb retorted, "Shit, you muthafuckas on the straight one-year program, ain't chu?"

Having already achieved a comfort level with the innocuous designation of muthafucka, I had no negative reaction to Cobb's language. The Air Force had lost so many fighter pilots in tactical operations that a Hundred Missions Program had been implemented to reduce fighter- pilot exposure. Once a combat crewmember flew one hundred missions in North Vietnam above the 17th parallel, his tour was considered complete and he was rotated back to a stateside unit. Over the period between 1966 and 1968, fighter pilots completed their hundred missions in five to six months, rapidly depleting the limited numbers of pilots who were trained or combat experienced. To retard the combat crew utilization rate, Tactical Air Command altered the tour criteria and eliminated the Hundred Missions Program and shifted to a straight one-year tour, no matter how many combat missions were flown. My F-4 class was the first group to arrive in Southeast Asia with the new combat tour definition.

As if feeling sorry for me, Cobb admonished, "If I had to be here for a year, I'd make them muthafuckas find me. I wouldn't volunteer for no missions. They'd find my Black ass at the bar."

I cracked up with laughter at Cobb's implicit admission he was not there to be a hero. Realizing he had touched me with his humor, he continued, "This is Whitey's war, man. There's too many brothers and Porta Ricans dyin' over here. This ain't my war. The only thing I wanted to do over here was get me a kill, a MIG kill. Just one and I'd be happy and outta here." *Wow,* I thought, *Brother Cobb is over here puttin' his ass on the line flying fighters, not believing in the war (just like me), hoping to shoot down a MIG while flying his hundred missions.*

From that moment I knew Bill Cobb was a brother I could relate to. He actually grew up in Harlem. His language and political sensitivity were of the street. He reminded me of Chico, my adolescent running buddy and political mentor from the streets of Muncie who lived in my mind like Black militant consciousness perched on the shoulder of my psyche. Bill was very dark complexioned, like Lorenzo and like Chico. He had an impeccably trimmed mustache and that bumpy skin condition that some brothers get from shaving irritation. He was short, about five ten, with big round bulgy brown eyes and nothing but muscle and bone, like a long-distance runner. Bill's rap made him sound like a student of Malcolm X. He was down to earth—no bullshit—and very militant, a revolutionary in a flight suit, a tamed radical.

Catching a slight chill standing there in the vulnerability of a towel, feeling self-consciousness sweep across me as Cobb rapped on, I asked him if he was heading over to the club for happy hour. I told him I had also met Lo. He agreed to meet in thirty minutes to walk me over. I felt great inside. I had hooked up with Lo and now Cobb to go to the club and meet the brothers.

At Da Nang the dress of the day and night was the flight suit. No one except weenies and ground-pounder office workers, usually contract types, wore nonuniform street clothes, civvies, to the DOOM Club. Stealing a little time for contemplation of the beehive of activity during Da Nang Air Base rush hour, I sat on the steps and sipped a beer. I had taken it from the community fridge situated in the open bay between the east and west wings of our quarters. I reflected on all the people and vehicles flowing in and out of the barbed-wire compound as I waited, sweating in the early October humidity, for Cobb to show. He soon emerged right on time wearing a form-fitting flight suit that seemed neat enough to have been ironed, inspiring me to say, "Damn, brother, that flight suit looks like it came from the One Hour Martinizing."

Not cracking a smile, Cobb bragged, "Shit, I got these mama sans pressin' my shit every day. Brother Cobb's stuff goin' always be tight—war or no war."

Once again, he had me in stitches. He had the Vietnamese maids who cleaned our rooms, made the beds, and washed our clothes also ironing his flight suits. Bill had his blue Air Force piss cutter (hat) perched atop his head, with shiny silver captain's bars, cocked to the side like a Harlem hustler driving a pink Cadillac. His flight suit was unzipped to the navel, not for relief from the heat or humidity, but to reveal a snazzy dark blue mesh undershirt that hugged and advertised his rippling washboard muscles. Protruding out of his lower left calf pocket was a fifth of VSOP Courvoisier cognac. Smiling in quiet admiration of his uniqueness, I couldn't help exclaiming, "Wow, man, you takin' the party with you to the club."

In full coolness, confidence, and justification, Cobb responded, "Shit, man, them tired muthafuckas at the club don't even serve my shit. I gotta bring my good thang wit' me."

I asked, "They don't allow you to bring your own booze in the club, do they?"

Again, Cobb had the answer. "Naw, but they can't stop what they don't see, you dig?" Walking down the burning-hot asphalt street that steamy October afternoon with Captain Bill Cobb, I perceived a connectedness with myself—a relatedness that reassured me I was not alone philosophically. I was not alone in my reservations about the war—nor my notion that U.S. participation in the war was facilitated by our systemic racism and justified by our Cold War mania over communism's spread. I felt a powerful sense that the bond among Blacks and people of color in general would be the ingredients abetting emotional and social survival in Nam.

With those thoughts permeating my mind as Cobb and I strolled toward the club, another rude reality presented itself. My buddy from F-4 training, Bill Smoyer, who had come through jungle survival school, and ridden on the C-130 with me to Da Nang, suddenly was approaching

from the opposite direction. Smoyer was a handsome blue-eyed guy with light brown hair,

a large nose, and big ears. He walked with a quick little shuffle, almost light in the loafers. Smoyer, spotting me at some distance with Cobb, yelled out from beyond normal greeting range, "Hey, Bee, what's happening?" I was gripped by a sudden uneasiness, as if I had been exposed that I had white friends.

"Hey, Smoyer, what you doin'?" I responded awkwardly and quickly, trying to make all of us feel more comfortable before introducing Smoyer and Cobb.

"I been over at the club having a couple and thought I'd go back and write Ginger a letter," Smoyer replied.

"Yeah, Captain Cobb and I are going over to meet some other cats now," I imparted, slyly letting Smoyer know it wouldn't be no white guy social. From all our soulful talks, Smoyer understood my philosophies of life. He knew I was a jock fighter pilot who despised bigotry and was not all teeth about shooting craps with my life in Vietnam. He also knew the civil rights struggle at home was not leaving me very patriotic about the flag or apple pie. Yet, even though we had connected, it was obvious he had limited experience hanging out with Blacks on a social basis.

I realized that even I had experienced discomfort at being in the depths of socializing with ghetto street brothers and sisters and occasional awkwardness just being around common, hardworking blue-collar Black folks. I selfishly assumed Smoyer would feel out of it sitting at a table full of raucous, heavy-drinking brothers and presumption prevented me from offering him an invitation to join us. I became Judas's twin. I felt embarrassed, phony, a hypocrite. I was manipulated by my preoccupation with being accepted as a brother. Smoyer got the subtleties and took his leave.

"Maybe I'll stop back over a little later, Bee. Nice meeting you, Captain Cobb." Heaped in guilt and a sense of betrayal, I sheepishly responded at Bill's departure, "Yeah, that's cool, man. Later."

Attempting to offer some ointment to soothe my sense of selling out on a buddy I liked, I told Cobb what a together dude Smoyer was as we resumed our stride toward the DOOM Club. It was a familiar déjà vu—rationalizing to a homey why I might have a non-Black friend. I was uncomfortable with the reality that we as Black people discriminated against white folks as much as they did us, the profound difference being that they were the majority. They had the power, the money, and the control. They had Vietnam.

Black folks were Americans-come-lately, trying to play catch-up in a society that seemed resistant to relinquishing the institutional barriers that denied full access to opportunity and dignity—a society that too often seemed to prefer keeping them out. How could any brother in Vietnam have viewed with a warm, fuzzy feeling the ubiquitous display of confederate flags brandished by American GIs from the South? It had always been the palpable symbol of the Civil War and by displaying this reminder of oppression and disenfranchisement, they registered their de facto desire to refight that war, inspired by some inner passion to reverse the results. Not all white military personnel felt this, but there was a haunting polarization between the races. It was not an easy period to have friends of the opposite race. For brothers to do so was to be vulnerable to the label Uncle Tom; whites got called nigger lovers for the same infraction. There was no possible time for relatedness and unity as human beings, despite the noble intentions of the sixties peace, flower power, and civil rights movement.

The bright sunlight outside the DOOM Club gave way to dimness. It was that familiar scene of entering a movie theater during the daytime. A gradual crescendo of laughter and chatter showcased a boisterous gathering as Cobb and I eased through the arched portal of the main bar. Instantly, my eyes fixed on one of many large round tables surrounded by wooden high-back chairs where six black Air Force officers sat crowded around each other. The noise from just that table was audible above all drinking activity at the other tables. Happy hour had a good start and obviously the room was full of early starters.

Three of the five brothers—two captains and a lieutenant—at the table wore green fatigues, regular Air Force issue. A quick inspection of chest pockets revealed non-crewmember status. Four brothers wore flight suits with stitched-on pilot insignia, one captain, and three lieutenants. The smallest one of the group leapt to his feet, raising his full glass to the roof as if making a solo toast to something or someone. One of the seated brothers shouted out, "Carl's drunk again." They all broke out in laughter. Carl shouted back, "Damn right, an' goin' stay that way too." Noticing Cobb and me walking toward them, Carl added, "And here comes that damn Cobb who got me drunk last night."

The brothers broke up again, bellowing hysterical laughter; some pounded the table with open hands. Being a sober outsider, I could only muster a sheepish grin, like walking in on a joke after the punch line was delivered. As Cobb and I approached, Cobb greeted the group. "Hey, what's happenin', brothers?" Gesturing with his thumb toward me, he announced, "This is brother Brian Settles. He's the new cat replacing me in the 390th. You know the Man can't have too many of us together in any place at one time for too long."

The brothers raised their beer bottles and drink glasses saying, "Hear, hear. I'll drink to that."

I cracked a big smile at the welcome and introduced myself to each one: Fig Newton, Alex Dawson, Denver McClendon, Carl Gamble, and Lo Pugh--all brothers, all U.S. Air Force officers, all at Da Nang in the Republic of Vietnam with their individual stories. I felt self-conscious and unsteady, shy and aware of an inner neediness to be one of the gang quickly, but a little awkward in breaking the ice of my own mind. A profound pride surged within me to be there among them, to see and hear them laughing in their social escape. The other ten or twelve tables in the room were occupied by white Air Force, Navy, and Marine officers, all toasting various causes, laughing and ordering more drinks from the cute Vietnamese bar waitresses in brightly colored traditional dresses.

Lieutenant Carl Gamble was one of the smallest pilots I had ever seen; it would be a stretch to say he was five foot seven. When he was smashed, he was also the loudest. He gulped Jack Daniel's from a medium-size water glass as if he was drinking Kool-Aid at a picnic. Before I could drag up a chair, he shouted, "Brother Brian, what's your poison?"

I almost felt like a newcomer in church. Strangely caught off-guard, in that throng of familiar strangers, I shyly announced, "Scotch and 7-Up."

Lieutenant Alex Dawson, feeling no pain, loudly announced he was the munitions officer for the 390th and also blurted out a teasing exclamation, "Damn, Brian, what kind of drink is that?"

I grinned and hesitated whether to defend my choice. I lamely proclaimed, "Hey, man, that's what I drink."

As if coming to my aid, Denver chimed in, "Yeah, nigga. That's what the brother drinks." Everyone roared in laughter again.

Carl Gamble was not only the shortest, but also the skinniest pilot I had ever met. His flight suit was the smallest available in supply, a small regular. Even wearing that size, his sleeves had to be rolled up and his pant legs were frayed and gnawed from scraping the floor. He was a handsome brother with that kind of brown skin that had an orange-brown hue when tanned by the sun. He wore a pencil-thin mustache and had a short Afro. He was an ROTC graduate like me, matriculated from Tennessee State as an aeronautical engineering major. Learning that, I instantly respected him just for his intelligence. He had a big broad smile that beamed with the shine of his pearly white teeth. Carl seemed to find humor easily; he laughed aloud in funny giggling sounds followed by snorting. I knew we would become friends because he broke out in laughter with most everything I had to say.

Carl was assigned to another squadron, not a fighter one. I don't think he wanted a fighter assignment and I was sure he wasn't excited about flying a C-47, the archaic goonie bird. His unit was designated the Psy-Ops Squadron—Psychological Warfare Operations. Their flying involved low-level sorties over South Vietnam dropping pamphlets printed in Vietnamese encouraging the peasant farmers to help the American effort against the Vietcong. They flew daily across the country supporting the Chu Hoi program to induce Vietcong to defect from their cause. We affectionately referred to Carl's squadron as the bullshit bombers. It was another mind-boggling folly that some Pentagon strategist had contrived as a program to help speed up victory.

And so the friendships began. That night we launched ourselves into bonding, sharing stories of background and life experience, the ubiquitous process repeated among Blacks in the military that tapped into the tangential relatedness that generates purely out of skin color. When meeting new Black officers, I often found myself surprised that there were so many other Black college graduates. I was perhaps an unwitting victim of brainwashing from my isolated experience at Laredo Air Force Base. Many talented, bright young Blacks were flying fighters and other airplanes just like me. I was as an ignorant savage in undergrad robe; my educational experience had left me with only a superficial knowledge of the struggle and extraordinary achievements of the Tuskegee Airmen. Had I been more aware, perhaps I would not have been so surprised at half-dozen or so brothers flying at Da Nang. But there they were, the best and brightest of Black America, huddled together, nourishing one another's psyche at the DOOM Club, doing their part to keep America safe for democracy and hoping to get back alive.

Carl Gamble and Alex Dawson became my closest friends at Da Nang, especially Carl. Maybe it was because we started out living in the same floor in the bachelor officers' quarters, what we called the Q, or perhaps it was because neither one of us had a problem starting the day with a beer and a shot of Jack Daniel's after breakfast.

Maybe it was because we had that invisible, intuitive connection that leaves one always feeling in a good place when one is in easy company—accepted, not threatened, even liked. Although I felt his flying assignment sucked (it would have never stroked my neediness), Carl was one of the few decorated war heroes I met who really deserved his Distinguished Flying Cross.

I recall that blistering hot fall afternoon when all inbound aircraft experienced arrival delays getting back into Channel 77. There had been an emergency landing on the north runway; a battle-damaged aircraft had come in on fire and closed that side of the airfield. As we landed on the south runway and slowed to turn-off speed, we cruised by the partially charred remains of a smoldering C-47 dowsed in foam by the fire rescue squad. It looked like a toy airplane that had been coated with pancake batter. The plane was badly charred; its exit hatches were open black holes. A bolt of horror shot through me, the same sense I felt a few years earlier turning our family's '55 Chevrolet Biscayne at the precise moment a speeding Buick Roadmaster ran the stop sign and slammed into the undercarriage of a fully loaded Selma Steel & Wire flatbed semitrailer.

My aircraft commander commented, "Wonder if they got out okay?" It didn't look healthy. We taxied in and shut down. Maintenance debrief could only say that the goonie had taken some .50-caliber machine-gun rounds south of Hoi An and came into Da Nang on fire. They didn't know if there were any injuries or fatalities. As we were leaving, the door to the command post opened and out walked Carl Gamble trailed by his copilot and gunner. I greeted him warmly. "Hey, brother, what's happening?"

Laughing with that big, wide smile, he said, "Man, I've had enough excitement in the last hour to last me a lifetime."

Catching his drift, I asked, "That wasn't you out there on the runway, was it?"

"Sure was, boy," he said, laughing. "I'll tell you about it at the Q."

Excitedly, I rushed back to the Q, opened a beer, and sipped it as I undressed to get in the shower, my mind stuck in disbelief that Carl was actually the aircraft commander of that charred C-47. He had narrowly averted a premature cremation. Ten minutes later, as I was stepping from the open-bay shower, I heard a screen door slam. It was Carl striding down the hallway.

"Hey, Bee, put on some clothes and come on down, man. We need a drink."

"Be right there, brother."

CHAPTER 5: LOSS OF VIRGINITY, AGAIN

Major Randy Billington was one of the smoothest white Air Force pilots I had ever met. He was wise and hip, like a street-smart brother. Brilliant with a raw intellect, he voraciously read science novels, periodicals, and newspapers, along with cowboy westerns. He was not familiar with the Black social experience, but had sensitivity born out of understanding the marrow of the civil rights struggle and he was sympathetic to the outraged factions. He grasped the benefit of violence and burning, the anarchic twins playing their part in a revolutionary societal movement. Unlike other white pilots who stood on adversarial or ambivalent grounds about racism, he didn't spend his time attempting to convince Black crewmembers he was okay or on our side. He didn't particularly gravitate toward us socially but he was politically correct before it was in vogue. Randy Billington had a dry sense of humor that would leave you in stitches or simply staring back at him in disbelief at what had issued from his mouth. He once told me early in our friendship, "Bee, my man, you are here to be a statistic—a dead one or a live one. Which is it?"

He was a rebel and a quiet outlaw. I was in awe of him because of his intellectual heaviness and ice-water-in-the-veins fighter pilot skills. Few knew him personally, but I did. He was the old head AC (Aircraft Commander/front-seater) assigned to break me in to flying combat missions. Brand-new GIBs were paired up with the same ACs during the first month of combat flying to improve survival prospects. The Air Force frequently lost fighters in Vietnam and Laos, even with experienced crews and so two new guys together in combat was a no-no in the F-4. That policy led me into the backseat of the Phantom with Major Randy Billington.

We first met on my sixth scheduled combat mission at Da Nang. I was relieved to finally be flying after getting the flu right after I arrived at the 390th. The macho shit had gotten to me. A so-called fighter pilot comes to war to shoot, maim, and kill and instead he's sick in bed after his second mission. I was medically grounded,

DNIF—Duty Not Including Flying. I was too sick even to be a duty officer, but I was anxious to get going, lose my new-guy status, and prove I could survive combat missions and wasn't scared of dying.

Three of my first five missions were in-country strikes with squadron staff pilots. Two were North Vietnam daytime strikes—easy missions to wet my feet, nothing hairy. In South Vietnam, we bombed suspected Vietcong tunnel systems, knocked out bunkers, and strafed a few water buffalo—pack animals that could be used by the Vietcong to tote ammo or rockets. The sixth mission was going to be different. It was my first night strike in North Vietnam, two big reasons for an elevated "pucker factor," a euphemism for a tightening of the sphincter muscle induced by the prospect of horror. It would be my first mission with my own assigned AC—Major Randy Billington.

We had a 0130 (1:30 AM) showtime at the command post for mission planning and target briefing for a 3:30 AM go. That time was scary enough, but we were fragged (scheduled) for a road reconnaissance mission along Route 1A on the east side of Bat Lake in North Vietnam. I recalled the MP at the entrance to the squadron telling me that Da Nang was affectionately referred to as Rocket City. Most rocket attacks happened between midnight and 4 AM. The night air was thick and pungent. My nose burned with the aroma of garbage dumps and sewage ditches; my mind was in uncontrolled wandering as if hop-scotching fearful notions, wondering whether a rocket attack was seconds away.

I had arrived at the command post at 03:15 to get a head start on mission planning and target study. I had never met him and did not even know what he looked like. No other crewmembers were present. Only silence inside and the muffled violence outside in the morning darkness. Identifying myself to the duty noncommissioned officer behind the counter as the back-seater on the sortie with Cutter as its call sign, flight mission B-320, I took the mission folder stamped with big black letters "Top Secret" and walked away from the counter and into the mission planning room. The folder contained the complete layout of the mission plan, where the target was, what it was, and what kind of defenses we would encounter. Major

Billington and I would be in Cutter 2, the second fighter in the two-ship strike. For rescue purposes, Billington was designated Cutter 2A, I was Cutter 2B. We would be on the wing of Cutter 1 who would navigate us to the target area and check in with the Forward Air Controller putting us in on the targets. On this mission we had it easy-all we had to do was fly formation on lead and follow his directives. But even as the wingman, we still needed knowledge of every aspect, every minute detail of the mission. Feeling safe inside the mission planning room was not easy; I could still sense the continuing rumble of the distant mortars. It didn't help that the walls vibrated and appeared to quake from the sound-wave concussions. A thought flashed across my mind: *What the hell am I doin' here?*

I glanced down at my wrist to glean some perspective from my black Air Force issue aviator's watch; Major Billington was late. I submerged myself in the stacks of up-to-date top-secret reconnaissance photos of the road systems running north and south along the coast of North Vietnam. The photos showed a web of road systems streaming southward from Hanoi through central North Vietnam toward the DMZ. After sunset, like clockwork, the headlights of the bumper-to-bumper supply-loaded truck traffic could be observed-armored personnel carriers, radar-guided 37-millimeter and 57-millimeter guns on flatbeds, and ten wheelers loaded to the gunwales with ammo and supplies manufactured in China and the Soviet Union.

Along the supply routes in North Vietnam were numerous emplacements of highly skilled antiaircraft gunners hosing .50-caliber machine guns on our low-flying aircraft. For high-altitude aircraft, sophisticated 85-millimeter radar-guided howitzers spewed shells as large as fireplugs up at us as high as thirty-five thousand feet, detonating on proximity and capable of blowing us out of the sky from an explosion half a mile away. My absorption with one of the gun emplacement photos was disrupted by the scratchy sound of flight boots on linoleum. Slowly shuffling into the room, baseball cap cocked back and to the side of his head, and wearing sunglasses at that hour in the morning, Major Randy Billington appeared. His nametag revealed in black-stitched letters only "Billington." Relieved and eager to break the ice and get chummy with the guy to whom I would soon entrust my life, I said, "Morning, Major Billington. Bee Settles, FNG back-seater for Cutter this morning." FNG was the commonplace acronym oozing the degradation affixed to fucking new guy.

He mumbled, "Fuck me! Glad to meet you."

As he nuzzled up uncomfortably close to my side to scan the mission folder, he gave me more than his greeting to produce distraction. His softly slurred words were painted with a thick coating of alcohol—too thick for that time of day. We were then equal. His body language bespoke uneasiness about taking a FNG on a night road reconnaissance to Bat Lake. I could not know his past experience with FNGs. Quietly, I was horrified to be going on my first strike at night with a front-seater who had either left the bar very recently or taken a belt of booze before leaving his room. Neither prospect offered solace.

Realizing in that instant that I was ultimately the only one I could count on for my survival, I made a quick assessment. The playground was no longer peacetime training where everything was done by the numbers, proper and tight. It was real, a "sho'nuff" war. Creating oneself, improvising, and being flexible were the keys to getting through it—a finely tuned survival sense didn't hurt either. I had to ask myself, "Is Billington smashed or just mellow?" Do I tell him, "Sir, with all due respect, I'm not going on the mission with you because I smell booze on your breath."

I knew drinking was generally a problem in the military. In combat it could be even more of a problem--like drinking and driving. Tension hung over the place like a dirty rug. People drank, flew, ate, and jerked off—anything to fill the time, anything to sooth or distract them from the madness of their mission.

I launched my own personal evaluation of Major Billington through a series of questions to discern his speech and clarity—to determine if he was fit to drive. But he was cool and professional. He briefed me on what he needed me to do and when. He emphasized that we were a team and that we probably would get shot at, that our survival could depend on one of us doing the right thing at the right time. The hair rose on the back of my neck; I was expressionless, but felt scared shitless. I was confident he could count on me, but could I depend on him? I couldn't believe he was wearing those shades. But since he was an old head in the squadron, if he were shaky and unsafe, he would have been discovered long ago. Or had he become an alcoholic the night before? I hoped not.

The intelligence briefing officer reconfirmed the details of the secret target study folders. "Gentlemen, Cutter flight is scheduled for road reconnaissance along Route 1A at coordinates N17 25.00 and E106 40.00 just north of Bat Lake. Heavy vehicular traffic will be moving toward the DMZ until daybreak. Your Seventh Air Force Clearance authorizes free fire at any and all observed traffic along Route 1A. The area regularly reports intense enemy antiaircraft activity of all calibers. If you get hit, "feet wet" is your best bet for emergency ejection and rescue. ("Feet wet" was the term we used for heading out over the South China Sea for the greatest chance for rescue). Are there any questions?"

I felt like barfing, taking a crap, or both. I glanced at Major Billington to check if he was wearing the same countenance of fear. A detached scowl made it appear he hadn't even been listening to the briefing. I was relieved. He wasn't sweating. He didn't seem like the frightened type. I thought maybe this cat has ice water in his veins. That was definitely who I wanted to be with, a good stick fighter pilot able to take the dish-off pass and sink the winning shot at the buzzer in overtime.

I remained uneasy about the booze smell, but had placed my assessment of him on the altar and given him the thumbs-up to trust him with our lives that night—my sixth sortie in Vietnam. Over the ensuing year, my willingness to trust others with my life was taxed dozens of times.

Following the intelligence briefing, we went to a crew briefing room with a small rectangular table in the center and four gray metal government chairs with padded vinyl seat cushions. A chalkboard was situated on one wall. Major Fosdick and Lieutenant Vogel were in Cutter 1. Major Fosdick conducted the briefing for our specific procedures: type of weapons scheduled for the mission—eight CBUs (cluster bomb units) per aircraft; time on station at the target, 0500 (5 AM); engine start time; parking spots of our birds; type of formation to be flown to target area; emergency abort procedures, en route abort, ejection procedures, fuel loads, and Da Nang return weather, including the type of approach for landing. It was all covered; we all knew what to do. My training had prepared me, but suddenly I couldn't feel my boots on my feet. I thought I actually experienced a quiver of trembling, but knew I was as ready and trained as I could be. It was now up to us to get ourselves back alive.

The personal equipment shop was always the first stop after briefings. There we picked up the survival equipment we would carry on all combat missions. We had the basic required stuff as well as individual, personalized items that were left to the imagination of each crewmember. Standard wardrobe consisted of a helmet with oxygen mask, G suit, a pocketed mesh canvas zip-up survival vest holding water purification tablets, an emergency pen-flare gun with spare cartridges, first-aid gauze, antibiotics, adhesive tape, a black leather gun holster for a .38–caliber long-nose pistol loaded with six live rounds, and a waist ammo belt with six leather buttoned-down ammo packs holding twelve rounds each. In the shock and trauma of an ejection, dehydration could be a critical element affecting prospects for survival. Crewmembers had an operational requirement to carry a pint of drinking water; I carried two plastic pint bottles, one tucked in each lower (specially installed) G suit rear calf pocket. A seven-inch Marine survival knife was also authorized and I carried it in a sheath strapped outside my chest vest pocket. Before leaving Muncie, my fishing buddy, Bemon Blythers, had given me a thick twelve-inch Marine knife to carry for good luck. I had it tucked into a leather sheath on which the personal equipment shop airmen had sewn a Velcro strip to wrap around my lower calf to prevent its loss on the force of an ejection. Bemon's big knife was a monstrously lethal piece of slate black steel, razor sharp, and beautifully crafted for slicing and killing. My private self prayed I would never find out what it was like to use it on another human being, but I still coached myself with reminders that my survival might someday require it.

Added to the twenty pounds of personal equipment was the ejection seat harness with padded back cushion containing a tightly packed hundred-fifty-foot length of nylon jungle penetration rope to use in letting down from branches if my parachute became hung up on a tall tree canopy. I also toted a dark blue vinyl map bag with two hand straps on each side of the zipper running through the middle. This map bag had the appearance of a square-shaped tacky pocketbook; it contained my own personalized laminated maps of frequently targeted areas and navigation routes to and from Da Nang. It also held the top-secret encoding wheel I checked out from the Command Post Intelligence Officer before each mission to decode and authenticate classified mission changes that might be transmitted to us while airborne.

After leaving the equipment shop, Major Billington joined me in the blue van that transported us to the flight line and our parking spots. With his cocked baseball cap, he looked goofy, but the two crisscrossed ammo bandoliers over his chest rendered him kick-ass ready for business. He reminded me of the Mexican revolutionary, Emiliano Zapata. I was dumb enough to think he looked frighteningly cool. The major had the same basic war garb as I. In addition to his bandoliers, he wore a second holstered pistol, an unauthorized .25-caliber chrome-plated automatic with an ivory handle.

We arrived at parking revetment number 13. The crew chief greeted us with a salute and briefed Major Billington on the bird's maintenance status. I climbed up the ten-foot ladder to crawl into the back cockpit to begin my preflight and get the inertial navigation system aligned. Ten minutes later, we started engines and taxied out on Cutter 1's radio commands over our discreet UHF frequency. Our flight of two was sent over to Da Nang ground control and taxied toward the arming area to have the safety pins pulled, making our CBUs hot and armed for delivery on target. Major Billington didn't waste words in chitchat; he answered my few questions and called for all checklists at the appropriate times. Prior to reaching the arming area, he upped my anxiety level when he asked over the interphone, "Hey, Bee, have you dropped CBUs before?"

Getting just a flash of a warm, fuzzy feeling hearing my nickname, I responded, "Uh, no, sir."

He came right back. "Well, you're in for a treat. They do a fuckin' job. We'll probably get some good BDA," he said, using the acronym for the "bomb damage assessment" normally received from the forward air controller after the strike's completion. "Only one fuckin' problem with CBUs, you drop this shit at low altitude, four to six thousand feet, wings and flight path level. If you jerk the airplane around trying to avoid ground fire while releasing the CBUs, you could screw up the bomblets and they might start cookin' off right under the airplane. If we get shot at while dropping this shit, we could be fucked."

"Jesus Christ," I exclaimed, wishing Major Billington had kept that info to himself. Jinking was the term for flying fighters in an erratic flight path with the control stick; those uncomfortable jerky motions made it difficult for ground gunners to track your flight path and lead you with their gun sights. Not jinking meant allowing ourselves to be an easier target for a gunner to track and shoot down, trolling with our asses as it were. It was the essence of being a fighter pilot and what gave richness to the job.

We switched over to Da Nang Tower frequency after our CBUs were armed. The next transmission signaled that moment of no turning back. "Cutter flight, cleared for takeoff Runway 35 left. Wind calm! Time 0330." It was precisely our takeoff time. Cutter 1 lined up on the right side of the runway centerline; we lined up on the left, slightly behind lead. We were tucked so snug to him that our wingtips appeared to be overlapping. Major Fosdick advanced his throttles to eighty percent of engine power, did a quick engine instrument scan, and smoothly went into burner, simultaneously releasing his brakes. Nestled beside them on the runway in the black of early morning, I was consumed by the awesome spectacle of the engines' jet nozzles spraying gallons of JP-4 fuel into the burner cans, causing twin fifteen-foot sky-blue plumes bordered in bright yellow to explode from the exhaust like giant flame throwers. The rumble was both deafening and blinding. I temporarily lost myself in the spectacle. Our bird and the concrete runway beneath us quaked and shook in an auditory chaos that vibrated our eardrums like sticks on a snare drum. The power, the force, the energy were mind blowing. It was complex aerospace engineering and physics, yet simple and explainable. Thirty seconds after lead rolled, Major Billington pushed our throttles up, paused, and then blam. We went to burner and felt the thrust of our healthy Phantom's engines pinning us to our seat backs. Ten seconds later, we were airborne, gear and flaps up, accelerating through 200 knots and banking right over the South China Sea, four eyeballs scanning into the starry blackness searching for lead.

Major Billington shook the stick and announced, "Okay, Bee, you got it." And just like that, with no warning, he handed over control of the bird. I knew it was up to me to catch up to lead and get on his wing, flying three-foot wingtip separation until we reached level-off. No words could adequately describe the rush of sight, sound, and force of that experience, pursuing at full throttle the tiny red flashing of Cutter lead's rotating beacon two miles ahead as we ascended into the clear night. It was the truest amplification of the exhilaration in simply being alive—the splendor of submersion in the unbelievable, the fantastic. This crystallized moment eclipsed the pain, struggle, and mediocrity of one's life, leaving one face-to-face with the unimaginable—the extraordinary. I glimpsed a flash of incredible clarity about life's magnificence that aided me in forgetting for a moment where we were going.

The area of North and South Vietnam is geographically compressed at the middle. Our missions were often less than half the distance between Indianapolis and Chicago and no farther than Philly to D.C. It was only sixty miles from Da Nang to the DMZ. Yet, in central Vietnam, that area consisted of a teaming bamboo jungle that extended westward to the jagged cordillera. Scenic river fords and waterfalls gave way to rectangular rice paddies outlined in lush green borders aligned in perfect geometric squares sharing the land with caribou and peasant farmers in balanced harmony waiting for Air Force fighter-bombers to show up and shatter the wee morning silence with war's rude wake-up call of flames and fusillade.

Flying formation at four hundred miles per hour to the target rendezvous point at Bat Lake in North Vietnam with Major Billington in my front seat that night was the ultimate macho warrior adventure. It made childhood bullies threatening to kick my ass on the playgrounds of Muncie laughable. Circling offshore at fifteen thousand feet above the pristine beige sand beaches hiding below us in the morning darkness, we waited in composed anxiety for the FAC (Forward Air Controller) to come up on frequency and direct us in on the target where big and small guns would have their sights set on us . It was another one of those inescapable moments where one is drawn across the line from reality into the surreal by the forces of exigency, where one's life is bet on one's skill and fate is teased.

Cutter flight arrived on station just as scheduled. We were on our second orbit off the coast when our FAC came up on frequency. His call sign was Nail 61. Lead checked us in on the discreet strike frequency and began his briefing. "Good morning, Cutter, Welcome to the show. We got a big truck convoy tonight; it's like the San Bernardino freeway down there. You got CBUs for me tonight, right?"

Cutter lead responded immediately, enthusiastically, "That's affirm!"

Nail 61 came back, with scratchy radio static in the background, "Charlie, Charlie. Recommend you fly right down the road and pickle at will (pilots used the term *pickle* to indicate pushing the bomb release button on the flight control stick) when you spot the truck lights. Should get a lotta action down there and you can expect reaction. Emergency bailout, feet wet." Out over the sea was the only area safe from bad guys, man-eating animals, and a place from which rescue helicopters could easily extract downed crewmembers.

Cutter lead took the reins. "Roger, Nail 61. Cutter copies and will get set up and call in."

Nail 61 acknowledged the transmission. Lead gave us our directive. "Cutter 2, lead's increasing speed; throttle it back for spacing. I'll call the base."

With that call, Major Billington pulled back the throttles and requested the Ordnance Delivery Checklist. In F-4 training, we had learned the discipline of flying racetrack patterns in the target area. Now it was real. We circled overhead the target with both fighters doing the same speed, ideally at opposite sides of the circular flight path. When lead releases his ordinance and calls "lead's off," Cutter 2 should be rolling in on the target, calling out on the radio, "2's in and hot." If the FAC has cleared the flight to drop its bombs, they are "cleared in hot."

Within moments, Cutter lead announced his position for spacing adjustment, "Leads turning the base. I have you, 2. Spacing looks good."

Major Billington came back, "Roger, lead." Just like that, the show was on.

I called, "Arming checklist complete."

Lead called in, "Nail, Cutter lead's in. Am I cleared?"

Nail 61, circling at five thousand feet west of the road we were about to bomb, gave the command: "Cutter lead's cleared in hot." We were opposite lead heading the reciprocal direction as he rolled in on final. Major Billington commented, as if assuring himself I was still with him in the back, "Okay, Bee, switches set. 'Bout to turn the base."

Not having anything more creative to say, I confidently responded, "Roger that, sir."

Major Billington banked the bird sharply to the left, descending from twelve thousand feet toward the road paralleling the beach, and said calmly to me over the loud background hiss of our accelerating respiration into our oxygen masks, "Hey, Bee, can the 'sir' shit. It's Randy, okay?"

What a cool thing to do, I thought. This dude was turning in to bomb the shit out of North Vietnamese military personnel who were trafficking weapons and ammo to their comrades south of the DMZ at five in the morning and he's taking the time to relax our relationship.

We rolled in on final and Randy transmitted to Nail, "Cutter 2, in hot."

Nail 61 responded, "Cutter 2, cleared hot." I called out degrees of dive angle, airspeed, and altitude to free up Randy's eyes to look out the forward canopy to pick up the glow of truck headlights on the road below. Arriving at three thousand feet, we leveled off and Randy said, "Pickling, pickling, pickling." Three times he pressed the release button on the control stick at three-second intervals and half our CBU load departed the ejector racks a few feet below my seat. Cutter lead's CBUs had glittered in the dark below like a thousand Fourth of July sparklers. The cluster bombs saturated the area on both sides of the road for a half a mile.

Lead called, "Cutter lead's off."

Nail 61 excitedly exclaimed loudly over the radio, "Wow, lead, d'ju see that explosion after your pass?" At that instant, bright yellow tracers began to spray up at our bird from the two o'clock position. Randy responded in mild panic, "Fuck me. They're hosin' our ass." The CBUs were away. Randy jerked up and banked us to the right and then quickly back left. Another barrage of a dozen or more red tracers spraying in single file streaked toward us from our four o'clock (to the right and behind us) in a quick burst. I could hear Randy breathing rapidly and heavily over the loud swooshing of my own exhalation. Sounding almost out of breath, Randy called out over the radio, "Cutter 2 off."

Lead remarked coolly, "Looks like you woke the gunners up. Lead's downwind."

Randy and I grunted in unison to counteract the heavy G load on the pull-out to gain altitude quickly in case we got hit. That was the only assurance for survival after a direct hit—get altitude and head east over the South China Sea less than five miles away. Showing me the first signs he was not out for any hero shit, Randy admitted, "Bee, we ain't doin' multiple passes on these fuckers. I'm unloadin' the rest of it on the next pass."

A side of me sighed in relief to hear his strategy; another side was horrified at the realization that, knowing the gunners were down there in at least two different positions, we would be going through for a second pass. What else could we do? Say we were scared and would rather take the CBUs back to Da Nang rather than tempt all those colorful tracers again? We were big bad fighter pilots and we had no say in the matter. You go for as many passes as you need till you run out of bombs, then you go home--not before.

The fighter-pilot lifestyle was blanketing me in a palpable sense of panic. I glimpsed myself for a brief instant, the ex-Muncie Bearcat would-be basketball star. I was scared to stiffness and fell back on the only reassurance I had—just do the frickin' job and don't crack on Billington. He had stared tracers down before; he would get us through it. Don't crack 'cause the word would get out and I'd be finished, defamed, disgraced as a weak sister, one who couldn't cut the mustard when the going got tough, one's worst nightmare. When you've chosen to compete in a world of bravado among professional heroes and warriors, you die rather than not live up to their expectations. It is the beguiling deception, the manner in which the old cajole the young into fighting their wars. The youthful bliss of naiveté is that fragile period of early adulthood when one can become enraptured by the nobility and honor in facing the mortal dangers of a questionable cause that may rip off one's life.

Cutter lead called in, "Lead's in and hot."

"Roger, Cutter lead, You're cleared hot." Just like that, the doom and danger of war were becoming routine. I was losing my virginity. Several secondary explosions had gone off, and fires could be seen on the roads below. I knew the supply-laden vehicles had to be burning down there; it flashed in my mind that military personnel with limbs on fire had to be running screaming into the jungle night aflame like escaping scarecrows. Our engines vibrated and issued their familiar whistle as Randy throttled back as we raced around the elliptical orbit maintaining our spacing on lead. The early-morning darkness illuminated once again with tracers as gun barrels opened up on lead just as he pickled his ordinance. This time, however, a third gunner woke up and sprayed his 23-millimeter shells accented with green tracers at lead from the east side of the road. Three different positions worked us over while we gutted out wings-level passes dropping our CBUs. It was madness and combat heaven rolled into one. I expected one of us to get shot down that night. Warnings from training flashed in my mind like neon signs in the red-light district in Muncie—"Never let the tracers stop moving on your canopy." As long as a tracer's light is traveling, it is not on a collision course with your aircraft. If the tracer stops moving, it will intersect your flight path. There may be only seconds available to initiate jinking to avoid being hit. The white sparkles of lead's second drop flashed and streaked, overlapping the road below. It was like witnessing the scene of a rock concert with ten thousand flashlights and candles waving above the heads of adoring fans.

As we watched lead getting hosed, the paralyzing thought hit me: *I'm being paid to do my job as an F-4 copilot. The North Vietnamese gunners on the ground are doing their job. There is no way out for any of us; we do our job until one of us gets killed. If we live through the mission, we go home, get more bombs, and come back again.*

Randy's voice over the interphone brought me back to consciousness. "Okay, Bee, turning base. You got lead in sight?"

"Firmative! He's pulling off now," I responded confidently, straining to stretch my neck muscles under the G load to look over my shoulder out the canopy window. Lead called off, "Cutter lead's off, Winchester." His Winchester call told us he had emptied all his ordnance and was out of bombs. Lead had dropped his CBUs in two passes to avoid the exposure of multiple attempts.

Randy jubilantly exclaimed over interphone, "Shit Hot, lead. Two fuckin' passes, and we're outta here." We called in on the road, "Cutter 2's in, hot."

Nail cleared us. "You're cleared hot, 2. Heads up!" Our engines surged as we descended on final, picking up the disarrayed truck traffic left scrambling from the detonations along the road. I made my usual call-outs, "Ten thousand feet, 420 knots, twenty degrees of dive."

At four thousand feet, Randy leveled the bird off and began gentle banks to line up right over the road for our release. "Okay, here we go," Randy mumbled.

"Pickling aaand pickling."

I made more call-outs. "Three thousand feet, 450 knots, five degrees of dive." Suddenly, from the right side bright green tracers pissed up at us from the high ground adjacent to the road. They headed straight toward us and fell off quickly behind as our speed seemed to outrun them. Randy had to hold the bird steady just for a moment to let the last CBUs gain separation from the canisters fixed to our ejector racks. An early pull-out could have been disastrous if we bumped into our released cluster bombs. The gun position on the left opened up with a vengeance. "Fuck me. Here it comes," Randy uttered with a groan in his voice. The aircraft shuddered for an instant and the engine compressor blades coughed, trying to catch up with the surge in thrust after Randy slammed the power levers full forward to escape the flak. Tracers were whizzed past us on both sides like dozens of meteors shooting through the universe. We were bracketed. It was a real-life video arcade.

The CBUs fell away; looking back over our left shoulders and grunting to counteract the Gs, we could see hundreds of detonations from the bomblets sprinkling the countryside lining the truck route. Observing the fireworks from his orbit, Nail 61 transmitted his approval. "Shit Hot, gang. You got two huge secondaries." Shit Hot, often softened to Sierra Hotel, was a combat exclamation of acclamation or approval—way to go, right on, yeah! Outta sight.

Randy, unimpressed that the results were equal to the value of our asses, simply noted in a hushed tone, "Fuck me." We called off the target and requested Cutter 1's position. They had climbed up after their last pass and were waiting for us feet wet. Checking the compass radial and distance from Dong Ha navigation radio that they had reported, we knew where to look to find their flashing red rotating beacon to commence our rejoin. I spotted them first. "Tally ho, Randy, up high above us to the left side five or six miles."

"Roger, Bee, Tally." Tally was the shortened aviator term for visually acquiring a target or object. "Tally Ho," I have the target.

With a huge exhalation, Randy shook the control stick and commanded, "You got it, babe. Join lead and take us home. You want a radar-controller-guided approach or a visual?"

Feeling like a seasoned veteran in that relieved instant, yet not confident we had really survived the mission, I offered the facade of the fearless copilot. "Roger that. I got the bird. I'll take a radar-controlled approach."

"You got it," Randy came back. "I'm going cold mic and taking my mask off." Immediately, I smelled cigarette smoke emanating from the front seat. In consideration of one another when we intended to briefly remove our oxygen masks, we positioned the interphone switch from hot microphone to cold mic to block out the annoyingly loud swishing noise in the cockpit. After the orgasm of cheating death, Randy was having an illegal smoke. Exhilaration and triumph surged within me as I rejoined on Cutter lead's wingtip. The orange glow of predawn light illuminated the dark blue distant horizon spreading into infinity across the South China Sea. My skin tingled from the goose pimples that frolicked, tickling the surface hairs under my sweat-soaked flight suit as I concentrated on creeping the two throttles in my left hand back and forth in half-inch increments to keep that two-inch green wingtip light superimposed on the emblem of the red, white, and blue U.S. Air Force star on the fuselage of the lead Phantom. That was the visual reference for perfect wingtip fighter formation with a mere three feet of space separating our aircraft. I stole a split-second glance at my airspeed indicator—320 knots. I couldn't resist the urge to showboat and impress Randy with my formation flying. I tucked it in real tight. I felt bold—cocky almost—as if I had just won the Muncie sectional basketball championship with a fifteen-foot jumper at the buzzer. Living through the first strike in North Vietnam was a fine moment in my life—that brief space, that stingy flash of awareness when one's very existence seems somehow vindicated, empowered, and worth it. The shallowest of victories was feeding my jubilation; I had merely survived a night combat mission in North Vietnam. The surging pride and glee erupting inside me instantly disappeared and was be replaced by a cold terror and loneliness in my heart—the realization that what lay ahead was the challenge of surviving these combat missions for another eleven months.

The radar approach controllers gave us vectors away from Cutter lead to set up the spacing for the landings on Runway 35 back at Da Nang. I flew a good instrument approach down to minimum even though the weather was clear, and made a grease-job landing, exchanging control of the bird shortly after touchdown so Randy could keep it aligned with the nose wheel steering. "Nice fuckin' job, Bee. You're gonna be okay over here," Randy said as we turned off at the end of the runway. We stopped at the de-arming area to have our ejector rack safety pins reinstalled, then taxied to the aircraft parking revetments, shutting down our engines on the signal from the crew chief standing on the ramp below us. Daylight was slowly creeping across the airfield.

After finishing maintenance debrief, Randy asked if I would like to stop by his quarters to rap for a while. I was pleased to receive his invitation--maybe it meant I had gained his respect. Despite the alcohol smell on his breath, which I had forgotten around the time we started engines two hours earlier, he had my respect for how cool he had been.

Wearily, we shuffled into his room after turning in our combat gear at the personal equipment shop. His room was neat and orderly. A dozen or so books lined a makeshift bookshelf. The walls were a light vanilla color--the Air Force must have gotten a good price on a few million gallons of off-white paint. Randy dragged over a chair from the corner and set it beside the other chair facing his desk, asking me with laidback cockiness, "How about a stiff one, Bee, before we call it a night?"

Without hesitation, I responded in rare white guy vernacular, " Fuckin' A-- sounds great!"

He grabbed a fifth of Smirnoff from his well-stocked liquor shelf, retrieved two clear water glasses, probably from the chow hall, and set them down on the desk. Pulling a quart of grapefruit juice from his small fridge, he apologized for having no other chasers. He lit a Marlboro King and leaned over to light my Salem. He filled our water glasses two-thirds up with straight vodka and politely handed me the grapefruit juice can to top off my drink. Fixing his own, he raised his glass to me and said, "Shit Hot job, Bee. Here's to helping get both our asses out of this fuckin' place alive."

"I'll drink to that," I exclaimed, feeling the relatedness and acknowledgment of a fellow fighter pilot being bestowed on me. Both of us took down half our glasses with the first gulp, finishing the swallow with that familiar *ahhhhhhh.*

With a twinkle in his eye, Randy looked at me in all seriousness and compassion and said, "You poor bastards have to be here for a full-year tour, right?" I nodded. " No more hundred missions program for you guys, right?" I nodded again. "Well, you know, Bee, if you sleep twelve hours a day every day, you'll only be here six months. If you drink the other twelve hours, you'll never be here at all."

I cracked up with laughter at the brilliance of his simple logic, and for the first time glimpsed part of his survival strategy for getting through the war. From the titles on the books he read, I could see he was deeper and more thoughtful than most Air Force officers I had met, probably an intellectual in disguise who drank a lot. As I composed myself, I echoed the words spoken between Humphrey Bogart and Claude Rains in the closing scene of *Casablanca:* "Randy, I think this is the beginning of a beautiful friendship."

CHAPTER 6: "GUNFIGHTER 5, COME IN"

The shift change on one gloomy rain-soaked evening in early November 1968 took place at 1800 hours (6 PM). The base had been pelted with heavy thundershowers throughout the day. All three gunfighter alert crews changed shifts at the same time. Each crew was made up of four crewmembers flying two F-4s. The alert crews were designated Gunfighter 1 and 2, 3 and 4, 7 and 8. The two F-4s assigned to the air defense command commitment, Gunfighter 5 and 6, also had a crew change. The incessant showers had dulled the twelve-hour-duty day; it was too nasty out for war. The Gunfighter crew to which I was assigned had not flown, and after work, we did our usual thing, signing off from alert duty, leaving the alert trailer, going to the personal equipment shack, hanging up all our survival gear, and checking in our .38-caliber pistols. On this rain-soaked night we went directly to the DOOM Club to have our routine lavish supper, a few drinks, and some evening camaraderie before returning to quarters for shut-eye. We would repeat the duty routine the next morning, checking back in for gunfighter alert for another twelve-hour-duty day.

Alert duty, as all the fighter jocks knew, could be a high-pucker ordeal of adrenaline and sweat or a mind-numbing incarceration in a protracted boredom of not getting dispatched on a mission. It was a static experience, being holed up for half the day in the dilapidated mobile home trailer referred to affectionately as the alert shack. It broke the monotony to fly at least once on a duty shift. The operation was finely tuned: the claxon phone would sound and the first crewmember to get to the phone would answer it and announce loudly which crew was being called up. The designated Gunfighter crew scrambled out of the shack and sprinted the twenty or thirty steps to the waiting birds, scurried up the ladder to their Phantom, cranked the powerful JT-79 Pratt Whitney engines, took off, flew the combat strike, and returned to Da Nang, normally in less than ninety minutes. Maintenance debrief routinely followed engine shutdown.

The airplanes were serviced and reloaded with ordnance. When the munitions and maintenance people finished recocking the birds, they called the command post to confirm that the alert birds were mission ready, at which time their crews were officially back on duty.

Earlier on in this day soaked in dreariness, Major Yale Davis and Lieutenant John Reilly were the crew tagged for the most boring alert assignment. They were saddled with the Air Defense commitment, Gunfighter 5 and 6, an alert mission rarely called to action. The likelihood of an enemy air attack on Da Nang was remote, but that was the precautionary role performed by Gunfighter 5 and 6.

The GIB in Gunfighter 5, Lieutenant John Reilly, had been warm and cordial in welcoming me to Da Nang my first night on the base. Major Davis was the maintenance officer for the 390th Tactical Fighter Squadron. On this night, a mission assignment had been issued from 7th Air Force Command Center in Saigon for a special sortie that sent them off to fly what was referred to as MIG Cap for the B-52s flying Combat Sky Spot Operations, the saturation bombings along the border between South Vietnam and Laos, the A Shau Valley. The weather in Vietnam was in the initial phases of the monsoon season deterioration and deluges were arriving more frequently. All returning combat sorties were forced to execute ground-radar-guided instrument approaches back into Da Nang. Bad weather and low visibility conditions frequently required military traffic controllers to guide flights returning from combat missions back to the runway utilizing radar scope information.

In the midst of the gregariousness at the officers' club over medium-rare steaks and burgundy, our evening was shattered by word from the duty officer who rushed up to our table. He announced that Major Davis and Lieutenant Reilly had mysteriously disappeared ten miles north of the airbase. It made no sense to any of us sitting there with gaped mouths, peering at one another incredulously. Reilly and Davis weren't on a strike mission; they weren't doing multiple bombing passes on enemy troops. They were armed with radar-guided Sparrows and heat-seeking Side Winders to defend against unlikely MIG attacks from North Vietnam on a high-altitude B-52 bombing mission. Yet, incredible as it was, they had somehow gone down. A buzz of chatter rapidly swept across the dining room. The gossip vine unleashed innuendo that made it sound like a Gunfighter flight bought it on final approach, coming back in for their ground-controlled approach to Da Nang, normally totally safe, but not this night. From intelligence briefs, we knew there had been sporadic incidents of arriving aircraft taking ground fire on final from miniature fishing boats referred to as sampans located in the bay on the approach to Runway 17L and 17R. The weather this night was dog shit; it was inconceivable that anyone, even the most zealous Vietcong warrior, would have been out there. But that was the only logical conclusion available we self-appointed Sherlock Holmes could arrive at that made any sense as to how Major Davis and Lieutenant Reilly had gone in—no chutes, no beepers. We were left with our informed speculations and wishful explanations on what could have possibly happened so close to the base, ten miles from landing. A few weeks later, the accident investigation board sorted it out.

After reviewing the voice tapes from the Navy Ground Control Intercept site, they determined that Gunfighter 5 had been given a heading change inland from the South China Sea for vectors to the final approach course. It was a heading that would take them directly toward the high terrain west of Runway 17L centerline intercept course. The approach controller also gave them a descent to three thousand feet. Tragically, confusion over a radio frequency change resulted in delayed contact with the final approach controller after they had been given the doomed clearance to descend and head west toward their demise, slamming into a high ridge just west of Da Nang.

In that one minute of radio frequency confusion, they lost their lives. John Reilly was a fellow student pilot from Laredo Air Force Base, clean-cut and sporting a flattop hairstyle—an Air Force officer. He was six foot, athletic, had a wife at home, and was a short-timer, close to completing his one hundred missions in North Vietnam, among the last lucky group of pilots on this program. Reilly had ninety-seven missions and was within weeks of going home. Major Davis and Lieutenant. Reilly lost their lives but left the rest of us behind alive, yet feeling more lost, lacking answers. The vision burned into my memory of a jubilant Lieutenant Reilly two days before the crash, euphorically swirling around the squadron, thrusting fat cigars at everyone he encountered, being the proud recipient of congratulatory slaps on the back over the birth of his son whom he had named Brian.

Despite being highly skilled, well-trained professionals, pilots still have a sad history of letting ego and neglect get in the way of safety, causing them to blow it too often in aviation mishaps. One of the occupational hazards a pilot always lives with is the possibility that a situation will occur that is beyond his or her means to control, a slightly greater consolation than a catastrophe caused by the stupidity of a dumb mistake. Many operating procedures have been compiled over the years for all the aircraft ever built, based on the mistakes that crewmembers and support staff made before others followed them in flying that equipment. It was always an eerie notion to be aware that many of the dos and don'ts written in our pilot manuals were placed there as a result of someone screwing up and learning the hard way what gets you killed or what happens if you fail to follow a certain procedure. No aviator wants to be the propagator of a warning, caution, or note. Yet that was the fate of Major Davis and Lieutenant Reilly.

After the accident board investigation was completed, it was determined that a radio malfunction had been the proximate cause of the crash. A new operational procedure for flying ground-controlled radar approaches into Runway 17 at Da Nang was implemented. It read simply: **No pilot shall descend below 3500 feet within 10 miles north of Da Nang until it is verified by radio navigation equipment that aircraft position is aligned east of the runway centerline**. With this guideline in place, given the high country just west of Da Nang, there would be no chance that the circumstances that killed Reilly and Davis would occur again. As simple as that, the problem was fixed, but at the cost of two fathers and a $2.5-million fighter-bomber.

CHAPTER 7: CHINA FANTASY

It was mid-November 1968. By reflecting on my geographical roots, I knew the fall chill was sweeping across Indiana, forcing the sycamores to shed the last of their summer bounty; Da Nang was hot with war. Two months had not yet elapsed since my arrival, but I was ready to pursue Bill Cobb's wise counsel to get out of Dodge every opportunity I had. I was busy making a break for going somewhere— anywhere.

My Da Nang bar buddies, Alex and Carl, had shared enticing yarns detailing their escapades with women and, oh yeah, shopping in Hong Kong. They schooled me on what to do when I hit the ground. I booked myself at the Astor Hotel, which was not like the Astor I imagined in New York, but a twelve-story four-star hotel, certainly finer than what I was accustomed to at Da Nang. The best feature was the absence of ground fire and not once did I worry about a rocket attack, but, strange as it sounds, the bizarre thought still crossed my mind.

The Da Nang brothers told me tantalizing tales of the best places for nightlife and made me promise to check out the Show Case Lounge. They described delicious details of the soul music played at the Show Case and the really hip Chinese chicks who hung out there, a lot of whom would be night ladies in waiting.

It was a soothing body shock to rest up after the hour and forty minute trip in from Da Nang, take a shower, and, uncharacteristically, lay out my civilian clothes on the bed. I hadn't even packed a flight suit. Following a mini-nap, I put on my civvies, stopped at the bar downstairs, had a couple of drinks, and then strolled down the crowded streets of Hong Kong city as if I were in San Francisco. There were very few non-Chinese on the streets, however, everyone was Asian or Oriental, with a mild mix of Africans, but few African-Americans. My feet knew where to take me; I quickly strolled the five blocks to the party destination. I also suddenly realized I was going out without Celeste.

I walked up the steps to the Show Case Lounge, arriving early, just as patrons were beginning to trickle in. My senses were blasted with classic R & B sounds of James Brown, "the hardest working man in show business," doing his thing, and, boy, was I glad he was working on that turntable. I delayed taking my sunglasses off when I was inside the club. The darkness was overwhelming; I awkwardly staggered into the tables situated just inside the entry. It is a challenge, looking cool while crunching kneecaps into lounge furniture. Realizing that safety might be a priority over being cool, I slid off my sunglasses and folded them into my breast pocket. The Show Case was an intimate nightclub with a beautifully finished wooden dance floor that glistened clean and reflective. Seating consisted of slick red or blue vinyl chairs with bright silver specks or cushioned seats with backrests spread circularly in cozy booths around the club. Tables were adorned with symmetrically placed pear-shaped blue glass vases that magnified the shimmering candlelight dancing above wicks inlaid in wax. A small stage at the head of the rectangular dance floor had a maroon velvet curtain drawn closed across it, for occasional live acts I suspected. In the dim light, I observed intimate enclaves of Chinese women, appearing to be in their twenties to early thirties. A few brothers were scattered among the cluster of patrons, having loud fun, some of them with sunglasses, laughing and acting pleasantly stoned. A Chinese barmaid quickly came over to the table where I sat and took my order—Beefeater and 7-Up—which often produced a response of gagging from my buddies. Sometimes I ordered scotch, depending on mood or mission, and it was a tasty, enjoyable drink. So I sat there and sipped my gin, thankful I had stolen away from for my four-day escape to a mini-R & R. The basket leave program was a fantastic loophole in the Vietnam military leave process that some enterprising administrative type had devised for crewmembers in Southeast Asia. Personnel were only authorized one leave and one R & R during the one-year tour. To permit crewmembers to get out of the war zone as frequently as they liked, a concept of basket leave was conceived; it involved filling out routine paperwork to go on leave whenever the C-47 or jet transports regularly took GIs to exotic places like

Bangkok, Sydney, Australia, Hong Kong, and the Philippines. The leave paperwork would be stacked in the in-box of the first shirt, as the admin master sergeant was called. He would cut travel orders for personnel to board travel aircraft for transportation to and from destinations with the formal travel requisition approval of the squadron. Upon safe return, one simply approached the first shirt and requested he trash the leave paperwork. You took leave, but you were never formally documented as having used a leave. Through administrative trickery, we created numerous escape possibilities beyond the two seven-day leaves authorized in Southeast Asia. It was one of those rare good deals ever to be experienced by human beings perpetually in search of a free lunch.

After a couple more drinks, a wonderful relaxation settled upon me. The music was grooving; couples strutted and bobbed in soulful sway on the floor. Some chicks danced with each other, moved by the hypnotic thumping of the percussion rhythms and melodic groove of their favorite discs. Gentlemen numbers were thin in the joint and several women had no dance partners, a condition a would-be-hip guy like me could quickly discern. I was born at night, but not last night. I spied a group of four women sitting together, looking real cool, chewing bubble gum wide jawed in similar manner to the sisters I met listening to Sly Stone's music in Berkeley before I left for Nam. These ladies were dressed to kill; they looked like pageant contestants. Their skin was a creamy smooth yellow. One seated at the end of the table began to make eye contact with me but thoughts of Celeste kept intruding. Eventually, a squeamish bravado fought its way through shyness and I mustered the courage to greet them. I politely asked if I might sit down to visit with them. It was a square approach, but I had discovered that humility and backwardness seemed to be endearing qualities, rendering women incapable of denying puppy dog eyes a request for socialization. How cruel and cold would one have to be? I was beckoned forward, following a split second of teasing giggles. So I sat down with the Hong Kong hotties and created conversation. To my shock, their names were Francine, Helen, Ruthie and Genevieve. I was puzzled that they would have these English names; I felt disappointment. I concluded the Americanized names were for the benefit of the visiting GIs.

The lady in whom I was interested called herself Jennifer. She wanted to dance to the first record the deejay played after I sat down. Never having particularly considered myself a James Brown level dancer, I shyly resisted her nudging until a song with a jumping beat that would not excessively challenge my dance prowess was played. Finally, with the booze continuing to flow and the crowd loosening up at the table, I not only danced with Jennifer, but also with others. It was a dose of heaven. I felt like a repeat winner of the Kappa Tau Cavalier Man of the Year honor bestowed upon me by the Kappa Tau Sigma sorority back at Ball State. The lovely ladies sported sexuality and smelled like rose petals floating in bowls of peaches. The intoxicating aroma of their perfumes teased my senses, suspended my spirit, and cast me upon them like a honeybee that had discovered an acre of hibiscus. Absorbed in the fantasy, I indulged my desperate self. The male side of me was constantly sizing up and calculating if I really wanted to invite Jennifer to be with me that night. In my inherent predatory greed, I didn't want to commit too early to a "selectee" and find myself looking over my shoulder in second-guessing that I might have missed a cutie pie at another table staring wistfully at me as I departed. But I went for the long-haired brunette wearing glasses; probably on a subconscious level I seemed to be attracted to the crazed librarian type.

It was going to be Jennifer; I asked her, being careful to avoid sounding too much like discussing business, if she would be able to leave when the place closed up and accompany me. She revealed to me in the sexiest broken English flavored with a Chinese inflection that arrangements had been fixed with the person who coordinated their activities. She was required to log a certain amount of time in the joint, making sure that interested customers drank a certain amount of booze from which these establishments made most of their money. GIs, being quite eager to indulge their fantasies, were unbridled in their spending and withheld no expense to have a great time. Jennifer reassured me we could leave in another hour. We had a ball dancing while waiting for the time to strike midnight. I savored the notion that I was going to have this sweet-smelling girl in my arms just as soon as I could get her out of there. The anticipation alone invited a great rush of euphoria for my tormented spirit. Life teaches us that the pursuit of ill-gotten pleasure often produces a greater deprivation of the spirit than the desperation that inspired it. The Lord was messing with my mind, rubbing my nose in my anticipated sinfulness. Like a magnet, images and thoughts of a faithful Celeste back home flashed across my consciousness. For an instant, I felt remorse that she had ever trusted her husband to love, honor, and obey. I blinked hard and shook off those thoughts.

Time passed quickly in the swirl of the R & B musical groove. Soon Jennifer and I were walking nonchalantly back to the hotel as if there were no mission, but simply strolling and peering into store windows—an unnatural act for me back in the States. We chortled over the subtleties of Hong Kong life that most visitors would never have tapped into through the insider advantage of cavorting with a Hong Kong native. Jennifer shared her knowledge of the small hidden shops where the best shopping deals were to be discovered—obscure, out-of-the-way places that Joe Tourist would never have found. The multifaceted benefit of our relationship was revealing itself out of simple relatedness. After our soothing connection during the stroll back to the Astor, there was little ice to be broken upon arrival at the room. Barely able to keep my clothes on long enough to give Jennifer a feeling of welcome, I languished lightly in the crudeness of my haste, but my lady fair was no child and had been through the drill many times before with many others. Judging from her hip language and black slang, it was an easy conclusion that a long line of horny brothers had bagged her—or rather, she had bagged them.

I had to overcome one iceberg of distraction before diving into the fantasy: disarming my anxiety. I was fearful that Jennifer might have been ruined for satisfaction with me by having had her horizons widened by the sexual prowess of a long line of studly airmen with whom she might have previously bunked. Would it tax her acting ability to conceal a burdensome disinterest in having sex with me? I scolded myself for being such a dork, so wimpy and sensitive. My ego reminded me that, before I was married to Celeste, I had been a special, carte blanche pet to a mature prostitute in Nuevo Laredo named Conchita. She had adored and loved me every which way but loose.

Within minutes of settling into the hotel room, Jennifer and I were hugging in pre-game petting. I had a desire, maybe even need, to kiss. In the automatic rush of communion and feeling the invisible reassurance of warm arms around me, it soon didn't matter how many men she had been with and that, ultimately, it really didn't matter if the welcome mat was well worn. It was quintessential mind over matter, and no fighter jock worth a shit would let anything get in the way of enjoying that delightful, long overdue fieldtrip into intimacy.

The next morning, after a night of marathon sex, I was so heaped with appreciation for the previous evening's dancing and lovemaking that I began to work on another agenda, which was to know Jennifer in a more personal way. I accomplished two things, one of which was to share and have her feel a special relatedness with me, not simply as a GI who came to her country to get screwed, but as someone capable of caring about her life and her future. Number two, through befriending Jennifer, I would ingratiate myself and be elevated to the list of those who no longer had to pay for her pearls. With that mission established, we went for a breakfast of American steak, eggs, and hashbrowns in a Chinese restaurant. Afterward, Jennifer invited me back to her apartment.

I was game for whatever amusement was available in that sociological arcade of cultural diffusion. We proceeded down the main streets of Hong Kong, hopping a taxi to a more remote section of the city where high-rise tenements nuzzled one another, cluttering the urban scene, much like you might see on the south side of Chicago. It was incredible-Chinese ghettos. Not slum ghettos, but humble neighborhoods where low-income Chinese folks, who could have easily been on welfare in the United States, lived with five family members in one-and two-bedroom high-rise apartments. The towering tenements created a skyline extending upward like brick-and-mortar fingers that seemed to be clawing at the heavens.

Jennifer's apartment was one of those fingers. As we ascended in the elevator, there was a gagging permeation of odor, emanating from the Oriental cuisine being prepared on floor after floor. Yet it paled in intensity to the sickening aroma of the daily lunches the Vietnamese maids cooked in the hallways back at Da Nang. It was strangely surreal to step out of the elevator and walk into her cluttered apartment on the seventeenth floor and be introduced to her mother in Chinese, not one word of which I spoke or understood. Stranger still was to have it seem important to Jennifer for me to meet her mother. Yet her mother exuded casualness and detachment about my presence, which left me convinced this was an oft-repeated experience. While Jennifer engaged in routine daughter-Mama catch-up conversation, I was being mesmerized by the television channel selected in the adjoining room-an ancient 1950s *Tarzan* movie starring Johnny Weissmuller, with actors speaking Chinese. It was a twilight-zone scene. After talking with her mother for a few minutes, Jennifer asked if I would like to meet her sister, Beatrice. I was naturally amenable to all invitations. We proceeded to the bedroom and walked in on Jennifer's older sister sitting on the edge of the bed in a light blue terrycloth robe. Upon being introduced, Beatrice put her hand out to greet me and invited me to sit down across from the bed, not more than four feet away-more twilight zone. It was as if I were floating through a deep space dream without drugs, but no less like Alice in Wonderland. I sat there in the chair across from the two sisters who animatedly cackled with each other in Chinese, engaged in a kind of sibling bickering. It was impossible to force my eyes away from Beatrice's open robe, the front of which had three buttons dangling idly, allowing an unobstructed view of the vertical wink of her private peach peering into my face.

I began to sense beads of sweat popping out across my brow. My breathing seemed to lose its rhythm. Where was I? No one in the world knew my location in that instant. I had no idea if they were all hookers-maybe I was being set up to be robbed and murdered. *Fight the paranoia, man,* I urged myself.

Focusing on how my time in Hong Kong was slipping away, I pondered my got-to-do list. The reality of returning to Da Nang in two sunrises left me with a frightening chill. I had shopping to complete for Celeste. Distracted by my errant distractions, I confirmed with Jennifer that we would hook up again that night. She assured me she would be waiting for me at the Show Case. To spice it up, I suggested we could perhaps go to dinner. Bidding everyone a bowed-head adieu, I departed the scene.

Leaving in a dazed disbelief at the human menagerie into which I had ventured, I strolled casually, enjoying the ten-block trek back to the Astor. Once contentedly to my room, I plopped like a fallen California redwood across the cool bedspread of the freshly made bed and sank into a deep slumber. The nap mission completed by mid-afternoon, I showered for the second time that day and decided to browse the streets searching for the widely touted great bargains no one could pass up while visiting Hong Kong.

Captain Andy Krog was a navigator who had accompanied me on the flight over to Hong Kong and was staying in a room just down the hall. He and I had made earlier arrangements to rendezvous for a serious shopping tour on the afternoon following the second day of our visit. Krog was a camera geek; he knew camera brand names like I knew fishing equipment companies. I was enjoying a childlike enthusiasm, looking forward to his support and expertise on our shopping spree. I was also savoring the titillating notion of hooking up with Jennifer again that night, treating her as if she were my date this time. It was the first respite from the horror of my war reality. For simple sanity, I needed to hang out, do some dancing, and generally make the best of a wonderful situation, safe and removed from Dang Dang by the sea.

I returned to the Show Case and discovered a completely different crowd from the one I had experienced the first night, but from their dress and manner they could have been the same people. The same drinks and cigarette smoke, the same merriment and replacement stoned GIs from another base in Vietnam there on R & R. I sat at a corner table alone, drank, and waited in amused observation. I did not dance but simply engaged in the rhythm, bobbing my head in contented unison with the beat of the music, feeling like I was the isolated artist twin of Toulouse Lautrec transfixed in an inebriated gaze at the showgirls in the Moulin Rouge who swirled and twisted with the patrons of the dance. Jennifer never showed. I sat there fighting disbelief, still sensing that we had actually bonded and tapped into an intimate connection. I was solitary, hanging out in my social limbo, seeking solace in dancing with whoever was available. I got pleasantly bombed and staggered back to my room alone at 2 AM, mumbling reassurances to myself that nothing was missing. The three-orgasm snug-fest I had shared with Jennifer the night before had quieted my roaring libido—at least for twenty-four hours.

I slept deep and long that night, awakening late the next morning. I scarfed down a great pig-out breakfast of mushroom-cheese omelet, ham, and the Chinese version of hashbrowns, toast, butter, and jelly. Another nap was in order after wolfing down breakfast. Awakening two hours later and feeling adequately reconstituted, I delightedly prepared myself with a long shower and got ready to meet Andy. Something about growing up as a young boy with money shortages being a constant conversation in our home made me uneasy about spending money. I lobbied myself with reassurances that Hong Kong was the bargain capital of the world. I would never find cameras and jade earrings or lamps and stereo equipment—anything the mind could imagine—as cheaply any other place. Relying on Mama's guiding examples of bargain hunting and stretching the wings of the dollar, I embraced the circumstances and granted myself permission to liberate my indulgence. Once I was committed to spending money on something I really wanted, I took it seriously and did my research.

Andy and I went to a recommended shop where I found an exquisite Chinese vase with a detailed history dating back to the Ming dynasty along with a second ornate green-gold vase that was an exact replica of patterns from Chinese antiquity for my finely cultured aunt and uncle, Marlene and Bill, who lived in Detroit. I concluded the agony of indecision and settled on a pair of jade earrings for Celeste and got my single-lens reflex camera over which I was absolutely ecstatic. As soon as my feet hit the sidewalk outside the shop, I instantly began snapping its shutters to document the experience.

With the weight of the shopping burden lifted, Andy casually suggested we go to the top floor of the Hilton, supposedly a great place to have lunch. When we arrived at the Hilton, he checked the directory for the precise elevator stop for the rooftop restaurant. It was the ritziest hotel I'd ever visited, appointed with pendulous glass chandeliers in the cavernous entry registration area. I followed Andy's lead, working diligently to keep my eyes trained on him to avoid tripping as I struggled with the hick-from-Indiana urge to gawk at all the overhead adornments and walls lined with artwork. After Andy confirmed our destination was the thirty-fifth floor, the express elevator shot us straight up at a rate just short of a rocket launch. Our ears popped from the rapid pressure change; it was impressive but strangely unnerving.

Our ascent stopped abruptly and the door slid open smoothly, exposing us to the exquisite ambience of the plush high-rise dining room. An explosion of sunlight blinded us; we departed the elevator and were enraptured by the spectacle of the ten-foot high picture windows that lined the restaurant exterior. We were seated by the attractive Chinese hostess at one of the last remaining tables situated alongside one of the massive window panels. Our table was parallel to the window with place settings and high-back chairs for two. I was facing a section of window that swerved off concavely behind Andy; he faced a couple at my back in a similarly arranged table.

Country boy exhilaration filled my being. I gushed with simply being there—me, a smalltown dude from Muncie, in the Air Force, in Hong Kong, on the top floor of a luxurious hotel having lunch with rich folks from all over the world.

We ordered two beers and placed our meal requests. The server arrived within a minute carrying our Heinekens on a round wooden platter. I noticed Andy repeatedly staring beyond my shoulder as we made small talk waiting for our entrees. Suddenly in soft voice, he suggested I do a slow pan to my six o'clock position to check out the knockout blonde seated behind me. In that moment of suggestion, I thought, *Big deal.* I had never been so keen on blue-eyed Doris Day–looking blondes, but I slowly swiveled my head to take a ho-hum sneaky peek at the babe Andy was ogling. My eyes finally fixed on the visage of the blonde as she centered in my view. *Oh, my Lord,* I thought. Andy was right. She was a goddess, seated with a short-looking dude wearing a business suit. I struggled to maintain the composure of nonchalance as her eyes made contact with mine. I did an Academy Award–winning repeat performance, rotating my neck just as slowly back toward Andy.

Grinning, he looked at me. "Fuckin' knockout, huh?" She was lovely and wholesome looking, like a cross between Hollywood starlets of the sixties, Marilyn Monroe and Kim Novak, with deep-set emerald-green eyes that easily convinced me she was a mythical enchanted temptress. I knew no conceivable occasion could present itself to talk to her, so why, other than masochistic predisposition, should I bother to frustrate myself with a second peek? The waiter brought our food. I consoled myself, gorging on a huge chef's salad; Andy splurged on a thick, juicy T-bone. Before we were half finished, Andy suddenly shifted his head to peer over my shoulder again, commenting, "They're leaving, Bee."

I turned my head indifferently to the left to observe the couple's departure. Luckily, the business dude led the way out, and we got a prolonged eye-filling view of her shapely exit. She sported a tight-fitting bright green skirt with a matching bolero-type jacket covering a satiny looking white blouse with a turned-up collar. For accents, she had a large gold bracelet on her right wrist, a large beaded blue pearl necklace, and matching earrings. The snug knee-length skirt hugged a very round, firm athletic bottom. Smoke-gray stockings covered her dancer's calves. Her perfection was capped off with medium-blue pumps that coordinated perfectly with her ensemble. She was a knockout, and her wardrobe skills made her a triple knockout.

Catching myself with my nose fixed on her departure like a kid's face stuck to a toy store window, I turned back. Andy unabashedly stared until they left the restaurant. I focused on the ferryboats in the harbor carrying tourists and shoppers over to Kowloon on their forays into consumer adventures. It seemed too often that the mere image of a gorgeous female spontaneously triggered ridiculous fantasies of attraction and conquest, another strategy used by God to remind me of how weak and trifling I was. In an instant, she was gone with her lunch escort, who I concluded was not a husband given the absence of wedding rings on either of their fingers. I was relieved. Andy and I were free to refocus on the minor cleanup shopping that remained.

The afternoon whizzed by. For once in my life, I had done some homework before leaping into my discomfort zone of spending money. I had a complete list with backups of stereo speakers, turntables, amplifiers, and tape decks. I permitted myself to transcend the poor-man mentality of spending to fully engage this once-in-a-lifetime shopping opportunity.

By late afternoon, our mission was complete. Fifteen hundred dollars' worth of bargains had been acquired, packaged, and set up for shipment to the States or back to the squadron. Contented and exhausted, I needed a serious drink and a nap before for my last night in Hong Kong, silently dreading the dismal rendezvous the next morning with the bird taking us back to the combat nightmare waiting for us at Da Nang.

After a rejuvenating nap and long shower, I was ready for my last supper in Hong Kong and a final visit to the Show Case Lounge, hoping to reconnect with Jennifer, my first-night lover, or any other volunteer. Preferring to be solo, I had bid Andy, an "I'll catch you on the bus from the hotel to the airport in the mornin' " type hasta la vista. I never liked hanging out in herds when I was carousing.

I took supper down the block from the Astor at a quaint little Chinese deli named Fung Yoo Too. To give my stomach a good liquor lining for the evening, I ordered sweet and sour pork, rice, and two huge eggrolls. I had been introduced to that strategy of coating one's stomach with greasy foods to raise the tolerance for alcohol from the older boys rapping about drinking on "the corner" in Muncie. Heartily stuffed, I left the Fung Yoo, sweating like I had stolen something, and was in the street by ten o'clock. It was too early for the clubs to be jumping, but I had to get my party started quickly if I was going to hang out and create bedtime companionship for the night. I headed on autopilot for the Show Case.

Three blocks later I was climbing the dimly lit staircase leading toward the darkened cavern where intimate clusters of early patrons sat around the scattered cocktail tables sipping libations and listening to the R & B musical mix. The hostess approached and invited me to a seat, but I asked to remain standing for a brief moment to assure myself that Jennifer wasn't stashed away in a shadowy corner with her girlfriends. Having convinced myself of her absence, I asked the hostess if I could sit alone at a table adjacent to the dance floor. As soon as my butt hit the seat, a colorfully dressed barmaid who called herself Ming appeared to take my order of a Beefeater and tonic. I plucked a Salem from my shirt pocket and lit it.

My drink arrived and I barely got the first gulp down when my adjusted eyes fixed in disbelief on a table that I had passed by on my arrival moments before. I could just make out the left side profile of what appeared to be an attractive blonde seated across from a gentleman wearing a suit and tie. While toying momentarily with the notion of how overdressed the dude seemed in a hip, quasi-Black disco in Hong Kong, my heart fluttered when I realized it was the same couple seated behind Andy and me at the Hilton earlier that day. *My God,* I thought. *It's her. What the hell are they doing here? Do I try to say anything to them? To her?* With all these questions bombarding me, it became clear that subconsciously I had wanted to speak to this superstar beauty earlier, but had been in denial. The notion of taking action horrified me, especially with the daunting prospect of rejection. But that invisible, depraved force deep within moved me to the conclusion that I had to say something. Was it a mystical sign or lesson? Was God teasing or teaching me? I at the very least had to talk to her, even if the utterance were as simple and lame as "You are beautiful. Please let me sit beside you and simply gaze upon the flush of your feminine pulchritude."

Spying on the couple as they sat there chitchatting across from each other, I observed the companion assembling a number of empty beer bottles before him. Ah-ha, I reasoned. Three bottles should inspire a not-too-distant trip to the head for bladder relief. That would be the occasion for my strike. The lounge was slowly filling with more patrons—a few Black GIs with Chinese chicks and small clusters of young women hanging out together. The decibel level of the music increased. I ordered a second drink, waiting like a lion poised to strike an unsuspecting prey. No sign of Jennifer.

Soon the gentleman friend rose from the table, awkwardly patted her on the shoulder and headed for the men's room. With shaky, stiff knees I pulled myself upright, crushed my Salem in the ashtray, and approached the blonde. I moved along her left side and, leaning over to get close enough for her to hear my words over Smoky Robinson's "Tracks of My Tears," I whispered, "Excuse the intrusion. My name is Brian, and I just wanted to say I regret not being able to spend my last night in Hong Kong with you."

As she turned her head quickly to look up at me, a look of shock came across her face and she instantly responded, "I beg your pardon."

Before she could think or leap up to slap me, I continued, "Please forgive the intrusion, but after noticing you at the restaurant this afternoon, I was so taken with your beauty that when I saw you here tonight, I couldn't help but tell you that I regret not being able to spend my last night in Hong Kong hanging out with you before returning to combat in Da Nang tomorrow. I sincerely meant no disrespect."

A countenance of compassion came across her mesmerizing face. I presumed she would say thank you and I would be on my way, having delivered my message in a bottle. To my shock, she stood and extended her hand, saying, "What a nice thing to say. I'm Donna." We shook hands for a few seconds; the tactile exchange sparked magic. The music shifted to another Smokey Robinson hit, "Going to a Go Go." She blew me away further, motioning in tempo with her body as if overwhelmed by an uncontrollable desire to dance. "Would you like to dance, Brian?"

Foolishly and feigning an absurd observance of manners and sensitivity, I hesitated, saying, "Well, I don't want to intrude on you and your date."

"No problem, Brian. He won't mind."

Huh, I thought to myself. She must know him well enough to realize he really is cool about that sort of thing or maybe she doesn't care what his reaction would be.

It was like a slice of ephemeral heaven spinning and twirling to the music inches from Donna as she moved and swayed rhythmically like a single pink rose suspended in a soft breeze, close enough that the fragrance of her cologne intoxicated my overflowing senses. Music was always wine to my soul. Donna and I became lost in our communion with the swirling reverie of the musical paradise. James Brown's funky cut "Popcorn" came over the speakers without a break from the previous number. We both noticed Donna's date finally return to the table with a sheepish grin cast our way. I had hoped he would have gotten mugged and dragged into the alley or perhaps noticed what a great time Donna and I were having and decided to go home. Donna issued a furtive wave his way, acknowledging his return. I loved James Brown songs, especially "Popcorn" and "Cold Sweat." Donna seemed to have a little soul herself. She hung right with me, not that that was such a feat of talent. Then, the deejay, as if answering my prayers, shifted the mood to Aretha's megahit "Do Right Man."

An infusion of guilt penetrated my conscious mind. By my actions and intentions, I had disqualified myself as a candidate for Celeste's "do-right man." The bizarreness of the scene was intensifying--I was convinced some supernatural power had taken over. I slowly pulled Donna to me for a third dance; this one was slow and called us into embrace. The dance gyrations of the up-tempo tunes had made us both damp and steamy and our bodies shared their wetness. I leaned my head close to Donna's and sang in a vibrating softness into her ear, permitting my lips and cheeks to guide her into a romantic trance with me.

Tasting Donna's perspiration, while holding her, was more than I could endure. Chivalry called--I had to be a gentleman. I furtively kissed her beckoning cheek, still caressing her gently, neither of us realizing that the music had stopped. Shaken back into the reality of silence as the deejay paused between cuts to permit the crowd to leave the dance floor, I thanked Donna from the bottom of my heart for so unselfishly sharing her time to dance with me. I escorted her to the table and she introduced me to her date, John. I apologized for briefly monopolizing Donna's time and acknowledged him for being so accommodating and patient. Before there was time for further interaction, I escaped the club and was off into the Hong Kong night.

I proceeded down the street for another bar, any bar, to choose a date for the remainder of my last hours in Chinatown. The streets were bustling with night activity; it was a menagerie of neon glitter, horns blaring, lights flashing in carnival-style rainbow colors up and down the streets. People, clubgoers, and dinner patrons filled the streets headed for their evenings of fun. Within a two-block walk I found a quiet bar nestled between a stereo shop and a jewelry store. It was named Sayonara Lounge. How appropriate, I thought. The place was like a mausoleum—friendly dead. A handful of American soldiers sat toward the backside of a cozy dance floor being entertained by hostesses with small talk. A half-dozen various-aged Chinese girls sat scattered about the lounge sitting in straight-back chairs as if waiting for company to show up for Thanksgiving dinner. And I was that company. Surveying the prospects for companionship, I fixed my gaze on a petite, long-black-haired cutie pie next to the jukebox. I approached her and said, in foreigner's English, "Hi. My name Bee," to which she responded, "My name Helen. You buy me Hong Kong tea?" I rolled my eyes in mild disgust at her question, thinking, *Jesus H. Christ, I ain't been in this joint two minutes and I'm bein' pumped for my money already.* My internal reaction to Helen's businesslike response added to the blues that had begun settling on me after my exit from Donna. The saving ingredient was Helen's attractiveness. Her diminutive stature made her look like a young girl and her hair extended down her back over her bottom to her hamstrings. It was amazingly sheer and shiny, gathered and neat like a show horse's tail.

I was distracted and felt swallowed up, sinking deeper into a bluesy funk that my time in Hong Kong was drawing to an end. I wanted to flee the joint with Helen right then. I asked her if she could go with me; she had to go see the Mama San. Before I could stoke a Salem she returned to my side, forcing her body to snuggle to mine, and reported she couldn't leave until I bought her five Hong Kong teas, a weak nonalcoholic beverage for which they charged top cocktail dollars. A massive faux crystal ball rotated slowly overhead, casting off multiple rays of light that covered the lounge in flashes of rainbow hues, generating the illusion that the room was rotating like a carousel. Where was the reefer when you needed it? Not in the mood for negotiation, I quickly okayed buying five Hong Kong teas upfront and asked how much. It amounted to just under ten dollars to purchase her company off the property. She took the money to her boss who smiled back with a nod of approval. Helen eased toward the rear of the bar to get her small sport coat. Returning shortly, she approached me, clasped her hand in mine, and said, "You letty?" Realizing she was saying "Are you ready?," I laughed at the pronunciation and responded, "Sho am."

A world record was broken getting Helen back to my room and another record in sliding into the rack for some headboard smashing. I was embarrassingly unromantic. Bliss, it seems, always has a short lifespan, but there in a calamity of clinging and in defiance of libido's release, I attempted to prolong the anesthesia of intimacy; I felt humbled by a sense of acknowledgment and appreciation of Helen for even gracing me with the embrace of her loving arms. Inexplicably, from deep within the cave of remorse from which my mind's eye gazed, she became my mother, my sister, and my lover— perhaps the singular embodiment of all the women of the world from whom I craved love. The flow of emotion was too much for my tear floodgates to retain; I sobbed uncontrollably. Helen did not know the origin of the tears, or for whom they were shed. She seemed connected with me in an intuitive awareness that was best expressed through silence. In the mix of emotion, I realized I was crying tears that would be my mother's tears if I didn't return from Vietnam. There I was, a six-two, athletic, 190-pound fighter pilot in the arms of a diminutive five-foot, twenty-five-year-old Chinese lady/woman/girl/prostitute who began crying her own mysterious tears in partnership with mine. It was a most obscure communion of seemingly dissimilar souls isolated in a sixth-story Hong Kong hotel room, clinging desperately to each other's need to block out the pain and challenge of being human.

Freed up by the power of connecting hearts, I shared with Helen my disillusion with the war, along with my disgust with the ugly American politicians in Washington and their racism, arrogantly pursuing a war that was costing thousands of lives monthly. I was a prime player in that war game—an absurd contest from which I might also not depart alive. Strangely, oscillating back and forth between the in- and out-of-body experiences, I was possibly never more confronted by the trilogy of closeness, vulnerability, and humility than in that last night of intimacy in Hong Kong.

After making destination-free love with each other, Helen and I filled the deep, old-fashioned porcelain bathtub with water to within inches of spilling over and soaked long and playfully. She bathed and caressed every inch of my body and shampooed my hair after which, finding her generosity irresistible, I returned the favor. Helen was giddy with discomfort that I reciprocated the pampering. It was a delight for me to wash her fine hair, glistening in silky smooth strands down her back to the top of her girlish bottom. It was a visual mind-screw gazing on her tiny body, having to remind myself she was a mature young woman, virtually breastless, with large brown nipples and barely the hair of peach fuzz adorning her nest. We made love on and off throughout the night in synchronized spontaneity as if the lovemaking volcano of a lifetime was building toward eruption in one glorious finale. It was incredible, palpable, and unforgettable.

Shamefulness fluttered overhead in the gray clouds of my mind like filthy seagulls. There was a psychological stench in the air. How could I do this gross, foul thing? I had cheated on Celeste when I knew in my heart I would have been ready to slit my wrists were she to have succumbed to such mundane inclinations for mere sex. The horror that clawed at my heart was the numbing thought that she also might have had the same need for closeness in the private eternities of longing into which we both had been thrown. I wondered what kind of hypocrite sleaze ball husband I was. How could I rationalize my longing for my newlywed bride in such a profound surrender to another woman? This is the burning question for any human being who has been unfaithful. Yet, over and over, sacrilege and conquest are rationalized by the crazed neediness for refreshing nectarine on the parched, cracking lips of longing and psychic depravity. As a frightened warrior, I was also an endangered species. I had rationalized away myself. I deserved to party and have a good time, get all the leg that was available because I could be dead the next week. And thus did I crawl through the morass of consciousness.

The alarm clock sounded with a rude indifference to our blissful tranquility, shocking me back into the blur of a fuzzy unreality. The bus would leave from the front of the Astor at 6:15. I couldn't be late. I leapt out of bed, urging Helen not to get up. I shaved with dangerous swiftness and brushed my teeth, opting not to shower to preserve Helen's lingering aroma on my body. Quickly leaping into my pressed khaki brown uniform, I set my travel bag by the door. It was 0605 (6:05 AM), the reality check for the Hong Kong fantasy to be over. Spying the two inches of Beefeater gin remaining in the bottom of the fifth sitting on the dresser, I walked over and unscrewed the top, dismissing the thought that I would be showing up for the flight bombed at seven in the morning. I turned the jug up, gulping down the burning liquid with a familiar *ahhhhhh,* exhaling loudly. Sans comment, Helen had jumped up, put on her dress, and tied her long hair into a single bun. She wanted to leave with me. Overnight guests like Helen were against hotel rules, but, again, what were they going to do? I was out of there. Helen had written her address down for me on Astor stationery and asked me to please write her. I promised I would. I gave her a long, deep kiss.

Carrying my bag in the left hand and resting my right arm around her shoulder, we walked to the elevator and descended back into reality. The bus was waiting outside at the curb with its diesel engine spewing black smoke. Having paid my charges the evening before, I placed my room key on the checkout desk counter and bid them a wonderful day. On the street, the bright early morning sunlight forced me to don my Air Force–issue sunglasses. I turned and wrapped my arms around Helen one last time in what was not perceived as a permanent good-bye hug. Before we had left the room, out of an awkward expression of heartfelt gratitude, I had attempted to slip a fifty dollar bill, five times her usual fee, into Helen's hand, and she refused it, not so much insulted by the generosity, but more to honor the authenticity of our connection. I had been acknowledged. I kissed her forehead, turned, and boarded the bus. She stepped rearward and walked trancelike back into her world. We had promised to write each other after my return to Da Nang, as if there were any possibility generating out of the power of that union, that divine intervention would procure a future for us. But it was an illusion. I was tripping on life.

The short bus ride to Hong Kong International was over just as I was being overcome with the need for a serious nap. The Beefeater had kicked in big time. I was floating in my own body. Departing the bus, the other GIs and I shuffled out single file into the military section of the airport terminal. Sunglasses on and blue piss-cutter hat tilted forward, almost resting on the bridge of my nose, I floated dreamlike through the swinging glass doors. An excited female voice rang out, "Brian!" I turned my head in slow motion. As I focused on the source, I embarked on another out-of-body experience. It was the exquisite blonde goddess, Donna.

"Hey, what's happening?" I slurred, too cool and feeling no pain or neediness. "What are you doin' here?"

"I'm a travel rep for Qantas. We fly military leave and R & R charters back and forth to Vietnam. You told me you were going back to Da Nang this morning and I looked up your name and flight info, so I could come and say good-bye. Where did you go last night after the Show Case? As soon as you left, we tried to find you but you disappeared. Where did you go?"

Feeling too numb to be pained by her announcement, I responded, "I disappeared into the void."

"What?" Donna exclaimed.

"I lost myself in the refuge of humanity," I responded.

My enigmatic responses seemed to enchant her. I stepped out of the procession of GIs as she nuzzled close to me. I confessed that I was bombed from an early morning shot of breakfast gin. Knowing an hour remained before airplane boarding, and realizing I was on a booze and fatigue-induced space trip, she grabbed my right hand with her left and said, "Let's go get you some coffee, Brian."

I blurted out, "Why bother to sober up? I'm going back to the fuckin' war!"

"Come on, Brian," she pleaded. "You'll feel better." I squeezed her hand tightly at her overwhelming display of mothering, dug my heels into the linoleum floor, pulled her to a stop, and swung her around, abruptly pulling her close to my chest. I said, "I wanted to be with you so badly last night. I melt simply looking at your angelic face and body. I don't care; I can't help it. It doesn't matter. I'm a fool."

As if plugging into my temporary insanity, she responded, "I knew from the moment you left the table, I regretted letting you walk out of there. I wanted to spend the night with you too." At that confession, we embraced and kissed each other like reunited lovers who had been without each other for a hundred years. It was like the beach scene with Burt Lancaster and Deborah Kerr from the film classic *From Here to Eternity.* We shamelessly plunged our tongues deep into each other's mouths over the crescendo of catcalls and whistles from the coffee shop packed with uniformed Marine, Army, and Air Force personnel returning to Nam. Looking good was at its apex. As Sly and the Family Stone had sung, I couldn't have gotten much higher.

Donna slowly moved her head backward to retrieve herself from our kiss. She gently guided me to an open table and told me to sit down while she confidently made her way to the front of the canteen line for emergency coffee. Quickly returning, she asked how I took it. I couldn't say. She put some sugar in the paper cup and urged me to sip. She held my hand again. Tears filled my eyes. Why, I thought, was all this happening? Where were these women coming from? Why was God continuing to thrust these mind-blowing encounters before me? A numbed terror swelled within me that I was losing it, maybe having a nervous breakdown. I wanted to fly away out of my body and its war ordeal to escape; at the same time I wanted to crawl inside Donna and be protected from the horror show of uncertainty that my life was becoming. Donna was so overtaken with the weight of my anguish, she leaned over and locked her lips on mine again. I couldn't help but noticing the audience of GIs unable to keep their eyes off the first lieutenant and the magnificent green-eyed blonde beauty in the starched white blouse and skintight olive-green skirt. I was reeling through outer space, dazed in disbelief.

Donna asked me to pull my sunglasses down so she could see my "beautiful brown eyes." She anxiously asked if I would come to visit and stay with her in her Sydney condo on my next leave. I couldn't believe my ears; the fantasy might have a future. I desired to leave for Sydney that moment.

"Sure, Donna, that would be a trip. I'd love to visit with you," I answered, thinking the war strain had robbed me of rational thought. I squeezed out thoughts of "being taken," a married man, an irresponsible scoundrel.

The terminal loudspeaker announced the boarding call for the Pan Am flight for Da Nang Air Base, Republic of Vietnam. I took a gulp of coffee and turned back to absorb one final gaze into Donna's eyes and record the last visuals of her Aphroditean countenance.

I snapped back to consciousness as Donna said, "Brian! Brian!! It's time for you to leave. I'm sick that you cannot stay another night." I put my arms around her and thanked her for transforming my departure into a magnificent farewell. I kissed her again, one last juicy time, clamping my teeth down firmly on her retreating tongue; she moaned. We were showered with another wave of catcalls from the peanut gallery. I knew every one of those dudes, the white ones and the brothers, would have given their right gonad to trade places with me. I could only wonder, *Why me, Lord?*

Looking down at Donna's face, I told her I hoped we would soon see each other again. Donna pulled at my hand, still clasped in hers, to turn me back around toward her, and whispered in a gentle breath that warmed my face, "I love you, Brian." I squeezed her hand tightly, remaining silent, and, like an ancient Mandinka warrior returning to battle, released my grip of her hand slowly and gently, sliding my fingers away from hers and departed through the door without looking back. It was a last hysterical gasp of machismo; its source was a complete and utter enigma.

Once aboard the 707 jetliner I quickly collapsed exhausted into my seat next to the window. I shut my eyes and reviewed the video replay of my mind-boggling voyage. I continually curled my upper lip upward to snuggle it beneath my nose to sniff the opiate of Donna's scent until I passed out into the intoxicating burnout of spaceless unconsciousness.

Two weeks after my return to Da Nang, I received a wonderfully perfumed love letter from Donna in Sydney beside herself with excitement over our planned visit. That very day I had also been shocked by the news that some lieutenant colonel down at Seventh Air Force Headquarters at Tan Son Nhut had ordered an immediate end to the basket leave program. Worse yet, he had ordered an inventory of all leaves that had been taken retroactive to October 1, 1968, which meant the Hong Kong shopping excursion would burn one of my seven-day leaves, allowing only one seven-day block, my planned R & R with Celeste in Hawaii in two and a half months. With no basket leave flexibility, the fantasy visit to see Donna was purloined by Air Force administrative red tape. She would not understand why I could not visit her with so many months remaining on my tour. My gut wrenched and I felt queasy and sick to my stomach. I would have to tell Donna the awful truth that her fantasy Air Force lieutenant was a married man with a young bride waiting and praying for his safe return.

I wrote the letter after a week of anguishing. I knew three pages of explanation, rationalization, and apology would fall painfully short of offering any useful level of consolation because the timing was horribly off schedule. It always is. It was the right thing to do, the only responsible manly response. Once again, honor, integrity, self-respect, accepting my punishment—all those dynamics were up for grabs if I failed to act. A month after I sent the letter to the Sydney address, I received a reply. It contained all the words of heartbreak I had hoped to avoid, although they were justly deserved. I pondered hard and deep how her reaction could be so intense from such a brief encounter. I lacked vision to understand the heart of a woman and the power of the human dynamic. I was making a lifestyle of trampling on trusting female hearts, perpetuated by justifications rising out of my own psychic devastation. Unknown to myself, like the albatross in "The Rhyme of the Ancient Mariner," I was proceeding through life with an invisible sign roped around my neck that read "Don't Feed the Animals." I existed in functional contradiction, along with the protracted morass of my unreconciled childhood angst, I had become the monster who was eating the young of his own village. It made me wince and turn from the image I saw in the mirror. Personal transformation would have to take a backseat to the challenge of surviving the war; I would fight for virtues of honesty, integrity, and fidelity in some other place and time.

CHAPTER 8: PROVING MYSELF

One insight I gained from being a combat pilot was the truism that pilots who are number one in their pilot training classes don't necessarily make the best pilot instructors. Likewise, all people with Doctors' degrees are not the smartest among us. One memorable aircraft commander I had the challenge to work with was a PhD in English who had managed to sneak into an F-4 assignment and get stationed at Da Nang in the 390th. We'll name him Major Henry Larson. He carried a macho, gung-ho fighter-pilot disposition but with a short, squatty physique like a fire hydrant. Soon after his arrival at Da Nang, someone stuck him with the moniker "Bullet Hank." He masterfully acted out the fighter-pilot stereotype. Bullet Hank chain-smoked Camels, was always ready to get a drink, and loved talking about his last mission. He was one of those guys whose story would always top yours, no matter how great yours was. He had that trait in common with Perry, my first roommate at Da Nang, a tee-totaling-born-again Baptist navigator from Tennessee. Like Perry, it was an obvious flaw in his armor—the chink in his personality. He worked too hard to impress others and seemed to have an emotional stake in being acknowledged and respected. This predisposition to want to look good and impress others was a dangerous lure for pilots in combat; it could get you killed or, worse yet, the wrong people—friendlies on the ground. The irony of Bullet Hank was that he was a good stick, a solid fighter pilot who was at home in the airplane. He was bright and articulate, but he cared too much about being perceived by others as a hot jock. Unwittingly, he robbed himself of the very reverence he craved from those around him who witnessed his obsessive pursuit of it. It diminished his stature and detracted from who he was, ironically transforming him into a needy man, addicted to praise and approval. Awareness of his hunger to impress supplied unlimited psychological ammo to play games with him whenever there was a shortage of amusement.

Bullet Hank had come into the squadron less than a month after my arrival. I was not yet an old head GIB, but I was close. One Sunday morning in late October 1968, the maintenance officer for the 390th informed us that crewmembers were free to spray-paint their names on the canopy railings of their designated F-4s. It was a neat esprit de corps opportunity to have Lieutenant Bee Settles painted on the same bird with Major Randy Billington, as if our names validated us as authentic or maybe even important like a nameplate on someone's desk. Like a group of excited children on the playground, we leapt into the 390th bread truck van and duty officer Lieutenant Wes Darrell burned rubber getting us down to the revetments where our birds were parked. Major Billington had painted his name on our bird with the tail number BS 592 the day before. Maintenance had just completed minor repairs to the radar on our bird and this would be my chance to get the stencil and paint the white letters of my name onto the dark blue railing of the rear canopy. I felt a shy embarrassment that I was excited about such a simple prospect.

Lieutenant Schlichter, another pilot back-seater like myself, was using one of the two cans of white spray paint available, and I asked him to be sure and hand it off to me when he finished. He gave me a "Rog, Bee," and I trotted over to the maintenance office to retrieve my personalized stencil. An impish excitement cruised through my veins just looking at the cardboard stencil with the letters of my last name cut out, *B. Settles.* It was a warm Da Nang morning. The dark blue sky was dotted with scattered puffy cumulus clouds. The flight line was the usual cacophony of chaos and activity, the loud swishing whine of electrical power units running, the deafening roar of flights of fighters taking off into the unknown, and crew chiefs racing up and down the flight line in pickup trucks frantic with aircraft repair assignments. In less than two minutes, I returned to Lieutenant Schlichter's parking spot only to sight him walking empty-handed away from the flight line. I immediately shouted out, "Hey Slick, where's the spray can? I'm next."

"Bullet Hank's got it," he explained lamely.

"Didn't you tell him Bee Settles was next in line?" I shouted in frustration.

"Yeah. I told the asshole you were next with the can and he took it out of my hand, saying 'That's okay,'" Schlichter explained. I was pissed. As I approached the revetment where the Major's airplane was parked, he was having the crew chief position a maintenance scaffold so he could get his pudgy ass high enough to do the spray job. Without so much as a salute, I barked out, "Major Larson, didn't Schlichter tell you I was next in line to get the spray can?"

Nervously looking over his shoulder as if annoyed that I was interrupting his work to answer such a disrespectful question, he proclaimed, "Lieutenant, you can have it after me." By referring to me as lieutenant, the major was pulling rank. Turning to walk away, I faced the reality there was nothing as a subordinate I could do. I mumbled aloud, "I didn't think nobody would be pullin' no rank shit over a can of spray paint."

"Watch your mouth, lieutenant. You get the can after me, okay?" he scolded.

I barked out "fuck it," mostly under my breath, having learned many years earlier that discretion was the better part of not getting your ass kicked. Given the Pavlovian phenomenon of condition/response in the context of racial discrimination, I pondered whether race was involved in Bullet Hank's snub. I was careful in my outrage not to play the race card on him. In my moral intuition, I knew from Mama's teaching about honesty and truthfulness and her use of fables like *The Boy Who Cried Wolf* that the race card could lose its value if applied with indiscriminate irresponsibility. To preserve its moral potency, it was to be played only in the face of overwhelming, irrefutable evidence and preferably when the outcome of its presentation was predictable.

Fuming, I walked off the flight line to hitchhike back to my quarters. If spray-painting names on the side of an airplane was a big thing to Bullet Hank, I chose to prove my machismo by passing on the opportunity completely. I never got my name on our F-4, but I knew I would have to make peace with Bullet Hank someday if we were ever going to fly together safely and professionally. A month later it happened.

Whether it was out of guilt, or a desire to get to know me, or to extend an olive branch, Bullet Hank finally seized the opportunity one afternoon a month later to ask if I had flown any particularly noteworthy missions recently. Not feeling like much of a hero over my sorties, I told him I hadn't. Informing me that he was the new awards and decorations officer for the 390th, he urged me to tell him about any missions I flew that got good BDA (post-mission bomb damage assessment reports from a Forward Air Controller) and/or ground fire. He assured me he would take care of the rest. A few weeks later over a marathon dart-shooting session, a high achiever lieutenant from Kentucky named Jethro Ballard casually boasted of having received notification of approval for a Distinguished Flying Cross (DFC) for a mediocre mission, details of which he had submitted to Bullet Hank. Ballard expressed gleeful dismay that those details had resulted in a DFC award. He confided that the write-up had turned his routine bunker buster into a harrowing mission of great personal risk and daring bravery to accomplish a critical military victory for the Air Force in the battle against communism in South Vietnam.

Being a professor of English, Bullet Hank had a natural facility with the language and creative writing and was putting it to good use as the awards and decorations officer. I reflected on the grave individual risk and danger Carl Gamble had undergone to bring his burning C-47 and crew back to Da Nang alive for his DFC. I wanted no part of what I perceived as Bullet Hank's profanation of heroism and bravery by glorifying bullshit missions to make them read like horrifyingly dangerous, war-winning engagements. In protest, I refused to submit any mission I flew, even the search and rescue ones, which were regularly fraught with great tragedy and combat heroics. The major remained puzzled by my perverse macho refusal and I soon became his personal project. He was dying to know why Bee Settles was a respected, even popular, back-seater, but a different kind of duck than he had ever come across among Air Force officer types. He inquired one evening at the bar where I had gotten my above average vocabulary and way with language. I told him I had been a Spanish major and an English minor back at Ball State. His eyes lit up with surprise and delight that he might perhaps find some common ground, maybe a little intellectual camaraderie. He suggested we socialize sometime by ourselves.

It took a month, but our meeting of the minds was finally set up after returning from my fantasy week in Hong Kong, I decided to give in and not put Bullet Hank off any longer and agreed to meet one night in his room for drinks and conversation. It was like a date with destiny, one of those mysterious encounters that may have had a purpose not understood by the participants. When the evening finally arrived, I was intent on diffusing any notions he had about being the professor and I the naive student seeking enlightenment. Our chat that evening danced around many subjects—from life on the streets of Muncie, my being a disillusioned sports jock, academics, and, inevitably, racism in America. It was pure delight discussing great writers like John Keats, Carl Sandburg, and Walt Whitman with someone who not only had heard of them but read their work and could participate in technical analysis of "Good Fences" or "Leaves of Grass."

I relished discovering that Bullet Hank held discomfort and closet intolerance of the civil rights struggle at home in the United States. Despite being a professor at a military academy, working with the young minds of future Air Force generals, he was unmoved and reluctant to embrace civil disobedience or militancy as viable manifestations of revolutionary civil protest for effecting societal transformation. My articulation of the proposal made him squirm. He nervously slid his wooden chair closer with a screeching sound as it clawed the slick linoleum floor. He seemed to need reassurance he was okay there with me as I proposed the theory that anarchy could actually serve as a catalyst for promulgating expedited social and political change in society. Beads of sweat formed on his upper lip; for a brief moment, it appeared to quiver. He pondered my words with an expression of disbelief at what he was hearing and again sought the anesthetic relief of nicotine, lighting another cigarette. He inhaled deeply and forcefully blew the smoke out of his pursed lips.

The crossover of our relationship occurred magically during a discussion of our literary heroes. As he listened to my impassioned description of the examples provided by the lives of some of American literature's greatest proponents of civil protest and disobedience, Ralph Waldo Emerson, Henry David Thoreau, and James Baldwin, a light bulb of revelation seemed to go off in Bullet Hank's mind. Maybe, just maybe, I thought, he had begun to comprehend the language from the "other country" within a country from which I spoke and its value in advancing a democratic society that secured and preserved the rights of all its citizens.

From the extraordinary encounter with Bullet Hank in his room that night, in the thick smoke of mind jousting, a dozen and more Camel and Salem cigarettes, and many cups of gin and tonic, I felt a modest vindication for enduring his arrogance and condescension. I oozed pride that I had persisted in stating my philosophies about the war, racism, and protest back home. His respect for me had been solidified, if not his agreement with my views. Perhaps for the first time in his personal and academic life he was face-to-face with an intelligent African-American Air Force officer who had different convictions and cultural experiences. I was a fellow officer with views that were born out of the authentic circumstances of a Black man who had emerged from the small, simple streets of Middletown America, as Muncie was dubbed in the sociological study conducted by Robert and Helen Lynd in the 1920's.

But, despite the apparent breakthrough in understanding from Bullet Hank, despite the ongoing struggle for a sense of wholeness, self-worth, and dignity, deep down inside where the mirror never lies, there remained a gnawing sickness in the pit of my stomach. I felt a betrayal that I had sold out on the nobility of my essence. I was caught up in the snare of proving I was "good enough" to white peers by whom I ultimately wished to be respected, maybe even accepted. I was being guilty of the same charges I had leveled against my own mother, always struggling to be good enough and accepted as a professional Black peer among her white coworkers back in Muncie at the public library. Whatever private, unresolved conflict raged within me, an infantile hopefulness was nourished that night by a fragile conviction that Bullet Hank got that the differences between us had only to do with where we grew up. He recognized that all members of the brotherhood of man will react to given stimuli in life in a similar, predictable manner.

The intimate communion with Bullet Hank was one of the few subsurface interracial interactions I had in Vietnam on race and civil rights that I felt might have had any lasting impact. With Bullet Hank, the potential intellectual, I dared to reach out and be myself boldly, an act of self-dignity that was superior to submitting to the oppression of silence. From that day forward, a new Bullet Hank emerged, if perhaps for the wrong reason. It was as if being "cool with Bee Settles" was his status symbol around other squadron members. We never had another visit like that first one. I went to him one other time six months later to share a poem I had written for my classmate, Vince, after he bought the farm on a high-drag pass and Bullet Hank continued his tour making a regular point of letting others know in public he was an insider with me. It was another one of Vietnam's small consolations that I could be true to myself, be respected for it, and also good at my job as a pilot in a combat fighter. For me, nothing over there was really important, other than survival.

CHAPTER 9: BONDING FOR SURVIVAL

None of us knows how we appear to others unless we ask. In the hood back in Muncie, hanging out as a sports jock was my winning formula to acceptance until I figured out how to present the rest of myself to the world for approval or at least self-validation.

Choosing the F-4 flying assignment out of Air Force pilot training, a choice that I knew would subject me to a combat tour in Southeast Asia, was mostly about looking good. I loved wearing that G suit; it must have been a similar thrill for the cowboys back in the wild wild West who wore chaps and spurs. We all want to be admired as someone worthy and special, but I was naively seeking to fill the hole deep in my soul where the pain of infant abandonment lived. How could I have realized I was a vindictive subversive on a lifetime mission to make Willie, Jimmy Mac, and David G. pay for their abuse and teasing? My achievements would make them regret-- or better yet be ashamed--that they had taunted a young yellow nigga who would transcend the menial existence in Muncie and become a fighter jock.

Up in the blue, tucked unsafely away in the Phantom over Southeast Asia, I was safe from the playground discomfort of Muncie. I was a real jock, goddamit. Within the chameleon act of surrendering who I was, there evolved a temporary shallow victory of feeling good enough, absolved and okay with the ugliness and suffering in the world, a brother fleeing from his demons.

Being a philosopher at heart, my most treasured times at Da Nang were spent relating to the enlisted brothers who were scattered in various support units all over the base. I frequently met people in the chow hall, after the drunken forays at the officers' club until three o'clock in the morning. The mess hall was always open for breakfast from midnight until 0900 (9 A M). There were many days when I consumed two breakfasts, one on the way home from the club and the other when I'd wake up and go back over to the chow hall before it closed to begin the lunch setup. I would encounter airmen from the

Bronx, Watts, Harlem, and Cleveland's Hough district. These were inner-city brothers, many of whom might have been militant college students, factory workers, maybe thugs, pimps, or dope dealers had they been back on the block. Some had lived in poverty back home, but now they were on their way to Morehouse, the University of Wisconsin, Bethune Cookman, or Hampton Institute. They were all there, all treading water in the war morass.

I don't know where I met Staff Sergeant Thomas Ervin, probably in one of those blurry-eyed, wee-hours chow-hall convergences for breakfast after he had left the NCO club and I had staggered in from the officers' club. I recall first hearing his loud mouth, talking trash in the cafeteria to the serving dudes behind the long glass counter as they sloshed ladles full of steaming scrambled eggs, bacon, sausage, and that ubiquitous gravy and chopped hamburger stuff called SOS over biscuits onto our plates. We greeted each other with a synchronized backward thrust of our heads. He attempted to shake off the hold of his inebriation and slurred out an exaggerated effort for a proper greeting, "Good mornin,' Lieutenant, ssssir."

His lower jaw dropped down when I responded, "Hey, what's happenin'?"

He relaxed, issuing an instant compliment, attempting an unnatural evocation of proper enunciation, "Wow, an officer that can be down. I can dig that." Ervin was feeling no pain. He was not alone. Picking up our food trays, I asked if he minded my joining him. In further shock at my request, he replied more stilted and proper, "Yes sir, Lieutenant Bee Settles," which he saw from my name tag. The room was filled with small clusters of boisterous servicemen either numb from booze and needing food to soak it up or midnight shift workers getting off duty. Most of the tables seated four and were covered with white cotton tablecloths, each with a long-stemmed artificial yellow flower stuck in a single clear glass vase. The linoleum floors glistened with the shine of daily buffing. We sat down to have breakfast. Sergeant Ervin was in a stunned state, caught embarrassingly off-guard by my deviation from protocol and the usual table segregation that took place between enlisted servicemen and officers. He was quick to boast he was with the Red Horse Squadron, civil engineering folks. That announcement went right over my head. We inhaled breakfast; Sergeant Ervin did most of the talking, recounting his good time over at the Airmen's club. He rambled on about who he had been with and how much he had drunk to explain why he was bombed, not realizing I myself was too shitfaced to listen to all the details or even care about them. Finishing breakfast, we parted company simply saying, "Nice rappin' with you; catch up with you later" but with no commitment on either of our parts to make it happen.

On a dusty Da Nang afternoon a few weeks later in late November 1968, I was walking back to the compound from the 390th, engrossed in the haunting visage of cordoned-off squalor of the ARVN personnel (the Army Republic of Vietnam) living in GI shanties skirted in concertina wire on the roadside. I pretended not to stare at the ragamuffin offspring, standing naked and idle, many with potbellies, stationary like cupid statues devoid of bows or romance arrows. A peculiar embarrassment ran through me as peasants staring back at me interrupted my rude gawking at the pitiful scene of Vietnamese women. They were squatting down and preparing food or sweeping with homemade-looking brooms with wire or string tied around the bristles at the end of a stiff stick. I mused at the sight of these ARVN families and their seemingly wretched lives, wondering whether the war was making things better or worse for them. I was convinced the peasant Vietnamese babies living in the villages and hamlets throughout the countryside did not have distended stomachs from malnutrition as did these offspring of paid ARVN soldiers.

I barely noticed a green army jeep screeching to a stop in a swirl of dust beside me and a tech sergeant brother in camouflage fatigues saying, "Wanna lift, lieutenant?" It was Sergeant Ervin. I don't think he knew it was I until he had already stopped and saw my face. Content with my private walk, for an instant I lamented the intrusion, but I was excited to see Ervin again and exclaimed excitedly, "Hey, right on. Thanks."

Not believing I would remember him from that drunken morning in the chow hall, Ervin blurted out, "I'm Sergeant Ervin, 366th Red

Horse Squadron. You remember when we had breakfast at the mess hall a while back?"

Irritated that he actually thought I didn't remember him, I retorted impatiently, rolling my eyes in pretend disbelief, "Yeah, man, I remember you from that night. Not much else though." I introduced myself politely, but more completely from our previous encounter. "Brian Settles, 390th Tactical Fighter Squadron. The Wild Boars," I responded nonchalantly.

"Are you a pilot?" Ervin asked.

Pausing for a suspenseful build-up, I responded casually, full of pride at the admission, "Yeah, in the fighters."

Seeming shocked and excited, Ervin said in disbelief, "The Phantoms? You fly the F-4?"

"Yeah, copilot in the Phantom," I responded with an inner joy that praise and admiration were near.

"Wow, man—I mean, lieutenant—that must be a trip," Ervin said wistfully.

Shunning Ervin's attempt at military protocol, I came back, "Yeah, man, it's a trip. My nickname's Bee, like bumblebee."

"Wow, sir, I never met one of you pilots before. That must be a real trip flyin' them thangs. I always wanted a ride in one," Ervin confessed, looking at me as if I might be able to possibly hook him up.

"Yeah, man, it's a trip all right," I replied low key and matter-of-factly. I shifted the focus, admitting my ignorance. "What's the Red Horse Squadron do, Ervin?"

He immediately seized the chance to make a speech. "Lieutenant, you ain't heard of the Red Horse? That's the nickname for the civil engineering squadron here in Da Nang."

"Naw, man, what do they do?" I said, truly interested to know more about his work.

"We build every damn thing on this base. Construction! Chow halls, barracks, and offices, even clubs. We built them stalls y'all park dem Phantoms in," Ervin stated proudly.

With knowledge of what being a skilled building craftsman meant from my construction days in Muncie, I well knew what Ervin was proud about and asked him, "Are you a carpenter?"

"Yep," Ervin responded proudly. "Sure am. I build cabinets, shelves, wooden lockers, hang Sheetrock, roofing, anything." With the buildup that occurred in Vietnam from 1965 through 1969, it was absolutely phenomenal what these engineering squadrons were able to accomplish. They did it all. While Ervin was not an engineer, he told me he was a natural at carpentry and his Red Horse unit had made him a construction supervisor. He read blueprints, took detailed measurements with surveyor's tripods, laid out foundations, and guided the construction of a twenty-stall covered latrine, a mess facility, and a wooden barracks with sidewalls made of pine studs and Sheetrock. Red Horse workers installed hinged pull-down wooden panels that could be lifted up by ropes on pulleys, exposing wire mesh screens on the upper wall portions that ventilated the quarters or could be lowered to keep out gusty winds and rain during storms.

Envious of anyone who could build anything, I was impressed; Ervin had me saying, "Wow." The deafening roar of a ten-wheeler Army troop carrier whizzed by, spewing black diesel smoke and almost blowing our hats off, adding to the layers of dust already lightly accumulated on my flight suit. Thinking about the stereo equipment I had purchased in Hong Kong, I asked Ervin if he thought he could build a stereo cabinet.

"No sweat, Lieutenant Bee. You need to come by and see mine; I built me a boss cabinet for my shit," Ervin enthusiastically responded.

"Right on. I'd like to see it sometime," I answered, thinking this might be a great guy to be friends with. "Of course, I'd be paying you to do it Ervin."

"Oh, no sweat, sir. I can do it for you anyway, and you a brother too." Pausing, as if realizing he had made a presumption that might have offended, he asked, "You don't mind me saying that, do you?"

"Naw, man, I don't mind. People don't always know what I am," I confessed, relieved we had that bit of awkwardness out of the way. It was an awkwardness that showed itself too often.

"Well, I knew when you got in the jeep you sounded Black, but I had forgotten you talked Black in the chow hall that morning too. When I saw your light skin and all today, I got confused what you were," Ervin admitted, innocently honest, once again shattering my ears with the touchy words I had been hearing my whole life.

"Yeah, man, I'm a soul brother and glad to meet another brother over here tryin' to get over and make it back home. I'm getting off at the entrance to the compound," I informed Ervin as the jeep approached the entry point where the snappy, sharp military policeman, a brother named Red from Cleveland, was on duty. Ervin and I made a tentative commitment to get together, but, again, left each other no means to make contact. I thanked Ervin for the lift as I got out, and we gave each other the ubiquitous brother handshake. We agreed to get together down at his barracks to see his stereo cabinet. As he put his jeep in first gear before driving off, Ervin proudly threw me a crisp military salute, saying, "See you, Lieutenant Bee. Wow! F-4 pilot." I gave him the clenched-fist Black power acknowledgment, and he returned it with an opened-mouthed, life-is-good laugh peeling rubber in his Red Horse squadron jeep. I was left with that rare *ain't it good to be alive* strut as I walked the short block to my quarters.

Two weeks later, Sergeant Ervin and I crossed paths again by pure coincidence. I was enjoying a day off from the flight schedule and just finishing a third straight pickup game win on the basketball court. The scene was typical of all the pickup games I'd ever witnessed in Muncie, Indianapolis, Anderson, Tucson, or Laredo. Players were hustling to be undefeated since it was winner-take-all-comers. Losers leave the court and beg to be picked up by the next team waiting to take on the winners. It was great exercise if you got on a team with solid talent and could win four or five in a row. Otherwise, you sat on the sidelines watching a lot of ball playing and absorbing the nonstop banter and signifying that was the verbal fabric of the lower economic social experience on playgrounds across America. Vietnam was a microcosm of that cultural reality. It made any of us who came from that, whose psyches were formed by it, feel at home anywhere in the world—even Da Nang Air Base. It was our thing, not just playing basketball, but a tribal ritual of socialization, camaraderie, and competition.

Walking off the court giving a brother from the Bronx named Mookie some skin for hitting the winning fifteen-foot jump shot for us, I heard somebody holler, "Lieutenant Bee." Turning, I spotted Ervin at the far end of the court in his green Red Horse jeep. Strangely, I was thrilled and embarrassed at the same time as I waved back. I had not been at Da Nang long enough to know the regulars at the court. They realized quickly that I was courtwise, but did not know I was an officer and particularly a jet jock. Most were young airmen hoopsters who worked on the flight line, the chow hall, or in administration. The hoop court was a unique place where eighty percent minority representation in Vietnam was not out of line with inner-city playgrounds in America, but the minority imbalance of GIs in Vietnam was out of balance with U. S. society's ethnic makeup. The astute young brothers knew it and discussed it in impromptu rap sessions along courtside. The pervasive sense of racism and victimization in America and the military formed the social glue that kept most of us over there bonded.

I waved at Ervin to acknowledge his shout and walked toward him. Sweat beads slid slowly down each side of my face, taking turns splashing on the ground from beneath my chin. I slipped my GI–issue green T-shirt over my torso to break the chill of the cool breeze blowing across the open end of the hoop court. The attention of a few players at the court suddenly focused on the greeting being exchanged between Ervin and me—the familiar ubiquitous handshake that had become a ritualistic liberation greeting shared among Black males. I could hear murmurs over my shoulder from the players behind me, "Right on. That dude's a brother and an officer too."

A cheap version of pride swelled within me hearing I was acknowledged as a brother, more so than an officer. But I was proud also for them. To be looked at as special was important to me, but to be admired and still be a part of the experience, avoiding any appearance of superiority, was the person who really resided behind the façade of ego and fighter-pilot arrogance. It was my private affliction—the split personality.

"How you doin', Lieutenant Bee?" Ervin beamed, grinning widely with unconcealed joy at finding me and showing the others we were tight, that we had a personal acquaintance. It was our own pitiful microcosm of recognition neediness and, unknowingly, we were all participating in it at various levels and intensities."Hey, brother Ervin, what's happenin', man?" I exclaimed with no intention of keeping it formal. Ervin had stopped by to see if I had some slack time to see his stereo cabinet.

"Hey, great timing. I'm off until tomorrow night," I responded.

"What time is cool with you, Ervin?" I asked as I slipped uninvited into his jeep, wiping the increasing flow of sweat from my brow with my T-shirt sleeve.

"How about sevenish, Lieutenant?"

"You can call me Bee, Ervin. When we're hanging out, it's okay to call me Bee," I scolded mildly.

Unable to shake the military conditioning, he agreed saying, "Okay, sir. Okay."

I asked Ervin to drop me off at my quarters to shower, and we agreed I'd come by his barracks around seven to hear his stereo and down a few. Anxious to make the visit right, Ervin asked me what my favorite poison was. "It don't matter, man, as long as it pours," I remarked.

"Whatever you want, Lieutenant Bee—Chivas, Jim Beam, Jack D, beer, whatever."

To satisfy his desire to be a great host, I said, "Hey, Chivas is cool."

Ervin grinned broadly with a pearly smile and a gleam in his big brown eyes and said, "Mellow. See you later, Lieutenant Bee."

It was a short walk from the compound down the main drag leading to the flight line. Rather than making the sharp turn to the left at the bend in the road two blocks outside the guard shack, I kept straight into the Red Horse barracks area. The evening darkness had settled upon the base, and the sky was dotted with an early sprinkling of stars. The noise and black exhaust of rumbling troop carriers had ceased. Traffic was down to a trickle. The intermittent muffled booming of distant artillery shook the pavement under my feet, spoiling the night tranquility. The flicker of flare light could be seen just above the treetops. As I approached the living area, I observed the Red Horse enlisted people were all housed in a one-story wooden barracks.

I purposely wore civvies for the visit with Ervin to preserve a slight anonymity and prevent generating overwhelming curiosity in his barracks mates. Entering the barracks door, I saw Ervin immediately, and he instantly shattered my efforts at low-key arrival. As if the louder than usual volume of the R & B tunes playing on the reel-to-reel tape deck wasn't enough to pique the curiosity of passersby, he invited everyone who peeked their heads between the splits in his entryway curtains to come in and meet Lieutenant Bee, an F-4 pilot from the 390th. Although I was okay with Ervin's need to showboat, I knew it annoyed and puzzled some of his white cohorts that this light-skinned officer dude was hanging out drinking with a tech sergeant. My rebel side delighted in unconventionality, disregarding certain applications of military protocol. I understood the need for superiors and subordinates on the battlefield, but never related to it in my concept of socializing freedom.

Ervin couldn't do enough to make me comfortable. I felt like I was Muhammad Ali or someone of commensurate royalty.

"What sounds you wanna hear, Lieutenant Bee? Aretha, James Brown, Otis Redding, BB King? I even got some rock," he said, cannily deducing that with my Caucasian-looking features, I might have some white-boy music tastes. Experiencing a flash of embarrassment that Ervin would have suggested I might prefer acid rock to soul music, I moved to greater endearment with him that he would have been candid enough to suggest Lieutenant Bee might have musical tastes outside pure soul. And he was right. I had always been puzzled why I did like different kinds of music—R & B, soul, blues, and all kinds of rock, even classical. My love of varying musical genres perhaps stemmed from having been a young musician who left the band in the ninth grade to play football and basketball. I had played trombone in the band and timpani drums in the junior high school symphony orchestra. Reciprocating the teasing for Ervin offering me the choice of rock, I asked him if he had Mozart's "French Horn Concerto No. 1 in D Major" for brass ensemble with orchestra. His eyes flashed up at me as he sloshed Chivas onto the side of my glass with an expression of horror. His mouth gaped for an instant out of shock at not having been able to meet my every delight on my first visit. I burst out in laughter at his seriousness and rescued him from sinking into inadequacy for failing to entertain his special guest.

Ervin's stereo cabinet was a work of art. He had obtained some beautifully grained indigenous Vietnamese wood to make his shelving and side panels, designed, cut, assembled, and stained it, and finished it in a glossy clear polyurethane. His design was exactly what I wanted for my stereo cabinet, but too unwieldy in size and bulk to transport back to the States, I thought. He claimed confidently it would be no sweat to ship it back home. I said that was cool and we could discuss details later.

Ervin told me stories about his life growing up in the Hough section of Cleveland, his family, and childhood. He showed me a picture of his wife, a heavy-set brown-skinned sister, and his three-year-old daughter. I could not resist the thought of how strange it seemed that little bitty thin men always took up with big rotund women. How did that work? But he was proud and rightfully so. We downed our scotches, and Ervin was quick to refill our glasses, as if the viewing of his family had produced a twinge of pain and longing that cried out for the numbing of another quick jolt of booze.

During our visit, enlisted members of Red Horse kept peeking between the gaps in the makeshift doorway of Ervin's bunk area. He shared himself honestly that evening. He was the kind of brother, the kind of human being, who had a caring spirit, predisposed to befriend all he encountered who would treat him with respect and dignity, white or Black. He was what people would call a good man, Sadly, he was trapped in the atmosphere of racial discord and militancy among Black folks in Nam whose hearts were full of reciprocated hatred and at times justifiable hostility. Blacks who were willing to get along with whites were viewed as Oreos and Uncle Toms. Sergeant Ervin bemoaned the grief he caught for his philosophy of goodwill, but didn't let it deter his smile. I admired that in him.

Ervin had some great sounds. We bounced around our musical tastes from blues to R & B and back to blues for a couple of hours, gulping Chivas, giggling and laughing through shared stories of the past and our hopes for life after Vietnam.

Ervin was a talented carpenter. I knew he would have a great future in or outside the Air Force. His expressions and mannerisms were funny. He reminded me of my fishing buddy, Bemon Blythers, who was not college educated, but very bright and self-taught in a lot of areas of which I was ignorant. Ervin was proud of our newfound relationship, and made me feel like a celebrity, at times to my embarrassment, but it was beaucoup nourishment for my ego. I was content to be available as a vehicle to elevate Ervin's feelings of self-esteem with his peers by being the brother lieutenant, fighter pilot no less, and his buddy.

Regrettably, for many of us, our past experiences have robbed us of the ability to stand tall in positive self-image and respect. In a way, Ervin and I were unwittingly using each other to feed our own inner needs, but it was okay. The by-product was mutual admiration, friendship, and companionship. It would be the foundation of our ability to survive the nightmare of being there and retain our sanity.

Throughout my tour, Ervin continued to be my change-of-pace social diversion. When I occasionally stopped by his quarters, rarely would there be another officer be in the barracks. Officers were only around was when someone was in trouble or an inspection was taking place. My light complexion might have led some to a misperception that I was a white officer coming down to enlisted quarters to hang out with Black airmen. That would have been a more onerous scenario than a Black officer hangin' out with other Blacks, lounging around in Ervin's room, drinking Jack Daniel's out of a water glass, no ice, with a Coca-Cola chaser.

In gleeful defiance, I hung out with Ervin and invited him to my officers' quarters to drink and listen to music on my roommate's stereo, which was crossing the line. Ervin ate up the drama and my predilection for rabble rousing. It was like having a taste of utopia, making up our own rules for socializing, having it our way sequestered in that small place. The grunts were out there in the bush fighting for their very lives, daily praying inwardly to make it back in one piece and sane as well. I could not shake the menacing feeling inside me. I imagined that were I out there with them in the bush, confronting that war on the terms they were confronting it--land mines, pongee sticks, rocket attacks, mortars, poisonous snakes, and malaria-carrying insects, watching friends and buddies being blown up on a daily basis--I'm sure I would have been a madman for the rest of my life. As self-appointed surrogate "partyers," Ervin and I honored their misery and enjoyed great visits, consuming large quantities of alcohol, chain-smoking, and basking in the richness of simply being alive.

I figured Ervin had a good shot at living through his tour at Da Nang because he wasn't in combat. He was in a combat zone where the major threat to his safety was a construction wall falling on him or being crushed by a backhoe in a trench. There was the remote possibility of a Russian-built 122-millimeter rocket landing squarely in his quarters, which did happen occasionally to a handful of incredibly unlucky servicemen.

And so it was that once having left the port of unlimited options for the greatest challenge of my life, there was no way to reverse my circumstances. I had to endure for a year, and I was determined to make the best of it and enjoy it whenever opportunity reared its unpredictable head. I liked Major Billington's counsel about being there for a year and drinking the twelve hours of the day that I was not sleeping. Beyond the sustenance of my isolated amusement, writing and reading, a special replenishment of spirit came out of commiserating with the brothers at Da Nang. It may have amounted to no more than psychological safety in numbers among people sharing common societal obstacles. The get-togethers were a blur of drinking, stories, laughter, cookouts while chowing down on ribs and talking about civil rights and racism in the service. Drinking was our collective anesthesia and our bond was deepened simply sharing ourselves.

Back in the States, civil rights unrest was the new kid on the block, receiving slow acceptance by increasing numbers within white America. Black servicemen were stuck in Vietnam supporting a war that too often looked racist. President Johnson had stated he wanted "Asian boys fightin' Asian boys, not Americans." To my continual diminishment, U.S. GIs uniformly referred to Vietnamese as gooks, zips, and slope heads. My ears always heard these words as *nigger*. Call me sentimental, but racial epithets directed at any class of people had left me vicariously dehumanized. To most U.S. servicemen, no distinction was drawn between North or South Vietnamese or Viet Cong; they were all gooks. All Black servicemen possessed was our sense of each other within the community of family to absorb the guilt of being there. Black was becoming beautiful, and anyone with just a modicum of soul was welcomed into the fold, including whites.

CHAPTER 10: GOOD OL' BOYS

Lieutenant Jethro Ballard broke the stereotype of good ol' boys. He entertained all who met him with a quintessential southern drawl, hillbilly manners, and few ideas that contributed anything positive to human relations. He was the archetypal fighter pilot protégé, gung-ho, patriotic, and he loved the ignominious label Yankee air pirate. Ballard, whom we called Jeth, took an immediate liking to me, maybe because he liked taking new guys by the hand, maybe because he desired a deeper contact with selected brothers around the squadron. Maybe I was a little easier to be with than some of the others because of my light skin. Maybe it was because Jeth was from Kentucky and couldn't resist the urge to bust my chops since I was an ex-prep school jock from Indiana—the hated sporting rival of all Kentuckians. Whatever the reason, ol' Jeth was a riot to hang out with; he was the comedian always telling jokes. He seemed to take special delight in passing himself off as just another dumb hillbilly Kentuckian who had escaped under the split-rail fence from the hills to fly airplanes. His hound-dog slow, deep Kentucky speech accentuated the hilarity of his stories. Jeth took delight in grossing people out, lifting a cheek off the chair to cut a fart that would stink so bad it would blur your vision or picking his nose with his right hand and reaching out to wipe his left hand on the person standing closest. People ricocheted off one another getting away from his extended hand.

He was one of those guys who seemed able to remember every joke he had ever heard. The gift of his storytelling made it instantly apparent he was different and special. His obtuse gross-everyone-out manner gained him an ironic acceptance by some of the brothers. He was one of the few white dudes I knew who got away with telling colored jokes, referred to as Rastus and Sapphire jokes, in integrated company and got guffaws rather than a shiv. That was special; it never would have flown in a crowd of enlisted brothers.

Jeth had a red hue to his complexion, with very white skin dotted with reddish-brown freckles and bright red hair, cut very short, kind of burr-headed like a Marine recruit. His voice had a nasal sound that flowed out of his large round nose. He had the biggest ears I had ever seen on someone not considered deformed. Jeth was respected and liked by everyone in the 390th. He greeted people he really liked, even captains and majors, with the endearing salutation, "Hey, you piece of shit." He had been my new guy escort when I was in-processed into the squadron; most important, he taught me how to shoot darts.

As likeable as Jeth was, his joy of being in Nam and killing gooks, as he referred to it, got in the way of any real bonding with him. I was a closet antiwar sympathizer, hanging out as a fighter pilot and always being thrashed by thorny reminders of the madness of my choice. My thirteenth mission was a sortie up to North Vietnam, a counter toward a hundred-mission total for Jeth who was flying in the lead aircraft backseat. That mission raised a permanent invisible wall between us. He was one of the last of the pilots in my squadron who got to go home after one hundred missions; that's how they came up with the term *counter*—any mission flown in North Vietnam.

Having flown a dozen in-country missions since the hairy CBU night strike with Major Billington along Route 1A where we got our asses hosed, the next mission had been scheduled for a daytime "recon" escort north of Butterfly Lake. Reconnaissance F-4s based at Cam Ranh Bay flew surveillance missions in the north, filming truck and troop movements toward the south along with weapons and missile installations being constructed along the coast. Our F-4s flew close support for the low-level RF-4 photographic runs and were free to retaliate on enemy ground fire against the unarmed reconnaissance aircraft.

Our flight identification name that day was Flipper. The flight, although in the danger zone, did not have that edge of foreboding and uncertainty as the first launch north, maybe because of my confidence in Jeth, an old head with ninety-one strikes. During pre-flight planning, he complained that these escort sorties really sucked because they dragged out in boredom, but at least they counted toward the hundred missions that would send him home. The RF-4s rarely got shot at since the North Vietnamese had no concern that pictures were being taken of their truck routes or missile sites and so there was no action for the F-4 escort aircraft. As the saying went, it was hours and hours of boredom interspersed with brief moments of stark terror. Ironically, this low-key blaze mission with no action became one of the most unforgettable flights of my entire combat tour. What happened during that flight with ol' gung-ho Jeth in the lead aircraft entrenched me deeper into the agony of my hypocrisy and disdain for the imposter wearing my flight suit.

As the RF-4 pulled off his last run down the sandy shoreline and headed his machine feet wet toward Cam Ranh at 400 knots, the Flipper lead aircraft commander expressed disappointment that we had not encountered any ground fire on which to retaliate with our Mark 82 five-hundred-pound iron bombs. In parting the radio frequency, the RF-4 jock uttered, "Maybe sumpin'll show up on the way home."

We closed our Phantom in to rejoin in tight fingertip formation on Jeth and his front-seater in Flipper lead just off the coast from Butterfly Lake. The South China Sea glistened beneath us in the mid-morning sunlight. The natural tropical beauty of the shoreline camouflaged the reality that war and killing were the hidden background to the soft waves tugging at the brown sandy beaches adjacent to the jungle paradise. From fifteen thousand feet, the ocean surface shimmered. The gentle sea breezes curled the waves that seemed to play leapfrog over one another, lapping peacefully at the mysteriously vacant beaches slipping into their conclusion on the pristine mocha-colored shoreline. My enchantment with the splendor of the North Vietnam coastline was shattered by a transmission from Flipper lead, "Hey, 2, throttle it back for some spacing. I got some sampans just off the beach at ten o'clock low. Maybe we'll wake 'em up with one pass of this 20 mike mike," he said, using the nickname for the 20-millimeter bullets we fired from our centerline-mounted machine gun.

My front-seater acknowledged, "Roger that!"

And just like that, we were in a rapid descent toward the sampans of North Vietnamese fishermen only a few hundred meters off the beach less than twenty-five miles north of the DMZ—peasants out to net the morning catch for their village. Flipper lead once again came over the radio, "Master switches—on. Pistol's hot." We were on our own, free spooling under no one's control. Four hundred and seventy knots and the altimeter read less than a thousand feet. *Bzzzzzzztttttt! Bzzzzzzztttttt!*, the buzzing vibration of our Su-16 20-millimeter machine gun that could fire at the rate of six thousand bullets a minute was the only sound that could be heard. I couldn't wait to corner Jeth and put his ass against the wall on how the United States could hold itself up to the world as some kind of moral authority if we could do some shit like firing on the water around those sampans.

After departing maintenance debrief, on the short walk to the personal equipment shack to hang up our gear, I tugged Jeth's sleeve and motioned him aside, protesting in frantic naiveté, "Jeth, how do we justify buzzing those innocent Vietnamese fishermen like that?"

Looking at me like I was the silliest, most naive dumb shit he had ever come across, in his slow Kentucky accent with an almost parental, reassuring tone, he consoled, "Bee, goddamit. The fuckers were stealin' fish."

Without a response to Jeth's indifferent deadly humor, I could only walk off, looking away so as not to betray my disgust. I was suddenly gripped by that same sick feeling I had experienced on April 5 back at the Air Force base during F-4 training the day after Martin Luther King Jr. was assassinated—a day of infamy for African-Americans across America. I recalled being in the fighter-pilot locker room, strapping on my G suit for one of my last F-4 training missions. From my position on the bench, I overheard the wounding words that would echo within me forever. In the brief exchange between a white major instructor pilot who was leading our training flight and the captain instructor with whom I was to fly, the captain asked in an *Oh, by the way manner*, "Hey, did you hear what happened to Martin King yesterday?"

I paused in zipping up my G suit to hear the response. "Well, he finally got what he was asking for," the major responded. I froze, staring trancelike into the linoleum squares on the floor until I became dizzy from prolonged focus on the tile design. I asked myself, "What the hell am I doing?"

In that instant the grossest insult to my race and what I as a Black man stood for had occurred and I couldn't react. The rationalization for my silence, not having the balls to run the risk of jeopardizing my successful completion of combat training, left me diminished, as if a chunk of my dignity had separated from me. In the smallness of the moment, like Dr. Faustus in the classic play by Christopher Marlowe, I had sold a piece of my soul to the devil to be with people I admired, but didn't like or wanted to be around. They were people who in too many instances were a major force of resistance in the United States, serving as obstacles to the civil rights of people of color all across America and perhaps the world. During my young life, I had experienced detached attitudes like the two F-4 instructor pilots had displayed many times—arrogant, cocky, condescending, and bigoted. For many African-Americans, choosing to be a fighter pilot meant forcing oneself to leave home to cavort with a few of America's homegrown racists who by definition were conservative, right-wing, and all for maintaining the status quo. Accordingly, any leader of color who really stood for changing American society, making it a better place for all its citizens with racial equality and equal opportunity, could be said to be asking for it, asking to be killed for a vision of freedom and taking a stand for it.

The gnawing question from that day forward was why and how could I possibly want to play these war games? I was on a team with insensitive, indifferent hired guns who were having a ball in Southeast Asia bombing the shit out of people of color because, quite simply, they were just dumb zips and gooks who, history has demonstrated, ran off every foreign occupier that tried to dominate their country, including the French and the Japanese. They dared to exist on their own terms of Vietnamese nationalism with their own

Ho-Chi-Minh guided politics and way of life and, in so doing, were they just asking for it?

CHAPTER 11: CULTURAL DIFFUSION

Like most military bases in Southeast Asia, Da Nang Air Base employed many Vietnamese civilians in menial capacities. Dozens upon dozens of Vietnamese females worked as maids in the servicemen's quarters and in the chow halls bussing dishes and sweeping floors. The parallel deployments of minorities in the states and the Vietnamese in Southeast Asia—unskilled, uneducated, and poorly paid--did not go unnoticed. Da Nang gave the ubiquitous shuffling of the seemingly unmotivated international flavor. They were the elite of the class. Compared to their racially oppressed American counterparts, the broad majority of Vietnamese workers were probably as well or better informed and politically astute.

Over time, to some of us, nationalistic optimism surrendered to mounting evidence that racist condescension was fueling the arrogance of U.S. policy in Southeast Asia. "America the Beautiful" seemed to have little respect for anyone or any country that was non-white, non-Christian, or non-American. The victims of discrimination and racial hatred perfected an animal-like radar that became finely tuned to pick up the subtlest manifestations of racism and condescension. Intent on not going to Vietnam as the personification of classic ugly American arrogance, I attempted to be accepting of Vietnamese customs and mores. During my entire year I remained eager to feed my curiosity and learn about their society and politics. Regrettably, my only regular opportunity for contact with any Vietnamese was through the daily presence of the maids. That is how I met Nguyen Thi Dao and May Thet Bong.

In February 1969, the F-4 squadron crewmembers moved into the newly constructed, two-story fiberglass dormitories that served as our officers' quarters. It was the creature comfort highlight of the tour to relocate out of the old, dingy concrete quarters for new facilities with two pilots per room and a shower and refrigerator shared between rooms.

With the relocation of quarters, we were assigned a new set of maids who were younger and more adventurous in intermingling with the crewmembers--or at least those who chose to reach out to get to know them. I wanted to massage their curiosity and at the same time learn about their lives and culture. I eagerly took on cultivating an easy trust with the new maids assigned to cleaning our rooms, washing our clothes—even shining our flight boots. Nguyen Thi Dao and May Thet Bong worked our room on the second floor north wing. My new roommate's name was Tim Bannon. He was low profile and kept mostly to himself, a refreshing change.

Dao and Bong were petite, with Bong the taller at five feet even. She had light yellow skin dotted with brownish freckles, mildly Oriental eyes, and slightly bucked teeth. She was shapely and athletic-looking. Dao was maybe four foot ten, with a slender athletic body like a fourteen-year-old Olympic gymnast. Although she was close to my age, her diminutive size made her appear adolescent. She had neatly trimmed hair and wore it in a short ponytail. Her honey-toned skin was silky smooth with an aura of golden cinnamon.

From my first meeting of Dao and Bong I made myself friendly. I avoided appearing aloof or superior, convinced that being friendly might help assure their trustworthiness not to steal or borrow things from my room. Within my private self I squirmed in doubt over trusting that they were not VC sympathizers waiting to sabotage me. It annoyed me that distrust got in the way of full freedom around them. Perhaps it was a survival instinct. During interludes of relaxed weariness, I indulged my sadistic predilection for teasing both of them, kind of like an older brother with a younger sibling. Bong had a melancholic dimwittedness about her that made her at times difficult to have fun with and was not as lively as Dao. The contrast in intellect was as pronounced as comparing the size of Moby Dick with a guppy. From the first day of our meeting, they wanted to know everything about me, asking in their broken, but understandable Vietnamese English whether I was married or had children. They had me in stitches with laughter. "Hey, Bee, you mallie? Got baby-san?" "Hey, Lieutenant Bee, you got picture you wife? Bee, you li' Vietnam?"

Amused and delighted with the exchanges, I would often answer in the same funny English that they spoke, "Yeah, Bee mallie. No got baby-san."

"Why Bee no got baby-san wit' you wife?" they would ask, puzzled. I would set them down, put my hands on Dao's shoulder, and deliver a convoluted explanation of why I had opted not to leaving a pregnant wife behind to whom I was just married. My response left them staring back at me with blank expressions. Something lost in the translation as they say.

They seemed fond of me and would often come to me with minor problems or challenges. With Dao a deeper relationship developed. She was curious and bright and desired to learn about America and its people. I wanted to take something home with me about Vietnamese society and what people there thought about the Vietcong and the war. Dao and I enjoyed a special bond that was difficult for me to keep from messing up. She was attractive and available every day. The perpetual unceasing ache of a starved libido made me want to caress and love her every time I saw her in the hall or when she came into the room to sit beside me on my bed, as if subconsciously tempting, but at the same time trusting my willpower.

Bong was shy and self-conscious. She seemed full of self-doubt and feelings of inadequacy. It made her an easy read. Her comments were mostly superficial and uninspired. Maybe it was just a language barrier, but Bong appeared to be boring even to her coworkers. It was interesting to observe how personality traits ran across racial and cultural lines. Bong seemed envious of the adoration Dao and I shared. Bong knew that Dao thought I was special, maybe even had a tiny crush, which she kept in check out of her own integrity and regard for the institution of marriage. They both appreciated that I treated them with genuine respect as people, beyond being Vietnamese and maids. I regretted fear and lack of opportunity for exposure to other Vietnamese restricted the potential for greater understanding of their country and its history.

One morning in the dull boredom of sitting in the starkness of my room with a hungry half-arousal, I glimpsed the barely perceptible twist of the doorknob. Like a figure in a dream, Bong emerged shapely and muscular, squeezing herself inside the narrowly opened door without knocking, which they were briefed never to do. She whispered in the softest voice, "Hi, Bee, you sleep? You tire." I was afraid to beckon her to me. There was that unspoken invisible knowing between us, like people secretly in lust for each other. I knew deep inside that, if pressed, she would acquiesce, perhaps out of a craving for acceptance, maybe to compete with Dao for my attention, maybe because she simply wanted to be loved. I resisted. I did not want to get caught with her, knowing that public knowledge by the other jocks would have created a sense of disgrace and ignominy for her. Avoiding the temptation, I pretended to be in deep sleep.

To keep our own impulses at bay and mutual attractions suppressed, Dao and I passed free time talking about Vietnamese customs. I shared stories about life in the United States, about racial strife and prejudice. It was cleansing for my psyche to discuss the Vietcong and Ho Chi Minh with her and hear her honest views on the American presence and the war. From her accounts of Vietnamese history, it was clear she felt the National Liberation Front had come with noble intentions. In simple language, Dao articulated her regret over the "by any means necessary" Vietcong policies that left no option of neutrality by the common Vietnamese citizen or peasant farmer in the rice paddies. We both understood the Catch-22 dilemma of the Cong coming into a peasant village and pressuring all able-bodied males to help carry supplies of rice, ammo, and rockets across the river or lose their grandfather or mother to execution. They helped carry supplies.

Airborne Air Force FACs circling over these peasant villages out in the jungle would spot the Viet Cong activity and supply operations and label the village as Cong sympathetic. I had witnessed the efficiency of our warfare. Often within twenty-four hours, sometimes only a few, air strikes would rain napalm and low altitude delivered bombs on the hapless families of the village. I imagined how easy it would be to acquiesce to the intimidation by the Cong. The devastation and suffering brought on by U.S. military retaliations stripped the peasants of their neutrality and indifference to the war and left them hating the Americans for their apparent indiscriminate killing of Vietnamese in their humble hamlets. To that reality, we add the random atrocities with names like My Lai along with many others that never made it to Walter Cronkite's lips on the *CBS Evening News* or the glossy black-and-white pages of *Life*. Dao knew that the rural Vietnamese farmers simply wanted to be left alone. Their only concern was a good rice crop, healthy children, and a growing caribou herd. Dao described in detail the suffering of her people. It diminished my honor, exposed my fighter-pilot arrogance, and shamed into frivolity my presence there in Vietnam. In my bones I knew their suffering was indefensible; an increasingly vocal minority back home knew it too.

Private chats on these subjects often got in the way of Dao getting her work done. In early exchanges, out of guilt or suppressed desire for forgiveness, I had held Dao's hand or placed my hand around her tiny neck. She shivered and reluctantly withdrew, as if not wanting to be with the sensation absorbing her, fighting the temptation to surrender to the intimacy. As much as I ached for sex with her, I never forced the intimacy. Thank God I had the decency and common sense to honor in this small way the heart of a woman and leave it intact.

Throughout the spring of '69, when returning to my quarters, I could always look forward to the excited greetings from Dao and Bong, their smiling faces and teasing antics. They loved listening to the R & B music tapes in my room, especially the Temptations. They thought I was weird to play Jimi Hendrix's "Electric Lady Land" repeatedly, and always loud, absurdly loud. My cultural students cleared out when it was Hendrix's time because the volume was always cranked up several decibels; both of them knew it was drinking time when Jimi's stuff came on the box—"Voodoo Child," "Crosstown Traffic," and the musical nature trip, "Moon Tide."

Dao would always scold, "Bee, you drink wickey now, you be good." She cracked me up, looking up at me through dark beady eyes like a cackling mother hen or Mama Settles.

At quitting time the maids would gather in a private area of the quarters to clean themselves up, even put on perfume for the trip to the guard shack and the daily military escort off the base. They gathered at the exit gate, resplendent in an assemblage of rainbow-colored native costumes in hues of pink, green, blue, yellow, and lavender. At the designated time, they were led out of our tightly protected entry. While they waited for the military escort, I often stepped out onto the second-story stoop to intercept Dao's enthusiastic ritualistic wave back at me, not concerned what her coworkers thought. I guess they knew from the grapevine that Lieutenant Bee was an okay guy, maybe not like the rest who had little to say and a lot of teasing. Bong would wave too. It was a simple, uncomplicated exchange, but it made me feel better inside, somehow connected—less guilty for what I was doing to some of their people on missions at night while they slept dreaming of marriage, family, and perhaps peace.

A southerner from Alabama, Lieutenant Champ Henderson, was assigned the room across the hall from mine. He perpetually ribbed me about poking the maids. He just knew that if it was a "colored boy" and women involved, there had to be some bangin' goin' on. Shamefully, a side of my needy ego delighted in Champ's presumption that ol' Bee was doin' the maids. He crossed the line with me when he began to tease Dao and Bong about it. It was as if Champ was jealous that Black Lieutenant Bee was gettin' laid by the Zip maids, as the whites referred to them, and he wasn't in on it

The day my spirit sunk to its deepest low came in early June on the occasion I discovered that the sudden unexplained detachment and reticence in Bong was due to her having succumbed to behind-the-door pressures one quiet afternoon while cleaning Champ's room when she jumped in the sack with him. I suppose he had banged her admirably. She was goo-goo, ga-ga over him from that day forward, but there was a veiled disgrace. Dao was heartbroken that Bong had permitted such an intrusion of her dignity to taint her world—our world. I was diminished and more deeply saddened knowing that Champ wasn't fond of blacks or gooks. To him we were just the same; she was a Vietnamese human being who, in his bigoted vision, was nothing more than a gook, a dumb zip, or a slopehead to him and most American fighting men in Vietnam. To my ears, those odious epithets rang loud and too clear as synonyms for nigger, jigaboo, jungle bunny, spear-chucker, terrapin, and Sambo. Sensitive people of color have never been comfortable around white folks who used derogatory references about other minorities. Incredibly, a lot of white folks never realized that.

The pain within me over Champ's conquest of Bong could not be shared with anyone. There was really no one to whom it mattered beside Dao and myself, or perhaps the base chaplain. Even he might still have found the depth of our outrage laughable. I knew that, for Henderson, Bong was just another dumb gook. Although she feigned good spirit, she was never the same and there was a palpable shift in the merry atmosphere of the quarters. Even Dao and I were different with each other, somehow vicariously, mutually, irrevocably diminished into disgrace that it would have been anyone but Champ. Our hearts were heavy over something that Bong didn't seem to grasp. It deepened my sense of struggle to survive the isolation, the deprivation, and now the denigration of the human spirit of compassion that war can rip from the very flesh of our souls.

CHAPTER 12: THE BEST DIE YOUNG

Trapped in a lethal limbo of uncertainty that created my passage through the labyrinth of the daily grind, I was never confident of my fate. Some were living to see another day. Some were dying early. I could not block out wondering whether a numbered body bag would be my coffin. Within the first month of my tour, as a distraction, I was inspired to document myself, log the history of my ordeal, be one of those self-appointed war journalists who would go down with the ship, cameras blasting and microphones recording. From the beginning of the Vietnam adventure, I was committed to writing everyone I knew. How else could I expect to receive letters if I didn't write? I was a captive author, compelled out of starved passion and an inescapable conclusion that I was the protagonist in the wildest ride of a lifetime. I had to share my ordeal with my loved ones, if only superficially, documenting what life was like there, careful to omit the unsettling details, the horror, the profound wrenching of enduring the grimness of daily existence—bored, bombed, and beleaguered.

Mama and my adoring sister Margerie tapped into the marrow of their strength to exude a veneer of bravery trudging through their routine paces in small-town Muncie. In the bosom of their hearts, I knew they were queasy with an unshakeable fear they would lose me. We were all locked in a private torment, feeding a familial collusion that perfected the art of pretense out of love for one another and to ease our collective suffering.

Mama had gained an early yet shaky trust in my ability to survive and triumph over challenge and adversity. She believed in my personal strength and will to prevail—to overcome. She also wished for me to invite Christ a little deeper into my life. During my college years, she had endured troubled nights over my attraction to the existential writers; I was after all a literature major. It was a comforting consolation to know I was in her daily prayers, but I rarely prayed in Vietnam. Naively, I operated more out of a quasi

Zen mode of meditation and finely tuned focus at the critical moments on which survival seemed most dependent on wit and concentration. It wasn't until many years later that I realized all credit for my fate and survival was due to the loving grace of the Lord God Almighty.

One quiet evening, early in my tour, hanging out within the refuge of myself, as mortar shelling rumbled the night air, I had a chat with God in which I acknowledged that making it out alive was not entirely up to me. Within the awesome crap shoot of it all, there was a degree of contentment's freedom in relinquishing responsibility. As Mama would say, "Let go and let God." I did. I considered every safe return from a mission as a blessing from God—an answered prayer for Mama.

In the midst of my numbing folly, bolstered by one-day-at-a-time calculations for getting through the tour, I regularly documented this once-in-a-lifetime bad dream. I bonded quickly with the airmen in the radio shop and had them modify my small reel-to-reel tape recorder to be compatible with the microphone jack in the Phantom so that all cockpit interphone and air-to-ground transmissions could be recorded on my tape set.

Early one morning during my second month, Lieutenant Sam Wilburn, a pilot GIB from Texas with six months in country, had just come back from an all-night gambling spree at the DOOM Club. From a mini duffle bag he produced a shiny new Canon 518 movie camera with a leather carrying case.

"Hey, Bee, right?" he shouted in a drunken tone, not sure if he remembered my nickname correctly. "You need a Super 8 movie camera?"

"Wow," I said, knowing I wanted to buy one during one of my leaves, but I was skeptical of getting stuff hot off the streets. In the absence of any other response occurring to me I queried, "Why do you want to sell it? It looks brand new."

"It is goddamit," Sam blurted with no intended disrespect but astonished at my incredulity. "I got this major so far behind the power curve shootin' craps just now that he ran out of money and started throwin' watches and cameras and every damn thing he had on the table tryin' to stay in the game. After six passes, I rolled my four and thought the poor sap would die. He was an asshole anyway. I already got recorders, stereos, cameras you name it. I don't need another frickin' camera. Besides, my ass is out of here tomorrow anyway, so I'll practically give it to you."

Getting excited by the plausibility of Sam's source of the camera, I asked, "How much, man?"

Sam came back like a New York City street hustler. "Spanking new off the shelf, it'd run you one hundred sixty bucks at the base exchange. It's yours for ninety. I gotta get packed." Frustrated that there wasn't time to consult *Consumer Reports,* but sensing it was too good a deal to pass up for something I wanted anyway, I agreed to the price. Quickly returning from my room two doors down the hallway with the cash, I slowly counted out the dough while Sam looked on, shifting from one foot to the other, simulating discomfort and showing impatience. When I finished counting, he handed me the new Canon 518.

Sam was slender with bright red hair, Marine cut, and a Texas drawl; I struggled with feeling if I could trust him. Uncomfortable as I was with his rush to get on his way, I couldn't help but asking, "Sam, why are you packing? Did you finish your hundred missions?"

"Shit no, man. I had to punch out for the second time day before yesterday. Over here, if you have to eject twice, they send your ass home. Tour complete. I guess it's Uncle's way of tryin' to save you from getting killed."

What a deal! I had a brand new movie camera and Sam was going home.

In the weeks that followed, I reflected on Sam's good fortune to be leaving early, but concluded that getting your bird shot out from under you twice was a scary price to pay. *Shit,* I thought. *People buy the farm from parachutes not opening after ejection.* It was all a macho dice game; you simply rolled the bones and hoped for the best. The worst fear was doing one's best and still falling short— fatally short. That was the feature that made office life different for fighter pilots, dozens of options for screwups for which there was no second chance.

I stashed the camera in my locker for two months before finally putting it into action just before Christmas 1968. In early December, Da Nang experienced record rainfall during the daily monsoon showers—almost two feet of rain in one 48-hour period. We finally got a clear day that offered us the gift of sunshine once again. I took the opportunity rendered from a free day off the flying schedule and grabbed my camera to record the ambience for posterity.

I positioned myself on the steps outside the officers' quarters on the side facing the flight line. Selecting the on button, I began my slow pan. The scene I observed through my lens as I scanned by the ARVN flight ramp brought on a cold chill that overwhelmed the comfort of the high seventies morning temperature. There in a small metal revetment, covered with a steep pitched corrugated tin roof, was the dark silhouette of a single F-4 Phantom, aircraft BS 391. It had no canopies, front or backseats. Through the lens before me sat the black shadowy carcass of an airplane on which I had flown two missions during my time at Da Nang. But why was it there?

Major Laird Bratton was the quintessential right stuff kind of fighter pilot, an Academy graduate, a bright, gung-ho professional aviator who knew his stuff. He was a jock who looked like the comic-strip character Steve Canyon, square-jawed, crew cut, and with thick eyebrows. Bratton worked out regularly and jogged for hours at a time marathon style around the compound where we lived. Aside from Major Bratton knowing me as a good back-seater from the two or three missions we had flown together, he had curiously been unable to resist stopping by the basketball court one day while running to watch me shooting hoops and fraternizing with a handful of enlisted brothers. They were brothers around whom most whites would feel uneasy. Witnessing that I was at home with this element, Laird Bratton got a new sense of me as a human being, a pilot, and an educated, light-skinned African-American.

Yes, Major Laird Bratton was arrogant and cocky. He was the kind of star performer who would make a fullback plunge through the opponents' defense and cross the goal line with a few ticks left on the clock to win the game. He had large rippling muscular calves that bulged out with their mass, comparatively small, solid thighs, a thirty-two-inch waist, and a flat, very hairy washboard stomach and pectorals. Typical of most fighter pilots, he had the obligatory grand ego. His knowledge of and skill in flying the Phantom had landed him a check pilot designation for our new crewmembers arriving in the 390th.

All pilots, to receive good effectiveness reports, had to assume additional duties beside their regular flight responsibilities; Laird Bratton had four such duties. He was destined for military stardom in the highest ranks, what the Air Force characterized approvingly as a fast burner. But that can-do machismo can sometimes prove to be one's undoing.

After Major Davis and his back-seater, Lieutenant Reilly, bought the farm slamming into a mountain on a rainy low visibility monsoon night just ten miles north of the base, there was a desperate need to temporarily fill the vacancy of squadron maintenance officer resulting from the loss of Major Davis. No one wanted the headache of being a maintenance officer. Colonel Foster was frantic to find an interim replacement, and who stepped forward to save the day? Laird Bratton, or Laird as he was affectionately called.

Taking on the complex responsibility of maintenance officer, which entailed overseeing routine maintenance of the twenty F-4s assigned to the 390th, directing the repair scheduling of broken or battle-damaged birds, and keeping up with parts orders and shipments from stateside was an awesome undertaking under normal circumstance. It was virtually impossible for any human, no matter how great his desire or competency level, to get a handle on that job within a week or two. On Laird's second day on the job as temporary maintenance honcho, after flying an early-morning sortie up to Mu Ghia pass in Laos that landed back at Da Nang before dawn, Laird left the post-flight debriefing and went to the office previously occupied by Major Davis. According to the senior master sergeant on day shift, Laird pored over volumes of Air Force maintenance directives, guidelines, along with policy and procedure manuals throughout the morning, skipping lunch. Airman First Class Clancey saw the major leave the office around 1800 hours (6 PM), saying he was headed back to the quarters to clean up for Colonel Gadfly's going-home party at the DOOM Club. Gadfly was the departing wing commander of the 366th TAC fighter wing. When honchos finished their tours, there was always a big shindig at the DOOM Club or their private trailer. It was the place to be for any field or company grade officers interested in earning a few atta boys or brownie points with the bigwigs.

Laird Bratton was reported to have had about a half-dozen chicken wings, some potato salad, and a small glass of white wine while at Colonel Gadfly's party. There was a brief ceremony of gifts and speeches by the new wing commander for Colonel Gadfly. Laird left the DOOM Club at close to 2200 hours (10 PM), hopped in the maintenance pickup truck, and drove back to the maintenance shop. The first shirt on the graveyard shift recounted that he spied Major Bratton sitting in his gray swivel chair in his office, head resting on his folded arms, fast asleep, manuals and policy notebooks scattered around him.

The duty officer at the command post logged the major in at 12:30 AM, his showtime for the Blackjack flight scheduled to take off in a two-ship strike over in Laos at 0230 hours. The two hours before takeoff were devoted to target study and mission planning followed by an intelligence briefing that detailed the nature of the target. An unnecessary post-strike refueling had been scheduled over the Mekong River in Thailand before the return to Da Nang.

Although not required on most of the sorties out of the 366th TAC fighter wing, Seventh Air Force honchos had altered our mission description to include pre- or post- strike air-to-air refueling. It didn't matter whether refueling was needed or not for mission completion; it was done simply to avoid losing the KC-135 tanker support for the infrequent sorties that required the gas to get back to base or for search-and-rescue missions. Frequently, we F-4 crews devised creative means of lowering the Phantom's gross weight after useless post-strike refuelings to decrease the bird's weight so that it was legal for landing at home base.

The Accident Investigation Board concluded from its evaluation of the facts that Major Bratton and Lieutenant Chris successfully led Blackjack flight, a flight of two F-4Ds, on a good mission to northern Laos. They had an on-time refueling rendezvous with their post-strike tanker, Yellow 1, and took on eight thousand pounds of JP-4 fuel that was not needed to safely return to Da Nang.

The airmen in the Da Nang control tower heard Blackjack lead check in for landing clearance after being handed off from Da Nang RAPCON (Radar Approach Control) at 4:13 AM. Blackjack lead was cleared to land. In Major Laird Bratton's zombified state, he had failed to notice, after the air refueling, that the right wing tank had a failed fuel boost pump. How two experienced, highly trained crewmembers were unaware, in the wee morning blackness, of the increasing difference between wing tank fuel quantity gauges was the gnawing question. Was it due to Lieutenant Chris thinking like a navigator and not a pilot? Or was he lulled down that primrose path of complacency because he trusted in the impeccable reputation of Laird Bratton, the *Right Stuff* fighter pilot who was the personification of the best and the brightest?

In those last few seconds just before touchdown, it appeared that Laird misdiagnosed the rolling action on landing as an asymmetrical flap, the procedure for which was to instantly raise the flaps to zero and execute an immediate go-around—the worst action he could have taken for his actual condition. Those of us left behind in déjà vu disbelief could only conclude in the comfort of armchair speculation that in the blurry-eyed return flight to Da Nang, Laird had unwittingly continued trimming off the stick pressures created by the wing imbalance. As with any competent flight lead, his mind was probably miles ahead of the flight, coordinating with radar controllers on the radio to get the flight of two F-4s safely back on the ground at home base.

Through the zoom lens of my new movie camera, I saw it there, recorded forever through the lens of my mind's eye, charred and solitary, still and lifeless, the silent Phantom resting in the caverns of the revetment as sunlight blazed brightly outside. In delayed recognition of what I was seeing, I thought, *My God, they parked the demolished bird across the street from my quarters, the bird that Major Bratton and Lieutenant Chris had flown back to Da Nang as Blackjack 1 at 0430 that dark fateful morning.* Lieutenant Chris had been airlifted to the burn center at Tachikawa Air Base in Japan. U.S. Air Force Academy Graduate, Major Laird Bratton, was burned beyond recognition, officially listed as KIA—Killed in Action.

Whatever his particular drives might have been, Laird Bratton lived his life in *Right Stuff* confidence that he was one of the best—a fighter pilot who could do it all. He met his fate, a fiery end that left us all more intimate with fear and our fragile existence when we exceed the limits of our capability with inadequate time to recover. In his drive for excellence and accomplishment, Major Bratton had pushed beyond his own envelope. He drove himself into the ground and took a crewmember with him by ignoring the simplest consideration of physiology: the limitations of the human body. Lieutenant Chris died five weeks after the crash at the burn center in Japan. He, like, Major Bratton, was listed, officially as Killed in Action. I guess that's true--but for their families back home the crash one week before Christmas Day altered that holiday forever.

CHAPTER 13: THE AGONY

The agony of the Vietnam purgatory seemed interminable. I was bound up in a psychic incarceration locked out of the world of my dreams, doing the time for my own folly, and bullshitting my way through each day. Without the thin threads of hope that I might be lucky enough to survive, it would have driven me to madness toughing out the deprivation-fraught agony of longing. The question was simply what activities to choose for diversion that would help numb the mind from too much heady contemplation. There were strategies for mental survival to live out the sentence and, ideally, join the lucky who would return home.

Malcolm X was dead, as were John and Bobby Kennedy and Martin Luther King, Jr. The idealistic spirit of camaraderie with my fighter-pilot team members was strained knowing that many of them never related to or comprehended why those slain icons were heroes to Black Americans. The cities were on fire at home in civil rights strife, and I was hanging out in Vietnam.

The surreal, yet palpable horror of surviving daily combat missions, dropping bombs, strafing enemy tanks, and dodging flak on missions, only showed up after returning safely back to the DOOM Club. Socializing often offered no respite. During quiet repose, the rumbling of fear would strike like delayed thunder following lightning flashes. My mind was not my friend; it teased me with wild notions. My anxiety involved harbingers of impending doom. Ominous visions of my demise would creep up on me during contemplative strolls down the concertina-lined streets when I was reclining upon the cot in the room after a nice shower, reflecting on what I had just experienced or was scheduled to face on the next day's sortie. For me, that was how fear lived, nestled next to me like my cat, Major, curled in my lap. It was a daily dose of posttraumatic stress syndrome.

To survive the insanity, I sought to lose myself in the distractions of the mundane. I played basketball with the enlisted cats down at the open-air basketball court in the compound. I learned to play handball with my jock buddies and spent hour upon hour of spare time taking slides and movie film of Da Nang's GIs trudging along in a death shuffle up and down the dusty base roads. I filmed the spectacle of the Vietnamese civilian workers clad in their signature black pajamas coming and going, checking in and out of the security checkpoints, wondering silently who among them might be Viet Cong. I logged entire days recording tapes for my music collection just in case I made it out alive for the future I imagined with Celeste and my family. My idle hours were dominated by thoughts and longing for Celeste's closeness and reassurance that life would become normal. The powerlessness was pervasive; the missing and longing were excruciating--they never went away.

The challenge of being perpetually in the grip of a lifestyle of uncertainty over getting killed and being among people with whom I disagreed about civil rights, the war in Vietnam, and politics in general made each day an exercise in social awkwardness. I relished my private escape into daydream constructions of my future with family, children, and Celeste. Imagination and fantasy, fueled by the streams of letters and tapes from home, were all I had to sustain the journey through the twelve-month ordeal.

The Temptations tape, *In a Mellow Mood,* that Celeste sent me was a mixed-blessing depression suppressor. I visualized a living out of my love for Celeste through listening to the tape, "Try and Remember," "Old Man River," etc. I submerged myself in the melodies night after night, clinging to anything that would sustain the fantasy and assuage the preoccupation over uncertainty about my future with Celeste. I was clueless as to how to escape paying the cost of our mutual neediness even if I had been intellectually capable of recognizing it. The disappointments from the pursuit of being liked and praised left me harboring doubts about our ability to get to a new place--one where we both could both be free to be ourselves and comfortable with life and its vicissitudes.

Celeste had a beautiful, athletic body, flat muscular stomach, nicely shaped symmetrically sculpted calf muscles, and wonderful full lips that I delighted in kissing. Naively, those were the primary criteria for my perfect mate. Unfortunately, I did not know enough of life and myself to take it other than personally when greeted with her reluctance about passionate kissing. My own insecurities spoke to me in a voice louder than her loving reassurances. I harbored notions that she really didn't love me; that she merely saw me as having the potential to fit into her vision of social acceptability, being a pilot—a fighter pilot no less. I wanted to have babies with her; I thought they could be beautiful, athletic, and bright. We were an ideal wedding cake couple—a Black Ken and Barbie.

Beyond the physical, perhaps my attraction to Celeste was founded in her sensitivity and creativity coupled with a powerful intellect and her amazing powers of observation. She had a deep appreciation for the arts, poetry, and music. With me being the renegade warrior poet, we were naturally drawn to each other. She was in awe of what she perceived as my wittiness and unorthodox style, which was out to deliberately challenge and unravel the comfort found in conventionality and conformity. It was as if she wanted to rebel from her own cultural conformity, but was instead locked in a private tussle with her self-doubts that led her to live vicariously through my fragile protest against uniformity and orthodoxy. This seemed to unnerve her but also to draw her to me. Her consolation and hope resided in the belief she would ultimately understand and assist in healing the psychic afflictions of my past that drove me into the clutches of a rebellious existence.

As an adolescent in Muncie confronting my manhood, I was guided by the fear of pregnancy and entrapment in a mundane, unfulfilled relationship with an untalented woman possessing few gifts other than the predisposition for rapid arousal and looking good. Cold-soaked fear of having sex with those chicks who threw themselves at me kept me petrified of getting someone knocked up and locking myself into a lifetime of "quiet desperation" as Thoreau dubbed it.

My young adult life was driven by my neediness to catch up on all the oohhing and ahhhing I had passed up, but Mama's face was always there in my mind with a plea not to disappoint her. She prayed I would not be a father at sixteen, not to screw up my future, whatever it was. My loving mother was always in me, begging me not to break her heart, to make her proud of my sister Margerie and me. In her infinite love, she had adopted two abandoned orphans and made them her greatest treasures.

The desire to catch up and recoup all the passed-up pleasures and reinforce the elusive sense of sufficiency fomented a tyranny of neediness in my marriage, which transformed itself into a conjugal oppression for Celeste. I too easily arrived at the debilitating conclusion that there was something wrong with me, that I was not satisfying my woman—any man's worst nightmare.

The greatest fear, beyond the sense of my self-imposed inadequacy, was the vision of some cunning dude stealing into the sanctity of the lonely, improperly attended boudoir and tapping a superior pleasure to which I aspired with my lover. These haunting phantasms suspended themselves over my consciousness and colored my expression to Celeste. My gut wrenched for the opportunity to return safely and realize the fulfillment of my dreams of love and family with her. But I was locked away in a foreign land, mind-grappling with myself in the sanctuary of concealment, suppressing my gnawing angst. I channeled my energies toward coaching the home front to stay strong for me and not add to my preoccupations by showing up weak at home and cracking under the strain of my voluntary embattlement.

I worried about Celeste's ability to get through the year emotionally. There was something in her emotional intensity that drew me to her, that made me want to protect and save her. I naively believed a life of love with me would be enough. We were a perfect match of insecurity and inadequacy. I was simply more proficient at concealing and camping out with my fears. Perhaps the symbiosis of our neediness fed our union. She needed and wanted a man whose strength and intellect matched her father's, a man she could admire and with whom she could feel protected. I was a delicate soul possessing a poet's passion, hiding out as a macho stud fighter pilot who needed and wanted a sexy mate who would love and adore him and over whom he could feel eternally superior in mutually agreed-upon domination.

I clung to the fantasy of living in an America where the color of one's skin no longer mattered and I desperately wanted only to love Celeste, to fill her up, to make her happy, to get her pregnant with a child who would offer immortality to our union, and to have her love experiencing life with me—no reservations. Many of my letters home spoke this presumption, this hope, this prayer of the future.

In Vietnam, the recollections of the challenges in our relationship and the uncertainties about making it into a happy fulfilled future together melted into a protracted fantasy of longing and articulated dreams of our life together. I could always hear Karen Carpenter singing, "We've Only Just Begun" above the din of muffled mortar rounds sounding in the distant hills around Da Nang as I wrote loving letters to my bride. I immersed my senses in smelling the perfumed pages of her letters of reassuring pronouncements. I would often lay back in my bed at night in the dark solitude of my room while my roommate was out flying and totally lose myself in the soft lure of her voice. The agony of the ache for Celeste in my loins was unbearable. I wanted desperately to be inside her, feeling the ooze and warmth of love's quintessential expression. I resided in the mental mirage of making love with her. Alone in Vietnam, the eros of love deprivation convened its own theater of desperation, offering routine performances of such simple, bestial satisfaction in a fantasy of being in Celeste's arms. It was all I had to shelter my sanity from complete derailment as month after month fellow pilots continued unabated dropping off into the abyss while I carried on.

CHAPTER 14: DRIVING WHILE DRUNK

The days dragged on like a life sentence. Seven months had elapsed, yet it could just as well have been an eternity. I was buried in melancholy musings on many a lonely night wondering how many other fools had been cajoled by the whispering voices deep within the dark holes of their souls—murmurs that made us willing to risk our lives just to appear to be fearless "bad mammer-jammers" and getting killed doing it. My imagination convinced me that rather than being remembered as a brave brother, flying fighters in Nam, it would be more like "What made that fool stupid enough to think dodging bullets flying an airplane was a good idea, even if he was doing it at five hundred miles an hour." White buddies could at least defend their madness copping a love-for-country plea, but I squirmed under the recurrence of my feeling that the war effort was ill conceived, morally wrong, and operationally misdirected.

Thirty thousand draft dodgers had fled to Canada rather than risk dying in Vietnam. Muhammad Ali had been jailed and stripped of his heavyweight boxing crown for refusing induction. Just as I was embarking for Da Nang, twenty-six thousand police and National Guardsmen had gone on an ass-kicking frenzy beating the crap out of antiwar protesters at the Democratic National Convention in Chicago. My fighter pilot charade made my daily existence seem senseless and indefensible.

Overdrinking was a professional concern as a pilot. Sure, a trained pilot could take a jet off the ground, fly it back to base, and land safely even while being a little smashed. But the survival equation changed dramatically when you threw in a high-speed abort on a wet runway with a full combat load of twelve 750-pound bombs. The horror of having to punch out in Laos or North Vietnam with a hundred angry villagers chasing your ass was enough to sober up anyone. But what, I imagined, would it be like if you were still shitfaced from the night before, got an arm broken or cut on ejection, and had to escape and evade enemy forces chasing you through a bamboo-thick jungle filled with tigers and deadly bamboo vipers? The prospect of crashing and dying or, worse yet, being captured, was scary enough to make it dicey for the bravest mutha. To die sober or buzzin,' that was the question. But what if having your wits about you under the trauma of ejection would mean not getting captured and becoming a POW? What if it could be the difference in getting fatally knifed in hand-to-hand combat by a vicious black-belt North Vietnamese regular infantryman who has lived the past month on the same amount of calories I consumed at the Da Nang officers' club the night before?

My general rule was to be disciplined, fly sober, and get decent crew rest before missions, but I wasn't always consistent in that responsibility. Sometimes the line got crossed. I just prayed to God, *Please, Lord, let me get through this one; I promise not to get shitfaced again before a mission.*

I think the Lord punished me one day to teach me a lesson about the irresponsibility of drinking too close to flight duty. I had left the USO show early at the DOOM Club after three or four scotch and 7-Ups, unable to suffer the sight of the sexy, half-naked Indonesian showgirls. It was a major challenge to resist leaping onto the stage and banging a bunny right there in front of the world. All the officers, white and Black, ate that dancing girl stuff up, especially the white ones. They often seemed absorbed in the fantasy of watching. I always wondered if it was mostly a Black thang that brothers would be trying to get some rather than being content to just look. Maybe it was just my thing; maybe I was guilty of stereotyping.

Fleeing the group exercise in voyeurism, I left the club and caught the squadron van outside the compound gate and went back to my quarters. Spookie C-47 gunships were orbiting and pissing red tracers down on potential sappers setting up crude rocket launchers off the base perimeter at the departure end of Runway 17. Recalling the relationship between Spookie activity and early morning rocket attacks on the airbase, I talked myself into stopping by the makeshift lounge area in the open bay for a little pre-rack camaraderie.

Fighter pilots are so resourceful and imaginative. The guys in my squadron had scrounged a refrigerator and built a wet bar with a shiny varnished countertop and storage shelves underneath. They stole three barstools and placed them tavern style in front of the decorated face of the bar counter. Pinups of a year's worth of *Playboy* centerfolds adorned the walls. A tacky wooden sign hung over the counter with words scribbled in big letters: **390th TAC FIGHTER SQUADRON DILDO AND SUPPER CLUB.** As I turned the corner, there stood Lieutenant Schlichter playing bartender with his elbows resting on the countertop and his front-seater, Captain Dave Cooper, sitting on a barstool. Witnessing my appearance, they drunkenly exclaimed almost in unison, "Bee, you piece of shit. Come on in here."

I bellowed out, "Bartender, I'll take a scotch and Seven." They argued over who was going to put the MPC, the substitute currency for piasters used by U.S. military personnel, in the coffee can to pay for my drink.

Coop scoffed, "Scotch and Seven! What kind of geek-ass drink is that?"

Instantly, I retorted, with the usual playful disrespect, "The kind of damn drink I like. I'll take a double."

They cracked up with laughter. Taking advantage of my seeming good spirits, Schlichter boldly came back, "Bee, goddamit, we open up the dildo club to niggers and you treat us like shit."

I couldn't resist getting my blow in for the revolution back home and jumped right back. "Shit, with all the riots and lootin' I'm missing back home bein' over here with you sorry dumbshits, I might burn this mutha down some night." One great thing about being in combat-- you could get away with saying almost anything.

Pleasantly bombed after two more granddaddy scotches, which Coop and Shlick cheerfully paid for, I staggered away, shuffling my way to my bed next door to squeeze in four or five hours of z's before brief time.

After arriving at the squadron building the next morning in bleary-eyed shock, I read the Plexiglas scheduling board that had a yellow grease pencil line crossing out Billington and the name Boswell written at the side. To my horror, there had been a last-minute schedule change. I wasn't flying with Randy; instead, it was the wing Deputy Commander for Operations, Colonel Lewis Boswell. Struggling for composure, gripped by the awareness there was no way out, I strode into the command post on wobbly legs for the pre-mission target study. Mild panic gripped me. At that point, I was in the proverbial box canyon and I was going to have to fake it. Appear to be normal. I was afraid that Colonel Boswell would discover or, worse yet smell, my inebriation. I knew if I were taken off the mission, there would be a delay replacing me with another back-seater for the colonel, and I would be in deep "kimchi" with Lieutenant Colonel Foster, my squadron CO. Explanations for the delay might filter all the way down to the Seventh Air Force Command in Saigon.

The saving grace was my reputation for knowing my stuff and being an experienced GIB. Luckily, I had flown four or five missions with Colonel Boswell. In fact, he routinely requested being crewed up with certain pilots and I was toward the top of his preferred list. His confidence and knowledge of my competency were already established. He would never have suspected that Bee Settles might show up slightly shitfaced for work. I should have gotten an Academy Award for what happened on that mission.

Flying with the deputy commander automatically meant being the lead in a two-ship strike. In formation flying, the lead aircraft had the weight of the mission on its shoulders; the bird on the wing simply flies good formation and follows the lead. The lead copilot is busy as hell with navigation, frequency coordination, and running all the checklists. Colonel Boswell was a good pilot. I didn't have to carry him like some of the desk-flying honchos who came over to recreate themselves as fighter jocks. He handled his lead responsibilities well. I was normally comfortable flying with him. The fact that I made it to the aircraft following the intelligence briefing without being thrown off the trip raised my hopes that I might skate through undetected. I knew once I was strapped in that backseat, got on oxygen, and encountered no disasters, I might escape being exposed as a derelict fighter pilot.

The mission went off without a hitch. Colonel Boswell put some good bombs on the target and expressed low-keyed delight over the

BDA report we received from the forward air controller working our strike.

In usual custom, after pulling off the target for the return to base (RTB) and feeling empathy for the GIB pilots locked in the backseat of the Phantom, front-seaters would often shake the control stick in short, steady jerks from side to side saying, "Okay, you got it," meaning the flying of the bird was handed off to the other crewmember. When Colonel Boswell shook the stick that morning coming off the target just west of Pleiku, I actually hesitated whether I was steady enough to fly back to Da Nang and make a landing. Glancing out the canopy of my backseat, I spotted our wingman bobbing into place alongside our right wing.

Fifteen thousand feet below us in the early-morning spread of yawning jungle, I glimpsed the narrow huddles of fog in the valleys tracing the winding streambeds. There, in the shadow of consciousness, loomed the disbelief of where I was and what we were doing as Vietnam awoke to another routine day of war. Even after an hour's resuscitation on one hundred percent oxygen, I was still shaky. The pressure of declining an opportunity to fly for a fighter pilot was tantamount to a sophomore on the varsity basketball team telling the coach when offered a chance to get in the game, "Naw, coach, I'd rather sit on the bench." Ego and not wanting to look bad or create suspicion made me respond to the colonel, shaking the stick back at him to confirm hand-off of control of the bird. "All right, sir, I have the aircraft."

Thank God the weather was not suitable for an overhead 360-degree pitch-out for a visual landing. From the ground looking up, seeing fighters come in with a tight formation, pitching out overhead the runway at fifteen hundred feet and with five-second breaks between birds flying visual approaches is a thing of beauty that will give any real pilot prickly skin. But when the weather was marginal, as it was that day, the return flights shoot ground-controlled radar approaches (GCAs). All I had to do was follow the controller's instructions right down to the runway for the landing. Usually steady and precise on my GCAs, that day I was all over the place: above the glide slope, below the glide slope, left of course, right of course. I was working my ass off for mediocre to inferior results. Rather than my normal smooth descent to the runway, we hit like we had landed on a Navy carrier. Bam! But we didn't bounce. Colonel Boswell took back control on the rollout as was routine, since the front-seater had the nose-wheel steering, without uttering a word. Embarrassed, but relieved it was over, I sheepishly confessed the obvious, "Sorry, colonel, about that ugly approach and landing. That's not my usual performance."

Sympathetically, and with a tone of puzzlement in his voice, Colonel Boswell registered his concurrence. "Yeah, you're right, Brian." I never flew drunk again.

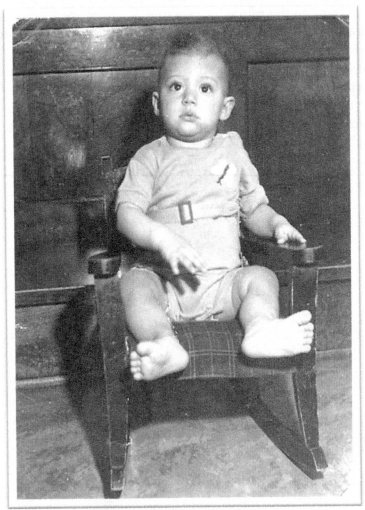

Brian H. Settles- an orphan
who would someday become
a fighter pilot

My first home- the Lincoln Nebraska
State Orphanage

The Mother who adopted me- Bernice Brooks Settles

Margerie and Mama Settles after Easter church service

B. Settles and JJ Winters, the high school chum who talked me into becoming a pilot.

F-4 Phantom returning to Da Nang from combat mission

B. Settles going up the ladder for a night mission.

F-4 Phantom refueling with KC-135 tanker in the soup

Major Randy Billington- My first assigned
Aircraft Commander in the F-4

B. Settles waiting to launch the next mission into the unknown

CHAPTER 15: ESCAPE TO CLARKSVILLE

Two months had passed since returning to the combat arena after my unfulfilled expectations of R & R with Celeste in Hawaii. It had not been a failure to be reunited with my new bride whom I missed dreadfully, but fantasy late-night swims in the warm waters of the Pacific and sipping champagne on moonlit beaches at midnight never happened. An unusual cold front whisked through two days after our arrival, turning the weather dismally cool and blanketing the skies with a gray overcast. An uncomfortable chill hung over the beach and rather than lying on a beach blanket, it was more comfortable lying under it. Only snowbirds would have dared sample the chilled waters.

The third night of our stay I rushed poor Celeste to the Serviceman's Medical Clinic at two in the morning due to a high fever, only to discover she had come down with a mild case of the flu. The last three days of our R & R honeymoon we were mostly confined to the room with Celeste taking catnaps while I sat on our seventh-floor balcony admiring gorgeous sunrises. I spent the time reading and sipping Mateus through the afternoons, comforted by the soothing musical groove of a classical jazz radio station. Relaxing in my patio lounge chair, I flowed in and out of stream-of-consciousness monologues rambling about my hopes for our future, Mama and Margerie. If I wasn't fantasizing about the future, I rendered updates on the latest events in the lives of my pilot training classmates as Celeste listened off and on, reclining inside on the bed. Celeste agonized about spoiling our vacation with her illness, forcing me into perpetual reassurances that stuff happens, people get sick, plans don't always work out, you adjust, stay tough, don't crack, keep on keeping on, don't boo-hoo about it. It was okay.

For that brief time, I felt good promenading along the clean, palm tree–lined streets of Oahu, browsing through exotic dress shops with Celeste. I mulled going AWOL, not returning to Da Nang, and heading home to begin our life together.

In what seemed a mere flashbulb moment for revitalization, Celeste was on a jet plane taking her away from Honolulu to Los Angeles and back to the frigid Indiana winter where a classroom of raucous third graders awaited. I returned to the misery of numbness in Vietnam to drop bombs and dodge flak for another six months. The isolation and deprivation of being locked in a lethal lifestyle gnawed at me. Daily drinking was the routine; it was my anesthesia for survival. I flew my missions when scheduled, read my books and ten-day-old Muncie newspapers, drank beer or booze every day, and wrote every person I knew to pass the time. It was difficult for many to write back consistently. Most people don't write; they are ashamed or shy or boring to themselves. Could I blame them? They were enjoying their lives. Who was I to bad-mouth them for being too busy to write my ass in Vietnam where I languished in my miserable hole, the hell for which I had volunteered. As Mama always said, "Sometimes you just have to lump it and like it." I accepted my penance, got loaded when there were breaks in the action, and left Dodge City every chance I could. The opportunity might come with bad weather or mechanical diversion to a base in Thailand or a boondoggle to Clark Air Force Base for refresher training in the F-4.

During the tour, pilots from the fighter squadrons were scheduled to go to Clark Air Force Base for F-4 systems review. It was a great opportunity to get technical questions or problems resolved by the expert enlisted personnel who taught F-4 systems. The ground school instructors respected the fighter pilots' way of life, and they knew, when we arrived at Clark, all we wanted to do was drink, party at the officers' club and chase skirts. Clark had dozens of isolated single female teachers from the United States in the on-base school system. The base was also a regular layover refueling point for the many military charters headed to and from Hawaii, Japan, or Okinawa.

On May 5, 1969, I scored my second boondoggle to Clark. The inspirational mileage from the fuel of R & R with Celeste had fallen off and again the daily routine was all guts and no glory. One afternoon in the squadron recreation room after I had waxed his ass at darts, and as a gesture of bonding or attempting to relate, Major Bullet Hank Larson pulled me aside and invited me to be his GIB on a practice missile shoot at Clark. The plan was to fly our Phantom to Clark, have a few days of refresher training, and shoot our radar-guided missile called the Sparrow at a drone target. Going to Clark with Bullet Hank wasn't my idea of fun, but I never passed up the chance to get out of the war for a breather, no matter whose backseat I had to fly to do it.

The first leg from Da Nang to Cam Ranh in the F-4 took an hour; the three-hour leg from Cam Ranh Bay to Clark was as ass numbing as sitting on a bus stop bench. En route, we rendezvoused with one air-to-air refueling tanker and took on two thousand gallons extra fuel. Our fighter-pilot butts were only accustomed to missions of an hour to an hour and a half at most. The ejection seat cushion in the Phantom seemed to turn into cement after two hours. I was never so relieved to land as when we crawled out of that bird on the ramp at Clark Air Base.

After checking into the visiting officer's quarters, in order to escape Bullet Hank's intention of coordinating our social calendar, I pulled a disappearing act by crafting the deception of meeting old buddies and intimating prospects of hooking up with him later for a drink or three at the officers' club. Observing his nervous shifting from one foot to the other like a baby elephant standing beside its mother, I agonized through the stoicism concealing his disappointment that there was anywhere I would rather be than hanging out with my shit-hot, roly-poly fighter jock front-seater.

"Sure, Bee, whatever you got goin'. I'll catch you around later," he assured me. I almost felt guilty. Almost.

Not fully dry from a quick splash in the shower, I shot over to the officers' club and ordered a T-bone steak dinner. There was something missing in devouring a delectable meal alone without some nicely perfumed company like my wife, but in the atmosphere of a good time, any skirted pinch hitter would have been welcome to join me.

The moral consciousness I inherited from Mama Settles whispered in my ear regularly while in Vietnam. I wrestled with the issue of fidelity to Celeste whom I trusted was pining away, thumbing the rosary praying that her fighter-jock husband would return whole to her. As a person of conscience who prided himself on thoughtfulness and sensitivity, I found myself in regular agony over the double standard confronting me, but I conveniently postponed analyzing morality issues. In that crucial but fleeting moment of my life experience, being on the doorstep of death every time I flew, I would not deny myself the gratification of feminine company, even physical intimacy. I clanked my eyes shut tight repressing how hurt my new wife would be if she were to know I was sharing what was special and sacred to our union with some—any—stranger I might meet. I had been with bar whores in Angeles City and Hong Kong. I would have been with the goddess travel rep with Qantas in Sydney had they not canceled the basket leave program.

Through the protracted suffering of longing, I was constantly haunted by fearful visions that Celeste was cracking under the strain of my absence and succumbing to the pressure from suitors to go out clubbing. But, in war, when people are far removed from home and hearth, when the person one loves is alone in the agony of waiting, all one can do is hope his lover is strong enough to resist craving attention from another. If she cracks under the weight of her own oppressive deprivation, she may acquiesce to the cunning reassurances of the inevitable player and rationalize away her fidelity. Her surrender to the transgressions of intimacy becomes her invisible albatross, a twin to the one dangling around my neck.

A predisposition for detachment lived in the breast of all my relationships with women. Perhaps my psyche was permanently damaged and I was emotionally set adrift by the haunting knowledge that my biological mother had given me away. Perhaps the key to my unfaithfulness and distrust of women was buried in the fertile Nebraska soil beneath the playground back at that orphanage. Or was it Daddy leaving Mama when I was seven? The unshakeable fear of rejection and abandonment was part of who I was. I had not been able to extricate myself from its grim grasp, but I had perfected a façade of machismo that would make it appear not so. I wanted to love Celeste with all my heart and soul, but I could not put together the confidence in my own self-worth that would free me to trust her with my heart even though she was my wife. That was the saddest note in our conjugal symphony.

Throughout the year, many of my letters to Celeste served a dual mission: to keep her spirits up for that day of reunion when we would commence the marriage dream of life together and to issue overt and subtle pleas for her to be strong and save her loving for me only. I knew there lived inside me a perpetual agony of fear that someone or something I loved would leave or be taken away from me again.

It is risky business to entrust another human with custody of the heart. Perhaps a bastard baby was vanquished in the battle to belong and good enough to be Black. Perhaps there had been one too many gang pisses in the tall weeds along those isolated, rhubarb-lined railroad tracks that carried the Baltimore & Ohio freight trains in and out of Muncie long ago.

Thursday night was teacher's night at the Clark officers' club Ratskeller. Stuffed to contentment after gorging on grilled mahi mahi at the pool bar, I looked forward to relaxation upon witnessing the trickle of patrons turning themselves into a large crowd that soon filled the tables. Looking much like one of those quaint Spanish bar room scenes from *The Sun Also Rises,* it was a cozy place for visiting, dining, and drinking; it was dimly lit and laid out in the shape of a D.

The musical entertainment was generally local Philippine musicians; occasionally, a traveling USO troupe of musicians, dancers, and singers would stop through on the way to military clubs in Southeast Asia. The club officer was adept at scheduling the best entertainment for the nights when the biggest crowds showed up, or maybe it was the reverse. It didn't matter; people came out. They never needed an excuse to party.

Most of the local acts were mediocre at best, with a lead male or female singer, generally Korean if not Philippino, who rendered borderline acceptable imitations of popular recording artists. Many of the renditions fell laughably short, given the speech characteristics of Asians pronouncing English words, but I always had a natural soft spot in my heart for any person with the courage to do anything creative or musical—talent or no talent. Besides, what the hell, I was easy to entertain. I had just gotten in from Da Nang; I was glad simply to be anywhere.

I ordered a glass of burgundy from the bar, knowing from volumes of empirical data not to switch to gin and tonics after the small bottle of Chianti with dinner. I was already a good candidate for Headache City the next day as it was. The good news was that the missile shoot wasn't until Monday. I had the whole weekend to "Yabba Dabba Dooo" and recover—any pilot partyer's dream come true.

Peering into the dim obscurity of the patrons seated at the tables, my eyes soon adjusted and I perused the crowd with the intense focus of a red-tailed hawk perched in the high branches, scanning an alfalfa field for fuzzy targets of opportunity. I fixed my gaze on a table that butted against a six-inch round vertical support beam. Three dolled-up chicks were at a table for four with a vacant seat--too good to be true. Judging from their colorful party attire and inspired makeup, I deduced they couldn't be school teachers--not conservative enough, probably airline stewardesses. Their hair colors were all different; one was a blonde, one a redhead, and the other a brunette. When jammed into the restrictions of time, I never let anxiety over race get in the way of socializing opportunities. Besides, I was learning more and more in my worldwide travels that brothers always seemed to get their fair share of play. But my light skin often obscured my ethnicity, put me in the category of "X" or "Other." People just didn't know what I was. Often feeling my lightness was a liability, I always clung fast to the Blackness inside me. It was what I knew.

Up on the stage, the musicians were tuning their instruments in preparation to begin right on the dot at 9 PM. I kept glancing back at the table of the three cuties, deliberating whether to rush them immediately or delay and do an end-around attack later, after the atmosphere was more alive and jumping. To delay was to run the risk of forfeiting a socializing connection to a jerk less deserving. But I was shy in a cocky sort of way. I routinely agonized over the intro— just getting started. Presentation from a stranger had to be finely tuned, no matter how desperate for companionship or a good time some women appeared. Gal pals out in public have highly sensitive antennae for identifying cockiness and shallowness, either of which will usually result in quick dismissal

I opted to gamble with the delayed approach, hiding out in the haze of smoke across the room. I stared like a voyeur at the three ladies, transfixed by the flickering candlelight rendering shimmering glows on their faces as they chatted between bursts of loud laughter. There was a repetition of similar scenes across the dimly lit club. The room had an eerie glow cast from a dozen winking table candles. Ownerless shadows glided and shifted upon the Ratskeller walls.

The music began and the lead singer was immediately identifiable as an Elvis Presley worshipper. The guy was good. "You Ain't Nothin' But a Hound Dog"—you kiddin' me, I thought. These people are desperate or, like me, a captive audience. If you shut your eyes and listened, you couldn't help smiling. He had Elvis down pat. In my momentary absorption with the Elvis reincarnation, I lost focus on the mission. Damn! I was too late. No sooner had the first notes filled the room than the vultures came out of the woodwork and hovered around the chicks' table as if sensing fresh carrion. In an instant, the brunette and redhead were up dancing their butts off.

The music was so square, I couldn't even have taken a whirl with a nude Miss Universe. The blonde remained seated, apparently declining the invitation of the diehard who was talking to her. I waited for him to succumb and fall, hoping to get an opportunity to break the code to her coyness. Soon the would-be suitor took his leave with a giddy look and bruised ego. The Elvis group broke into another up-tempo number, "Jail House Rock." If the blonde had turned the other dude down for a dance, I reasoned, what were my chances? Her friends were still dancing; the table was empty of an audience to witness my possible humiliation, so what was there to lose? I took the plunge. Wiping the moisture of my palms on the side of my slacks, I approached the table and saw her look up. Good Lord, I said to myself; she is more beautiful than what I had spied from across the room.

I had rehearsed several introductions but had not chosen the final one. I decided to break with routine contrivance and go for the straight-out, honest approach. "Hi, I apologize for the intrusion, but thought you'd appreciate some good, sane company to chat with and assist you in fending off the riffraff. Your beauty seems to have brought unwelcome attention." She looked up at me with a stare of disbelief wondering, who would use such stilted loquacity.

She responded, "I'm not really in a party mood like my friends. I'm just sitting here, kind of out of it."

"That's cool, if you don't find it a drag, I'll sit here with you and support your mood. My name is Brian. I think my mood is similar to yours," I said, feeling as if I was pushing it.

To my amazement she said, "Yeah, okay, sit down. My name's Eva. Eva Burg, Brian."

I extended my hand; she shook it. Her hand was cold, mine hot—hot like it had been in a pants pocket all day.

"Wow," I said, looking straight into her incredible green eyes, "your name and voice sound Swedish or maybe German."

She responded, "Ya, that's correct. Svedish." The candlelight was doing a ballet on her cheeks. Mesmerized, I apologized to her again for intruding, but explained my boldness with the excuse of having to go back to the war in three days so I was not being held back by shyness to say hello to people who welcomed my friendliness.

Eva was breathtaking. She had short, fine, golden rust-colored hair and a light sprinkling of freckles on her tanned face, which revealed she was logging lots of sun time, somewhere. Her green eyes hypnotized. When she leaned forward, her low-slung turquoise halter offered a peek at the top part of her freckled chest, the sight of which raised the hair on the back of my neck. Our conversation flowed in surprising freedom. Bar conversations so often got mired in the awkward boredom of misspeaks, but not this one. Her face was exquisite and I had difficulty looking her in the eye. When I did, I wanted to kiss her mouth, hold her in my arms, or just kneel down and beg.

After many dances, but too soon, her friends returned. Their eager dance partners loitered briefly, inspired to cliché question-and-answer chitchat. Eva nonchalantly introduced me as Brian, a nice guy who had come to the table to offer reasonable conversation and protect them from corny creeps. They paused briefly, expressionless, wondering if they had heard Eva correctly. Simultaneously, they tilted their heads backward in guffaw, and issued a tongue-in-cheek thank you for sacrificing my time to save them, each shaking my hand. Relying on shallow cleverness to alter the subject matter, I revealed I was a fighter pilot on tour in the F-4 in Vietnam. The ladies quickly confirmed they were all stewardesses for TIA (Trans International Airlines), a West Coast charter carrier that was getting rich off the war in Vietnam hauling GIs. Their crew was laying over at the Oasis Hotel just off base from Clark. They were on a rare extended two-day stay.

Eva and I chatted into the beginning of the next set and once again her gal pals were swept away to the dance floor. Eva shared with me that she was having relationship problems with a guy she really liked but who had become possessive and had begun a pattern of physically abusing her back in Oakland. They were supposed to get married, but hadn't yet set a date. He was pressuring her to act quickly, but she had become unsure of her feelings and their future relationship. Having a penchant for philosophizing and naturally intrigued with relationship counseling, I attempted to coach Eva about her fiancé and asked her to think about what buried perceptions she might have about herself that would make it okay to hang out with anyone who would abuse or disrespect her. We began to bond; she expressed appreciation for my detached objectivity. I had no vested interest in the outcome; I was free to relate and respond. She confessed being confused over what to do and was impressed I was helping her gain clarity.

On the podium, Elvis suddenly broke free of the up-tempo repertoire for a moment and played a slow oldie but goodie, "Love Me Tender." The recording held some strange appeal for me. I prayed Eva would say yes to my first initiative that night for a dance. She rose slowly from the table as I extended my hand, opting to bypass a verbal request. As we entered a slow dance groove, the smell of her perfume, her petite frame in my arms, and her fine copper hair strands tickling against my cheek made my knees feel like they might buckle. I melted for the second time. The tactile immersion made me want to hold her for the rest of the night. She

159

gently placed her arms around my shoulders in an acknowledgment of our conversational intimacy. She relaxed into me, surrendering to the sway of our embrace. I could feel the warmth between her thighs on the sides of my right leg, which was properly placed for the kind of slow dancing my childhood mentor, Chico, had attempted to teach me back in Muncie when I was a clumsy adolescent. She moaned softly into my ear as I made a risky best effort to hum in tune with the melodic ballad. What possessed me to sing, only God knew. I gently kissed Eva's temple and thanked her for making my evening more special than it might otherwise have been. She confessed to being glad we had met.

We danced three decent songs in succession after which, without warning, she announced she was going to be leaving the club soon so that she and her crewmembers could get up in time for early sunbathing around the pool the next morning. Thinking it gentlemanly and tactically prudent, I didn't press Eva for more time that night. Instead, I asked, "How about I drop by the pool tomorrow for a visit, maybe a little lunch?"

"Ya, Brian, that vill be great. Whenever, I'll be at the pool." The first part sounded enthusiastic; the last part had a ring of blasé indifference.

"Cool. I'll walk you out," I replied, feeling like Mr. Big Stuff sitting at their table all night, with many an envious male's eyes upon us, and now walking out with a finalist for most beautiful woman in the club. I thought to myself that, for a bar scene, it didn't get much better than that night. After escorting the threesome to a cab, I returned to the bar to savor the sweetness of the encounter and wallow in the fantasy of what Eva and I would look like twenty-four hours.

Fuzzy visions wrapped in anticipation swirled in my head throughout the night, remembering the sweetness of Eva's fragrance that lingered locked in my senses. The titilating tickle of inhaling her fine, wispy hair strands into my nose as we slow danced replayed constantly. Why did her green eyes hypnotize me so? An excruciating longing within me yearned for something from her—amorphous, inexact, enigmatic. It had to be more noble than lust.

Maybe it was her love; maybe to love her. Was it something so base as the simple taboo of pursuing the untouchable "white thing"? Could it have been some unnatural mystical calling from a buried Oedipal desire to connect with the whiteness of my biological mother? Once again, craving something invisible, lacking tangibility, that could not be possessed, I was unable or unwilling to resist the challenge of seeking it—of filling the unfillable void that lingered deep within me crying out to be cuddled.

The following day, the refresher class on F-4 hydraulics and electrical systems let out by noon, thank God. All six of us in the class were still hung over from the prolonged evening of self-abuse the night before. Bullet Hank, unable to tame his curiosity, asked me what I had done that night. I responded with a vagueness bespeaking boredom, so as to leave the impression there was no party hanging out with me. I did not want him to know I had met a copper-haired Swedish fox who had approved of my stopping by the pool at the Oasis to see her that afternoon. It seemed selfishly cruel of me, given there were other stewardesses with Eva, to deny Bullet Hank the invitation to join me. He surely would have thought he had died and gone to heaven just sitting around them sniffing their perfume, goo-gooing in audience with the "round eyes," the term white guys (and a few politically unsophisticated brothers) so fondly used when referring to white chicks. Perhaps experience had taught me it was a rare white dude who could be thrilled with white chicks preferring to hang out with brothers. Pretentiousness, it seemed, always succumbed to hypocrisy. I left Hank, allowing him to think we might hook up later at the club, a deception that soon backfired.

I stopped by the officers' club package store to get a jug of something for the pool visit and for sipping later in the day. Inexplicably, I chose to buy a bottle of creme de menthe liqueur, which was a first-time impulse purchase to help pace the drinking groove for the day, given the clinging fuzziness from a late night and little rest. The creme de menthe was a rich, dark green color, soothing to my eyes. I figured I could offer some to Eva with a little club soda, rendering a creative poor man's spritzer that would make a great poolside imbibement.

I placed myself at the pickup point just outside the package store to catch the hotel van, which made regular stops at the club on the way to the Oasis. Within five minutes, the bus turned the corner right on schedule, and, with the large jug of liqueur stuffed down into my left flight suit pocket, banging against my leg with every step, I excitedly boarded. Anxiety crawled all over me as the bus proceeded through the front gate security checkpoint toward the hotel.

What adventure, I thought. It occurred to me I didn't even know what I was doing, simply trekking into the unknown, driven, compulsive, like chasing an addiction. My angel side was questioning my motive for pursuing this gorgeous stewardess. No moral justification was available. The devil side was making a great speech of rationalization. "Shit, man, you over here layin' your life down for some bullshit war you might not come back from. Why shouldn't you be all over Eva if she welcomes you? Go for it."

As I stepped off the bus in front of the Oasis, a single word in neon lights flashed in my mind: *Madness.* The hotel had a lush tropical ambience, rows of well-trimmed palm trees, along with soothing green broad-leafed banana trees nestled among exotic flora splendidly accented by radiant purples, yellows, and reds. Brown geckos frolicked and skittered about in the bushes, pausing briefly to puff out their bright orange throats in their mating rituals. The scene was the paradise that honeymooners and lovers dream about, thick with humidity and jungle fever palpitations.

A sign at the front entrance had an arrow pointing down the walkway for the pool. Following the winding brick pathway through the lavishly manicured foliage, ducking to prevent the armlike ginkgo tree branches from ripping away my flight cap, I came to the Oasis pool. Two women appearing to be in their late twenties splashed idly in the pool, clinging to the side and giggling in conversation. Directly above them was Eva, lying in the sun in a lounge chair. I surmised the girls in the pool were also some of Eva's crew but I did not recognize them. As I approached Eva, I could see her eyes were closed beneath her sunglasses. Her hair had a damp, stringy appearance, indicating she might have just gone swimming. I took advantage of her slumber to scan her gifts as her skin deepened its golden red glow in the hot Philippine sun. A sea green micro bikini hugged her small frame and cupped her young girl's breasts. She looked so young, so small, like a girl of thirteen. A month shy of twenty-five, I seemed to dwarf her, but she was two years older; she had confessed it the night before. As if sensing my visual feasting, her eyes suddenly opened to behold me standing over her. "Hi, Brian," she said in a soft, drowsy voice that made me want to nurse on her right there. Eva was angelic, the embodiment of the purest, whitest, most beautiful rendering Sweden could offer the world.

Maintaining all possible cool, I casually responded, "Hey, lady. What's happening? You lookin' too cool out here."

She chuckled back, saying, "You say the neatest things."

I asked politely, "Is it okay if I hang out with you for a bit?"

"Sure, vee can visit for a while, but the girls and I are going shopping in about an hour." My heart sank; my face seemed to crack, like a marble wall being slammed with a sledge hammer. There was something else she would rather do than get to know me? Damn! *Recover,* I thought. *Don't panic. Keep your cool; be with her agenda—remain accommodating. Never appear to be desperate for company. And, for God's sake, don't give her any cause to think you might want to make love with her before you go back to Da Nang.*

"Yeah, no sweat, I got some stuff I need to do too," I responded, lying though my teeth. Going to get another drink at the club maybe, I thought, feeling small time.

Eva and I sat by the pool sharing lightweight stories wrapped in superficiality, me being very careful about any slip-of-the-tongue mention of a wife waiting longingly back in the States for a jive-ass husband to return alive. Amazingly, Eva went for the idea of the crème de menthe and soda. I strode over to the brown metal ice-making machine tucked in a cubbyhole to retrieve some cubes. Plastic cups for pool guests were neatly stacked on top. It was brief slice of heaven being there with Eva, looking into her deep green eyes when I wasn't staring trancelike into the glimmering greenish-blue water of the swimming pool, feeling like a character in a romance novel.

In less than half an hour, Eva's friends interrupted our exchange to remind her it was time to get dressed to go shopping. She actually invited me along. That was pushing my zeal; I wanted to hang out with her, not her gal pals ooohing and aaahing over monkey pod statues and native jewelry. I politely declined—one could sacrifice but so much, even if the most treasured example of feminine pulchritude was at stake. Eva kept the door of the fantasy open by asking if I wanted to get together later for supper. She explained that it would be the last night of their layover before heading to Tokyo. A premature feeling of loss and desperation for more time with her overwhelmed me. Maintaining my cool in a feigned indifference was challenging. Ultimately, there was only one thing to say, "That's great. What time's good for you?"

"Seven o'clock be okay. I can't be up too late'n. We have da early go," she replied. Feigning unstoppablility, I shook off the potential obstacle of an early good-night foreclosing on a groovy evening.

"No sweat." I beamed, kiddingly adding,"Your place or mine?"

After a brief but seemingly deliberate consideration, Eva replied, "Your place. Yeah. I'll come over to the Plaza."

A sudden display of mature sophistication from Eva made me wonder if she was playing me more than I was playing her. Was it privacy from the others she sought? I thought. I fought off my suspicions, rationalizing, *"Come on, man, this ain't no time to get bogged down in details of why it's your place rather than hers."* Waxing into a bit of Don Quixotic chivalry, I sought her reassurance that it was not a problem for her to come over alone to the Plaza Hotel. She assured me it was no sweat.

Gleeful over the prospect of dinner with Eva, I returned to the Plaza, whistling a happy, unrecognizable tune. Upon arrival at my room, my all's-right-with-the-world euphoria inspired me to commit an unnatural act. I called Bullet Hank to see what he was up to. I was shocked and somewhat moved that he was in his room alone, sipping cold Sam Miguels, reading his book and listening to television. My intellectual wanna-be side whispered into my ear that Bullet Hank was spending his leisure time doing what real intellectuals do, reading novels and scholarly periodicals rather than chasing skirt tails around the globe. He acted delighted that I called to suggest we do something together. To my surprise, he came up with shopping as an acceptable diversion. What the hell, I thought. At least it would give Hank a sense we did spend some time hanging out. What a great act of altruism. Stealing short swigs of the creme de menthe, I jumped in the stall for a quick shower, slid into a tight-fitting pair of gray slacks to match a black Banlon shirt, and hurried downstairs to meet him. We caught a jitney taxi to take us down to the strip in Angeles City where all the tourist shops spread out block after block.

As fate would have it, while we were browsing over knickknacks (far from my favorite thing to be doing), who should come strolling into the same shop but Eva and her entourage. I was all teeth as Eva spotted me standing by the monkey pod carvings next to Bullet Hank. I thought, *Oh boy, this is going to be interesting.*

"Brian, what a coincidence?" Eva shouted across the store.

"Hey, Eva, what a gas," I said, acting casual and nonchalant. Bullet Hank looked up at me with a raised eyebrow expression as if he had just busted me, saying, "Hey, guy, what you been holding out on me?"

"Naw, man, I just met them briefly last night at the club," I assured him.

Naturally, his curiosity took over and a surge of bravado induced a request for me to introduce him to these honeys. In an instant, after exchanging introductory pleasantries, Bullet Hank attempted to strike up a conversation with Eva and her crew. They did not seem interested in being entertained by his wit and humor for very long. I was suddenly struck with pity for Bullet Hank--he was too square and out of it to know how to relate.

Excusing themselves, Eva made my day by whispering to me in front of Bullet Hank, "See you around seven."

Being quick to catch Eva's words, he looked wistfully at me, exclaiming, "What do you have going, Bee?" It seemed as if he was entitled to know as my superior whatever I had going might be against policy or, at the very least, some of his business. I knew I didn't have to reveal my social calendar, but not to tell him would haunt his mind even more. I sloughed off his interrogation by responding that Eva was good people and we had shared some personal stuff the night before and were just tapping into a little human relatedness.

"Yeah, Bee, I got your relatedness, you slick fucker." My response had given him a lot of territory to wander over, being the intellect he was. I took some degree of sadistic delight in knowing he was squirming inside, presuming this brother was banging this magnificent creature, this white woman that he, the white man, wouldn't get to touch. But brother Bee was stepping out into the forbidden zone and, since the Emancipation and the civil rights bills had already been signed, there wasn't a thing he could do about it except be envious and perhaps regretful.

Feeling elated from the encounter with Eva, I returned to my room for a mini-siesta after the shopping foray before showering again in preparation for dinner. Taking regular hits of the creme de menthe, I could feel my raging libido clawing at me with the strength of a lion as I showered. I could hardly contain myself. I ached for the tubular tickling of orgasmic release, but struggled desperately for self-control. My sense of who I was assured me that Eva thought I was unique, perhaps stimulating and easy to be with. I hoped she would want an indelible memory, an isolated groove, something to take home in her recall bank that would make life seem a little more precious. It would be a cherishable reminiscence—a fleeting interlude of magnificence with a sensitive man who spoke like a poet-philosopher.

The loud ring of the phone startled me. It was Eva.

"Hi, Brian, it's me," she whispered in the softest voice.

"Hey, lady, I'm glad you're early. You want me to come down and we go to the bar or cool out in the room for a while?"

"I can come up'n and vee can talk'n. I don't feel like being in da crowd'n with people tonight," she responded in a half-dejected tone. A moment later, she was knocking softly at the door. After my third shower of the day, I had again donned my gray khaki pants, but this time slipped on a red Banlon sport shirt to render the deception of a wardrobe change. Even my boots were polished. My stomach had been gurgling throughout the afternoon, leaving me woozy and feeling somewhere between an impending massive gastro-colic reflex and preparing to take a big final exam. I wasn't sure if the intestinal roulette wheel was major butterflies over seeing Eva again or food poisoning. I had been sipping the crème de menthe off and on all afternoon; maybe that was the problem.

I unbolted the door and opened it slowly and deliberately, wanting to pan Eva's figure standing there. Anything for greater dramatics. Hands crossed in front of her, she was holding a small navy blue purse and wearing a bright green form-fitting dress that stopped just above her knees with matching green flats. She seemed to know exactly the proper colors to magnify her golden tanned radiance. Her blonde hair looked freshly washed and blow dried to a fine sheen, hugging her head. She had squared-off bangs across her forehead like Cleopatra. She was radiantly aglow, as if dolled up for a big date. But she was there to see me, Brian Settles from Muncie, Indiana, former Bearcat and reluctant fighter jock. That instant, tangible and real, was the brief encapsulation of what looking good felt like. I was fresh and clean wearing my sporty duds. She resembled a finalist in the Miss World contest. I welcomed her into my room and placed my hand gently on her lower back, just above the curvy musculature of her left buttock.

Immediately I confessed, "Eva, you may never know how thrilled I am you honored me with this visit before you leave tomorrow."

"Jeeps, Brian, don'tn be so modest. Vhat girl vouldn't vant to hang out with a looker like you and you seem to be a great guy too."

"But you don't know me, really. You just met me at the club last night. I could be Brian the Ripper. What makes you trust me enough to come to the room of a stranger?" I asked rhetorically, perpetually intrigued with making the simple complex.

"Vhat you vant to do, Brian, scare me and make me vant to leave?" she said, flashing a bit of vulnerability and imprudence.

"No, no, I'm sorry. I was simply moved by the trust you have for me. I mean to be here together like this—in my room. I am the perfect gentleman. We shall have no experience that isn't mutually agreed upon," I said, attempting to assuage any misgivings.

I invited her to have a seat and asked if she wanted to go to the restaurant or order room sevice. More shock: She voted for room service. I phoned down to the kitchen. She ordered a small Kobe beef dinner with baked potato and steamed carrots. I ordered the chef's salad with blue cheese dressing and rolls. Eva decided to have a glass of burgundy and I opted to stay with the crème de menthe, which I had quietly begun to spike with a touch of Beefeater gin. Somewhere along the road, I had come to discover that, for me, gin was inexplicably a great poor man's aphrodisiac, especially Beefeater. I didn't know where the evening with Eva would lead, but if making love was to be a part of it, I surely wanted to be ready for action. Room service arrived quickly, and the gleam in the eye of the dapperly dressed Philippino waiter seemed to say to me, "Right on, brother san, you bang bang pretty girl for me too."

After our cozy little meal, Eva settled back in the lounge chair beside the bed; I kicked back on the bed, slipping my boots off, feeling quite at home in her company, rested against the hand-carved mahogany headboard. I ordered another burgundy from room service. My stomach's rumbling seemed to be intensifying, but struggling to ignore it, I remained committed to the gin and crème de menthe.

Sharing stories about her experiences being constantly pawed at by men in her job as a stewardess for TIA and my strange career in the Air Force flying fighters in combat, I glimpsed a sadness in Eva and I decided to explore her melancholy.

"Eva, your extaordinary beauty does not conceal the distraction in your gaze. You seem to be harboring a heavy heart about something or someone. Would you like to share more of what life looks like for you?"

"You're very smart, Brian, maybe too smart for me," Eva confessed. "I'm have da very inside crushed by dis'n guy I thought'n vas anxious for marrying me back in Oakland. He's quite da handsome Italian, and athletic, but now he vants to put off to engage me. Like he vants to punish because I have trouble vit' being treat badly. He does not have the honesty. He von't talk'n me about the things deep, of da feelings or vhat's in the heart. Meeting you make me think he probably not the right man for me." Sitting up on the bed at her admission, I reached over and grasped Eva's hand, squeezing it in firm reassurance. Tears began to run down her golden, tanned face. I left the bed to hug her while kneeling at her side, my knees burning in agony from the hardwood floor.

Our deepening communion grew ominous. To the degree that I was capable of sensing her pain and disappointment, I felt a vicarious sadness for her. I was sorry that women were subjected to the insincerity and exploitation of men who were experts at playing on their weaknesses and naivete. I looked Eva in the eyes and said, " If you are in love with someone who is not right for you, someone who does not hold honesty and your happiness as a priority, it is better you find out quickly and get the pain dismissed earlier rather than later."

"You're vight, Brian. You're vight. It just hurts so much to give da love and be da good person, not vanting to hurt people, and then be hurt by da ones you vant to love," she said, sobbing. As if Eva and I were both lost souls perfoming in our own existential version of *Little Miss Muffet,* I leaned toward her and began to kiss away the tears on her reddened face. Then, slowly, I began to kiss her thin salt-coated lips. The verbal outpouring of pain and disappointment had served as a catalyst to unleash the passion of a woman who was not being loved frequently or properly. Having earned her trust as a wise and sympathetic ear, Eva began to free her soul to fully immerse herself in me and in that moment, in the microcosm of that obscure room outside Clark Air Force Base, the Philippines, far away from Oakland, California, and Indianapolis, Indiana.

We kissed and kissed; she began to suck on my tongue with such force that a masochistic euphoria overcame me. I wallowed in the pain she rendered from her passion's desperation. Increasingly more passionate, we turned up the intensity of our submersion in hugging and squeezing, forcing the intimacy to teeter on frenzy, at the edge of out of control. I gently and patiently fumbled my way through unlocking her bra clasp, hoping not to derail the spontaneity of our absorption. Undoing her blouse buttons, I could feel the heat of her chest as I lifted her tiny bra cups above her breasts, exposing her hardened dark red nipples. I exhaled heavily as I took her left nipple to my lips before softly pulling most of her breast inside my mouth. She moaned in acknowledgment and submission to the pleasure. I could feel the blood rushing to my groin as I stiffened in the throb of arousal.

The gurgling utterances of my stomach made it easy to believe there were three of us in the room. As if suddenly competing for attention in the emotional chaos of the moment, I began to bear witness to the duelling sensations within my body that might force a quick dash to the bathroom. Both knees, too long imbedded in the hardwood floor, wrenched in throbbing pain. What a masochistic price was being paid clinging to Zen control over pain in the mania of the pursuit. I pulled Eva up with me as I guided her onto the bed. Clothes still on, and Eva with an open blouse and crooked, drawn-up bra, I laid down on top of her wanting her, to know and feel my stimulation. I struggled in a juggling act to stay focused on the mission and ignore the incessant colonic disruptions. Maneuvering her skirt hem up her legs, I spread her heated thighs with my good knee to introduce the erection clawing through my pants to her beckoning nest. She squirmed and moaned softly, indicating with her body she wanted me to have her then and there, thrusting herself toward me in surrender. Thoughts—errant thoughts—bombarded my consciousness. It was too good to be true. I was on the verge of cracking under the rush of euphoria. Was I really going to get laid in the Philippines on a brief escape from Da Nang?

With the ultimate in gentlemanly sensitivity, I suggested to Eva we slip her skirt off to avoid excess wrinkling, to which she responded, "Yeah, Brian, good thinking." I pulled back the clean fresh sheets and Eva placed herself in my bed with only her pink flowered bikini panties, her tanned body looked like it came straight from a dream—surreal and absorbing.

As I slipped off my slacks, feeling my erection departing, I was overwhelmed by a massive intestinal surge that forced me to excuse myself and step quickly and lightly to the bathroom. I was suddenly flushed with discomfort; Eva was writhing in ectasy waiting for me to make love with her and I was running for my life to avoid destroying the ambience with a scene unimaginably gross. What a trip.

I shut the bathroom door and had barely lighted upon the oval throne before my sphincter relaxed, releasing the unstoppable green flood. Good Lord, I thought, my stomach's churning like a Mixmaster; I swabbed myself back to freshness and stood to partake in the unexplained human ritual, like cats do, of viewing the deposit before flushing it. The toilet bowl was polka dotted with a marvelously hued dark green goosh. The prolonged sipping of creme de menthe had painted my insides bright green. I returned half-stunned to the side of the bed. Eva said in a concerned voice, "Are you feeling okay?"

Good Lord, I thought, *did she hear me through the paper-thin walls?* I felt like an idiot. I responded, "Yeah, I just had a little stomach upset, but I'm better now."

Since the mood had been radically altered, I took on the challenge of regenerating the ambience. Eva repeated her lines that she really thought I was a neat guy and wished she had met me earlier. I thanked her for the compliment, and soon we began to peck tenderly at each other's faces. A few shudders later our tongues were probing each other's mouths again. I soon maneuvered myself back atop Eva's mountain and was again feeling her wetness calling to me through her panties. The steamy eros of Eva's readiness (and the Beefeater) had left me fully ready. In that moment of overheated frenzy, that life-sustaining connection between human spirit and longing for intimacy, Eva and I knew we suddenly had no say in the matter. Our communion had crystalized into unharnessable passion. With both hands I gently lowered her panties down her legs and off one foot. My shy erection throbbed in the sequestered silence. I experienced tightness at the entry to Eva's paradise as the love probe poked and gently endeavored to push past humble resistence. In the increasing flood of humidity and stimulation, I could feel Eva's warm breath puffing against my face as I eased gradually, sliding through the snugness into the sanctity of her being. The sensation was gripped in tintillating power, intoxicating, juicy, and beckoning, warm and wonderful, heaped with that human essence that dominates all of us with such a simple satisfaction—that magnet of biological pull.

Unexpectedly, gripped in perspiration and panting, Eva whispered in my ear, "Brian, I'm tinkin' I'm falling for you big time. I vantin' you to know'n that I don't use'n d'birth control. It is a time that I could get pregnant, but I can't make myself care in this moment. I need you so badly. I'm vantin' you inside me."

Bam. Just like that, an avalanche of bricks, cold water, and stampeding elephants came down on my consciousness. My mind flashed back to the conversation I had with my T-38 instructor, Captain David L. Ramsay, the only Black instructor pilot in our training squadron at Laredo. The subject was whether Celeste and I should try to get pregnant before I left. I had embraced the ultimate manifestation of caring advice in following the wisdom of his recommendation—"Don't leave behind an attractive war widow who would have the additional burden of raising a child alone as she went forth to create new relations in going on with her life."

Hovering above Eva, I was ready to submerge myself in unbridled love-making. I rationalized the appropriateness of doing so because I was a Vietnam fighter pilot who might be dead next week. But the more powerful grip on my conscience was the paralyzing horror of telling Celeste I was the father of a child I had sired while on a boondoggle from Vietnam. I was slammed with the icy glacier of guilt and a ponderous sense of dishonesty and betrayal. My body's weight slowly relaxed onto Eva. I was struck silent, motionless, face-to-face with my selfish, reckless behavior. A behavior that was guided only by the present moment and the panic created beneath the skin of the flesh within me that I might become a casualty of Vietnam—that I might never go home alive or, even worse, be maimed and dysfunctional in some way that would alter my relationship with Celeste for the rest of our lives.

Sensing my shift, Eva inquired, "Brian, did you hear what I said?"

"Yeah," I replied solemnly. "Yes, I did."

Eva's intuition began to serve her better; she struggled against my weight to sit up in bed as she seemed to grasp I had suddenly hit a wall. "Don't you still want to make love to me?" she said wistfully.

"Yeah, Eva, in the worse way, but I can't," I confessed, feeling the heat of the connection cooling as quickly as the Arizona desert upon sunset.

"There's something you haven't told me, isn't there, Brian?" she retorted, sensing an awful truth. At that moment, I was free to utter any lie to get off the hook, to concoct any explanation I could have dreamed up. I didn't have to run the risk of freaking her out after she had already shared the heartbreak and disappoinment of knowing that her would-be fiance was an imposter, playing her along because she was gullible and perhaps an easy prey for any seasoned predator.

Daring to stand for some modicum of truth and mercy, I said apologetically and ashamedly, "I cannot be dishonest and take advantage of your feelings, Eva. I have not been completely open with you about my life, and you are too nice and deserving of a human being for me to treat you otherwise."

Eva interrupted, "You're married."

It seemed eons passed before my mouth would work, before I could respond. "Yes, Eva. I have a wife," I admitted, not knowing what to expect.

Quickly pulling herself to her feet, trembling as she fidgeted to slip on her skirt, fasten her bra, and button her blouse, she turned, heading for the door, and said, "Godbe-damn you, Brian. You bastard. And to think vhat I vould have surrendered. Tanks for da truthfulness and tanks for nutting." Eva launched herself forward, having slapped her clothes on speedier than Clark Kent before he turned into Superman and slammed the door with an abrupt bam that vibrated the wall. I stood there, silent, in the middle of the room gazing briefly at the empty steaming bed that had seconds earlier been a would-be love nest. My head swiveled back toward the door. I was convinced I had just experienced an out-of-body phenomenon. I was stunned and feeling very green—green with envy to be anyone else but myself in that moment, in that miserable place of pristine deceit and immaculate deception.

CHAPTER 16: WIDOW'S HERO

The words that magically come to us for writing poems are like loaded seeds of creative inspiration that drop rainfall-like upon our minds from the universe. Whenever these literary kernels visit our minds, they must be written down or we lose the opportunity to capture a speck of life's fleeting quintessence.

"Widow's Hero" was one of the few poems I wrote about combat in Vietnam. Unlike my brilliant poet Vietnam vet brother in Los Angeles, Horace Coleman, who published an entire book of Vietnam poems entitled *In the Grass* generated from his experience, I wrote mostly desperate letters. "Widow's Hero" was, strangely, a eulogistic poem for a golf instructor buddy who was also my classmate at Laredo. He was a gung-ho Virginia Military Institute graduate.

I had survived eight months flying the F-4 in Vietnam; four long months remained. The intelligence briefing on that warm night in April 1969, before going on Gunfighter alert for a twelve-hour graveyard shift, contained a summary of in-country activity and downed aircraft for that day. A Phantom had gone down on a napalm pass along the Cambodian border in the area called the Triangle west of Phu Cat Airbase. The briefing officer uttered the too-often-heard infamous phrase, "No chutes, no beepers." The Phantom crew had gone in with the bird. I was stunned once again by the twin disbeliefs of hearing and then knowing that inexorable avalanche of horrors tumbling down on me as the crew's names were read. The copilot was Vince Scott, my pilot training classmate.

Vince was as different from me as a lion is from a leopard—an electrical engineering major from VMI, right wing, conservative, crew cut, who believed in the Vietnam War. At first encounter, I didn't particularly like him. He possessed a cockiness honed by academic success and white middle-class privilege and had cultivated a witty albeit dry, nerdy personality—so intelligent he was borderline boring. Until meeting me, I didn't think he had ever been around a

Black person. Despite our differences, his having graduated with honors in electrical engineering impressed me and I took him on as a project to school him on Black culture and sentiment. Ironically, in Air Force pilot training he took on teaching me the rules and techniques of playing his favorite pastime, golf, a game I had always avoided, not wanting to be confused with the bourgeois fairway folks who played it. I generally perceived them as a self-centered lot who voted conservatively, resisted integration, and simply urged colored folks to be patient about civil rights advancement.

Vince had a gorgeous blonde wife named Michelle who fronted a figure that would stop traffic. It was not easy being around her and Vince together because you didn't want to get busted struggling to take your eyes off her. Lame as Vince seemed, I just knew some suitor would be chasing the daylights out of her back in the States while Vince was away in Vietnam making the world safe for democracy. It was paradoxical that I was moved so deeply by the news of his becoming another Vietnam combat loss statistic.

After completing the preflight checks of the birds we were assigned for alert duty that night after the flight line activity had subsided around 2300 hours (11 PM). I took leave of my squadron buddies in the alert shack and slipped into the comforting solitude of the late evening breezes. Drawn inexplicably to the concrete reinforced revetment where our lethal sleeping Phantom was bedded down for the night, I eased under the six-foot-high left wing and plopped myself down on the concrete ramp and snuggled my back against the left main tire for support. The auxiliary power units were shut down; the revetment was illuminated by huge bright floodlights with circular aluminum hoods to help direct the light beams. The intensity of the lights shining down on the F-4 cast a silhouette of the bird on the concrete beneath it. I was seated where the light shone on my yellow legal pad but not on me directly.

After a meditative pause in the hypnotic midnight tranquility, as if conducting my own private wake, I wept and reflected on what I may have omitted saying to Vince that would have let him know, despite our differences, we were really just the same and that I admired him. Words began to flow across my consciousness like stock quotes printed on a ticker tape and, as if I were a poet stenographer, I transferred the words to my pad. I wrote "Widow's Hero" in dedication to Vince and myself.

WIDOW'S HERO

Black pervaded night as thick as coal,
Another sojourner to the rudiments retires,
Where once again his nature an element becomes.
No doubt that it's right, but for widows untimely.

From his fresh lover's womb to the cold crust converge,
When warmth of springtime had yet to show the dark side of
    scourge.
No more promise of the great trip to the West,
Now only eternity in the chilled Phantom's nest.

Returning, still burning, to the basics repair,
Man strapped to machine, both rusting to ashes.
For one, last red fluid drips unslowed from the tubing,
While for better half-dried plasma no more hope does it offer.
Engines now seized; no Hawaii revisited,
Lonely maiden sob to regroup—as of yet still forbidden.

Dubious slaughter, one against the other,
Bullshit engagement—more fucked-up the marriage.
Sinister masturbation flowing from Macho perturbation,
But on goes the scramble; three cheers for the nation.

A long time no see. Well, I've been returning
To a lush foreign land not mine to be yearning,
And so sorry, now, to clutch the rich sod of another
As I lay dying on the land of my slant-eyed brother.

Insanity's roar was that which provoked
And led me to lunacy on untraveled shores.
So don't sweat the small shit; life is too short,
But expect government condolences arriving at your door.
   "OVER."

CHAPTER 17: THE GOLDEN B B

Air Force undergraduate pilot training had been my first grassroots exposure to college graduates from the deep South. Indiana had its rich sports rivalries among the Boilermakers, the Hoosiers, and the Kentucky Wildcats. But teams in the Midwest never received national attention as did the big schools like Louisiana State University, Texas, Texas A & M, Ole Miss, Florida, and Miami. My classmates at Laredo Air Force Base mostly came from these southern colleges, graduates who had by choice been thrust into a lifestyle of allegiance to the history of their alma mater and the myriad jokes and name calling that were all part of it.

My classmate buddy, Lieutenant Virgil Grant Stewart, was a Louisiana State University grad. Like me, he was a distinguished military graduate (DMG) from his ROTC program. With DMG feathers in our caps, upon arrival at Laredo, Texas, Grant and I shared duties as class leaders for our pilot training class of 68C. I was assistant class leader and Grant was class leader.

Being responsible for much of the communications between the training squadron and our classmates, Grant and I shared the workload of getting the word out, organizing social gatherings, and meeting with training officers. Grant was special. Although he had grown up deep in the boondocks of southern Louisiana, he had been molded into a compassionate spirit and evolved into a genuine people person, able to relate to people whether rich or impoverished, Native American, African-American, or Cajun. His open-mindedness and acceptance of others broke the stereotype of southern good ol' boys, I could honestly say he lacked the overt prejudices that most carry away from the legacy of the Confederacy and their hometown experiences. Grant had an uncanny sensitivity and support for the racial struggle in the South. One didn't need to convince Grant or school him about race relations--he understood. He was distinct from a lot of white folks who couldn't (or wouldn't) comprehend the depth of the discrimination experienced by people of color in America. Liberated by the numbness of a half-dozen Cuba Libres, Grant would actually defend the minority struggle at home. Was it guilt? It didn't matter. Full of a good ol' boy wit and omniscience, he browbeat his racist southern cohorts who listened to his exhortations in shocked disbelief that Grant had traded in the views for which the Confederate flag stood to carry the flag of human relatedness. In some circles, behind his back, he was called a nigger lover.

I admired Grant for his intelligence and willingness to stand for something beyond the preservation of the southern past. He had a gift of common sense. Like me, he sometimes struggled academically with the rigors of the pilot training program, but his desire to be an Air Force pilot kept him always inspired to do whatever it took to succeed.

Grant was skinny as a rail. He chain-smoked Marlboros and loved to get shitfaced at the officers' club. He would get loaded on his rum and Coke, shoot craps with field grade officers in the back room of the club, play poker until 4 AM and be up at noon overhauling the carburetor on his souped-up '56 Chevy. I admired anyone with that natural mechanical know-how, people who could figure out how to take something apart, add a new piece, and put it all back together without ever consulting an auto maintenance manual. Grant had that talent.

Judy was Grant's wife. They were college sweethearts at LSU. She had a full figure, a great Louisiana accent, and loved to cook and entertain their friends. Anyone could tell they had a salubrious marriage. It was not exempt from upsets and breakdowns, normally brought on by Grant's spontaneous, cowboy like zest for having a ball with the richness of life. At the drop of a hat, he would stop anything he was doing to go off fishing with me. With backwoods experience in hunting, trapping, and fishing, Grant was like a modern-day Daniel Boone. My bland accounts of night fishing for bullhead catfish along the banks of the Elkhart or Wabash rivers in Indiana couldn't hold a candle to Grant's stories about encounters with cottonmouths and rattlers and gators while camped out deep in the swamps of the Louisiana wilderness. We had a closeness that made our race differences invisible. Deep inside, where the heart of hope pumps out its dreams, I secretly wished all people were able to be as free and generous as Grant. I regularly basked in the warmth of welcome in Judy and Grant's apartment, even when I was a bachelor. They shared an equal empathy for the bachelor pilots in our class who had to eat all their meals at the officers' club or the open mess and I turned down many invitations from them for dinner or a barbecue. It was common knowledge to those close to Grant and Judy they were trying to start a family. Judy seemed to be having difficulty conceiving and would share her wifely frustrations with Celeste when she joined me in pilot training after our marriage.

Most of my classmates in 68C were outwardly ecstatic to receive notification of their F-4 assignments—pipeline Southeast Asia orders to war in Nam. Grant, being the essence of fighter-pilot zeal and desire, was euphoric about flying fighters for his country. His wife, while happy for her husband, walked around their small apartment fretting over the inevitable separation that would have to be endured as part of a military officer's duty to support the Air Force mission wherever it led him.

Celeste quietly agonized over my behind-the-back move to bid for the F-4, knowing it would take me to Vietnam. She kept her thoughts to herself. But, unlike the other wives whose husbands were overjoyed, Celeste did not understand why I was volunteering to fly fighters and risk my life—her husband's life—in Vietnam. She never knew at the time that I didn't either.

And so it was that Grant, half the class of 68C, and I (over fifty of us) graduated from Laredo Air Force Base in October 1967. Many of us set out for F-4 training after getting our Air Force pilot wings that wonderful day. Grant and Judy returned to their home in Louisiana to enjoy thirty days' leave and continue working on having that first child. For me and Celeste, that car ride in her little red Falcon Futura across Texas toward the Midwest and Indiana was the most glorious basking in the warmth of achievement I had ever experienced. In my mind I had overachieved--had accomplished the incredible. Brian Settles, half-breed from Muncie, lazy B-minus student, ex-Bearcat, and coulda-been collegiate hoop star, had reached beyond his comfort zone of possibility to achieve what had never existed in his wildest dreams. I had made the starting five on the ultimate sporting team. I was going to be an Air Force fighter pilot.

Occasionally, there are those brief, fleeting moments when the sense of peace and joy is bursting within us—a moment, an experience in time that one wishes could be locked in forever, as if one had just found the closest connection to Heaven on Earth. I shall never forget the freeway sign reading Texas State Line—Welcome to Oklahoma. A grueling year at Laredo was in my rearview mirror. The radio reception in that moment was excellent as the long-play version of the new Doors hit, "Light My Fire," filled the car interior. Celeste, in a rare state of relaxation and inner solitude, slept obliviously with her head resting on my right thigh. I was bursting with the pride of personal accomplishment. Grant, the rest of class 68C, and I were returning home. I was going back to Muncie to see Mama, Margerie, and all my friends and relatives who would honor me with congratulations on becoming a pilot and express their disbelief that I was going to fly jet fighters in the war in Vietnam.

EIGHTEEN MONTHS LATER

I was lying on my bed with the door gapped open, reading old issues of the *Muncie Evening Press* at 1600 hours (4 PM). It was mid-May 1969 and my partying spirit had temporarily abandoned me. Celebrations for special occasions had become anticlimactic and replaced by numb listlessness. Instead, I was choosing to lose myself in the revelry of silence on the day I had turned twenty-five, once again delighting in pulling off the macho challenge of not bringing it to anyone's attention.

A sweltering, unrelenting heat hung over Da Nang; there were three months remaining on my tour. I heard the bang of a door slam at the entry to the officers' quarters. Someone was slowly shuffling down the linoleum hallway. The sound of the steps became louder and, spotting a shadow, I glanced up to see Captain Bill Nelson standing in my doorway; we affectionately referred to him as *The Admiral*. He was short in stature, maybe five foot seven, and rotund. He sported a silly-looking mustache, thin and scraggly, just like mine. He was sweating profusely and he had a beer can clenched in his stubby hand. The air-conditioned quarters seemed to advance his sweating. The perspiration patterns on his light gray flight suit revealed he had just come out of his survival vest and G suit.

"What's happenin', Admiral?" I asked.

"Looks like you're happenin' lying on your ass while the rest of us are out there fighting the war," he replied.

"You got that right, asshole," I retorted with a big grin, knowing I had beat him with my remark. I noticed that he was clinching a small cassette tape recorder in his other hand. Many of us carried recorders to tape our combat missions. Admiral was a front-seater who had volunteered for the Stormy FAC program when Tactical Air Command decided to use F-4s as forward air control aircraft for air-to-ground strikes over Laos. It was open season on U.S. jet fighters every day in Vietnam and especially Laos. There wasn't a North Vietnamese Army Regular or Vietcong who wouldn't sacrifice his life to be able to shoot down an F-4. Flying the F-4s down low to the ground, looking for targets of opportunity that fighter-bombers could bomb, was like trolling hot dogs through a school of piranha. Admiral and the other Stormy FACs were always getting hosed down by enemy ground fire, particularly in Laos.

My eyes left the recorder at Admiral's side and back up to scan his face. He looked whipped with fatigue. "D'yall have a rough one out there today?" I asked.

"Fuckin' A, man. A four-hour fuckin' search and rescue at Mu Ghia. We hit the tanker twice."

"Damn," I responded, if for no other reason than just knowing how hard that F-4 seat gets on an hour-and-a-half mission. Admiral seemed subdued and pensive. Inviting him in to sit down, I inquired further, "Who went down?" He began to slide his pudgy frame along the wall by the door to sit on the floor but abruptly stiffened his legs to stand erect.

As if it were an afterthought, given the effort it was going to take him to slide his ass to the floor, he asked if I had anything to drink. Beer in Nam was like Coca-Cola. Booze was one commodity that didn't have long life expectancy around fighter pilots. Luckily, I had a jug of Beefeater in the fridge, and I invited him to help himself to the unopened grapefruit juice chilling on the shelf beside it. I never moved from my repose on the bed. He filled an eight-ounce water glass one-third with gin, topped it off with grapefruit juice, and returned to repeat the athletic challenge of slowly sliding down the wall, using his boot soles for traction.

Not knowing if he was deliberately keeping me in suspense before his reply, I waited patiently for him to get settled. After lighting a Salem, he pulled his knees up toward his chest, rested his right elbow on his right knee, and exhaled the account. "Yeah, it was a Phantom out of the 8th from Ubon. Fucked-up shit, Bee." A foreboding crept through my insides as I grasped the reality that many of my classmates from Ball State and F-4 training were stationed at Ubon Air Force Base, Thailand, in the 8th TAC Fighter Wing. It was the very same fighter wing, the Wolf Pack, made famous by MIG killers Colonels Robin Olds and Daniel "Chappie" James, the latter an original Tuskegee Airman.

"What happened, man?" I inquired, sitting up, feeling intensity beginning to take over my face as Admiral relayed the details of the search-and-rescue (SAR) mission. These were often the scariest missions because they were always conducted under dire no-holds-barred circumstances, and every crewmember in Vietnam gave a hundred and fifty percent to rescue a downed airman. It was the one mission we were authorized to "hang it out," "get down in the weeds," and "press the target" to save a buddy. There were often multiple aircraft losses on SAR efforts and it was also the one occasion when fighter pilots abandoned their usual bombing safety precautions. From experience, we knew enemy ground fire could be intense in a rescue zone. The area of a downed aircraft was always swarmed on by enemy soldiers like maggots on a carcass, knowing there would be major attempts made to effect rescue. Downed crewmembers always attracted a sky full of fixed-wing fowl to shoot down.

Admiral began his account. A FAC out of Nakhon Phanom, Laos, with a Nail flight call sign, had put a flight of fighters out of Ubon and one flight from Da Nang in on a mining mission. They were dropping 500-pound land mine bombs along a river ford extending out of North Vietnam just across the border into the dense jungle of Laos near a place that was notoriously well defended by Level 5 and 6 antiaircraft gunners, the best. It was called Mu Ghia Pass. Many a fighter pilot had bought the farm there. Yet, as long as it remained one of the primary road accesses into South Vietnam, there would continue to be combat sorties to Mu Ghia every day and we could always count on deadly antiaircraft emplacements being there. This day was different for the fighter jocks committed to this mission. There was a very low overcast cloud ceiling obscuring the drop area, which required visual ordinance delivery beneath the cloud cover, the worst possible conditions for a crewmember.

Admiral told me the first flights that were put in mysteriously took no ground fire. It was only the last flight, Bronco Flight, two F-4s from Ubon, that got flak. The clouds were so low that some gunners were literally shooting down at their Phantoms. They had made the last pass and Bronco 2 had just released when a 23-millimeter shells hosed them, scoring a direct hit in the underbelly, beneath the rear cockpit. Admiral went on, "The GIB's ejection seat evidently fired upon the impact of the direct hit to the fuselage floor directly under him."

"Fuck me," I responded in disbelief. That was your worst nightmare: A direct hit and you get ejected with no time to position your body or prepare. Just like that, your ass is hurled into the air four or five hundred miles per hour. It was a miracle if your limbs weren't ripped off their hinges just by the sheer force of eight to ten instantaneous Gs on ejection.

"The front-seater of Bronco 2 was able to loiter over the downed airmen for a few short orbits, helping with initiation of the rescue effort, but had to leave to return to Ubon due to low fuel. The back-seater was ejected just east of Mu Ghia," Admiral said with a low, soft tone in his voice that added to my intensity. "We finally got radio contact with Bronco 2 Bravo and told him to hang tight. We had the Jolly Greens approaching to pull him out." Admiral went on, explaining that the back-seater's chute had snagged on some jagged protrusions of karst on descent and he was suspended in his harness, dangling about fifteen hundred feet above the river ford they had been attempting to mine at the pass. Admiral told me they heard him pleading on his survival radio, "You gotta get me quick, guys. My arm's cut wide open; I think it's broken. I'm bleedin' bad." Admiral told him to hold on, he was sending some A1E Sky Raider flak suppression aircraft in to see if they took any ground fire before dispatching the rescue Jolly Greens. "Goddamit, Bee," Admiral asserted in a regretful tone, "The A1E Sky Raider support birds got hosed; we had to put another set of fighters in on the gun placements. I encouraged the downed back-seater to hold on; I told him over the radio we were about to come in,"

The sound in Admiral's voice was ominous. The three fighters made single passes, each dropping six 500-pounders on the enemy gun positions. Admiral said that he then called in the Jolly Greens immediately to pick up the back-seater. Swarms of rescue support aircraft were circling the area low on fuel with fingers crossed, praying they would get Bronco 2 Bravo out. One Jolly Green slowly descended into the killing zone and hovered above the karst as the paramedic went down the jungle penetrator cable. The fighters seemed to have suppressed the enemy ground fire. Within an instant, the paramedic came over the radio. "Pull me up. He's gone. I can't get him out. We're too late."

Admiral seemed to be feeling that he personally failed one of our comrades, confessing, "He bled to death, Bee, by the time we got to him. The rescue crew had to leave him; it would have jeopardized their lives to try to get his body out of the ejection harness and onto the penetrator seat."

"Damn," was all I could say. "Did they know the name of the crewmember?" I asked, almost afraid to hear the answer.

"Yeah, Bee, It was a Lieutenant Virgil Grant Stewart. I got the whole SAR effort recorded here on my cassette."

"Oh God," I mumbled.

"Did you know the guy, Bee?" Admiral asked solemnly.

"Yeah, man, I knew him. He's my classmate from Laredo."

"Jesus Christ, man. Do you want to listen to the tape?"

I got up off my bed, refilled Admiral's drink, and fixed a bigger one for me. The ponderous magnitude of the incredible was slamming into me full force. How did circumstances come together like this? I wondered. What was the message from God? Why did my buddy from Laredo, one of the nicest human beings I had ever known, die on my birthday, fatal victim of that freakish enemy round we called the "Golden B B."

A few weeks later, the sound of Grant's voice on the recording that Admiral had made of the rescue was still ringing in my ears, begging the rescuers to "Come get me quick 'cause I'm bleedin' bad." I'll never forget his pleas on that recorder. Word came to us from the States just weeks after Grant had bought it that his wife Judy had conceived their first child while they were on R & R in Hawaii, two months before he was killed. The good news had arrived in a letter from Judy that was placed in his squadron mailbox the day he went down. He never got to open it.

CHAPTER 18: THE GLORIFIED HEADACHE

It was mid-June. I had stretched survival out to ten months. Captain Jerry Titmus and I were teamed up to be number two in a Loran-guided strike over northern Laos, where, of course, no air strikes were being conducted according to the official Pentagon position. The navigation precision of Loran guidance enabled accurate saturation bombing even when cloud cover prevented visual contact with ground targets. Bombs were released relying on an audible cue received through the helmet headset when the fighters were over the precise target zone. It was neat and safe, but a wimpy style of bombing.

The takeoff and join up out of Da Nang were normal, except on this particular mission we were a three-ship formation rather than the usual two. Since the strike was unusually far into northern Laos, a pre-strike refueling tanker had been set up. The weather was overcast throughout most of Laos approaching the Mekong River. The river snaked its way from the undulating jungle canopies of Cambodia through Laos up into the rice paddy deltas of eastern Thailand. The heavy spring rainfall had turned the Mekong a light muddy brown, like coffee with half and half, accented in a visual esthetic against the greenery of the jungle on both sides of its banks. I marveled at the raw lushness of the jungle topography; the panorama always reminded me I was in a foreign place with a history that called for respect.

The KC 135 refueling tanker on the northern Yellow Route was right on track at the designated 1045 rendezvous time. Within a few minutes, we were in radar and voice contact with Yellow Anchor, our Boeing 707 refueling tanker. We were the first fighter to hook up for fuel.

"Flamingo 2, this is Yellow Anchor; how do you read?"

"Flamingo 2 reads you five square, Yellow," responded Titmus in his soft voice.

"Roger that, Flamingo 2, you are cleared to the pre-contact position."

We could now ease forward slowly behind and below the tanker to a position twenty or thirty feet away from the refueling nozzle, called a boom, that protruded like a bull elephant erection from the tail of the Boeing 707. Once the boom operator was assured the pilot being refueled was stable in the pre-contact position, he cleared the refueling process.

I could hear Titmus's respiration rate increasing as we approached the pre-contact. Titmus announced, "Flamingo 2 stable."

The boomer, being in agreement with the transmission from us commanded, "Flamingo Two, you're cleared into the contact position."

Titmus wiggled our Phantom's two throttles forward gently, less than half an inch. We moved too far forward on the tanker and watched bug-eyed as the massive tail section of the aircraft's rudder slid directly over our heads shadowing us like a mammoth airborne metal whale.

The boomer's voice emerged again, "Stabilize, Flamingo 2! Back five."

Titmus simply had to settle down and fly formation frozen in a precise position and the boomer would do the rest. I respected his sense of precaution and clear thinking. He wasn't going to kill us attempting the impossible or something stupid like trying to become a hero. We waited in the contact position for the boomer to extend his boom and feel the bang clank bump of the boom nozzle inserting into the refueling receptacle just three feet aft of my canopy. The swishy sounds of Titmus and me breathing into our oxygen masks were interrupted by the boomer's baritone voice, "Flamingo 2, check refueling door switch on."

Damn, I thought, Titmus had missed a step on the checklist. He confirmed the door switch was in open. For the safety of the operation, Titmus came back to the boomer, "Roger, Yellow, Flamingo 2 returning to pre-contact to check switches."

"Roger, Flamingo 2, cleared back to pre-contact."

As Titmus inched back the engine throttles and we eased slowly aft of the tanker he cursed, "Shit, I know I turned that fuckin' door switch on." After positioning the plane safely behind Yellow, he confirmed it after checking the refueling panel, "Damn, Bee, we got a problem. The switch is on." I keyed the microphone button, "Yellow boomer, confirm you observe our refueling door closed."

The boomer acknowledged, "Roger that, Flamingo, she's cracked partially open." Titmus recycled the switch. "How does it look now, Yellow?" Titmus queried.

"No good, Flamingo 2; she's still slightly cracked open."

"Fuck me." Titmus sighed in resignation. "No gas, no mission."

In the automatic thinking response that is engrained from pilot experience and training, I inquired almost instantly, "Fuel check."

Titmus responded after a pause to confirm the correctness of his answer, "Sixty-five hundred pounds, Bee."

Shit, we were below our Bingo (return to base fuel). We didn't have the fuel to do the mission and now we discovered we didn't have the fuel to make it back to Da Nang.

Flamingo lead came on the radio. "Hey, 2, what's your fuel? You got enough to RTB [return to base] Channel 77?" he said, indicating the radio navigation number for Da Nang.

"That's a negative," Titmus answered. "We're going to have to head toward Udorn or Takhli to get some fuel."

Not wanting to leave a wingman distressed, Lead asked, "You got any other problems, 2?"

"Negative, Lead, we just got the door. Go on with the mission. We'll be fine."

Lead rogered our transmission and called for Flamingo 3 to go ahead with radio contact with Yellow Anchor. Although we still had the reassuring daylight of the late morning broken cloud deck, it was no less ominous a feeling departing the safety of the flight for an uncertain destination somewhere in Thailand. Just as Titmus was sighing "Well, Bee," I declared over the interphone, looking at my navigation charts of Thailand, "Tit, it looks like Udorn is the closest shot."

"Yeah, okay, I just hope it's not raining," he responded with reservation.

In an instant, the meaning of his concern registered. "Damn, we can't land on a wet runway with this shit, can we?"

"That's right."

We received flight clearance and an altitude change from the GCI controller to proceed toward Udorn Air Base. We were in and out of turbulence and rain showers in the descent. Titmus and I discussed our options, which brought on a new rush of mild panic. Seventh Air Force directives dictated that no fighter aircraft were to be landed on a wet runway with MK-82 land mine ordinance. The canopy was being intermittently pecked by peanut-sized raindrops that reminded me of Muncie Boys Club summer camp, sleeping in the woods while thundershowers pelted our canvas tents. The ordnance-free jettison zones were either in hostile Laos or just off the coast of Da Nang. If we didn't have the fuel to return to Da Nang, we surely couldn't get to the jettison areas. If we got clearance back across the Mekong and blindly tried to follow jettison rules, we would risk getting shot down and captured by the Pathet Lao who didn't take prisoners, just tortured them to death. Out of convenience, we could attempt to jettison over sparse jungle in an unauthorized zone and hope no one got hurt. We could land on a wet runway, ideally without incident, and lose our wings for disobeying an operational directive. Or, if the runway at Udorn was wet, we could run out of gas and punch out because we couldn't land with land mines. There were few options, and most of them sucked. We were face-to-face with that familiar creeping terror that leads to reflection on our stupidity for daring to think flying fighters and routinely toying with disaster was a great idea. We would have to make a decision soon. Even though both of our asses would fry, the call and, ultimately, the responsibility was on Tit. Maybe that's why they always say it's lonely at the top. The fuel quantity counters seemed to be on a steady spin toward empty. Soon we would be flying on fumes.

The GCI radar site handed us off to Udorn approach control for vectors to the air base. I dreaded the prospect of being forced to elect one of the frightening options facing us. Pilot clichés played peekaboo with my thinking. It was the proverbial box canyon, between a rock and a hard place.

"Udorn approach, Flamingo 2, due north of airfield forty-five miles, over," I called out loudly over the UHF radio. The pause before approach answered us seemed like waiting for the coffee to brew after a night at the club. "Flamingo 2, radar contact; say intentions."

"Roger, approach, we need vectors for landing Udorn. Say runway condition and latest weather." We couldn't have been any more puckered in that instant. If it was wet, we were as they say, up a shit creek without a paddle. "Roger, Flamingo 2, latest weather fifteen hundred broken, five miles, wind calm."

They hadn't answered the important question. Titmus got annoyed. "Ask him if the fuckin' runway is dry, Bee." I got pissed at Titmus getting frustrated with me.

"I was just gettin' ready to, Tit," I exclaimed in an irritated tone. "Udorn, is the runway dry?" Another agonizing pause.

"Affirmative, Flamingo 2, dry runway. We had showers earlier but brief sunshine dried us out a little." Tit and I simultaneously exhaled.

Obviously relieved and feeling apologetic for snapping at me, Tit said, "Thanks for your help, Bee, in getting us here. Looks like we dodged one."

"No sweat, Tit," I came back coolly as if I hadn't even been fazed. I was becoming a great actor.

At three thousand feet, we broke out of the dirty overcast into the clear. The Thai countryside was a brilliant contrast of brown hues, multiple shades of jungle green and rice paddies. Visibility was what we commonly referred to as "severe clear."We were vectored to final approach for landing on Runway 35 and handed off to the tower for landing clearance.

"Flamingo 2, cleared to land on Runway 35," the Udorn tower controller said loud and clear. Despite receiving clearance, we didn't rest easy until Tit turned off the runway after a grease-job landing. The Follow Me vehicle intercepted us on our turnoff and guided us to the special de-arming area where our undelivered lethal cargo was made safe with six-inch metal safety pins that prevented them from being inadvertently jettisoned. After de-arming, we taxied to the parking spot, discussing how long it might take to get refueled and on our way back to Da Nang. We had plenty of crew duty time remaining. In wishful thinking, I said, "Maybe we can find something wrong with the bird that will keep us here for a few days for maintenance repairs."

Tit chuckled before taking off his oxygen mask. "Yeah, right, anything to get a day away from fucking Da Nang."

The crew chief gave us the stop signal and crossed the wand in his right hand under his chin in a horizontal motion, for us to shut down the engines. He quickly moved to position the long yellow ladder up to the canopy rail so we could descend the ten-foot distance from the cockpit to the pavement. The assistant crew chief hollered out from beneath our bird, "Chocks in," which was our clue that the blocks were placed around the wheels to prevent the aircraft rolling forward or backward when the parking brakes were released.

My flight suit was heavy with sweat from the heat and humidity of the landing and the weird ordeal from the refueling track. I was unstrapped and out of my seat in a flash. I scanned the serenity of the airbase that was devoid of the too familiar distant boom and rumble of artillery strikes. I hesitated going first down the ladder to defer to my front-seater out of simple protocol and good manners. Tit, noting my gesture, said appreciatively, "Hey, thanks, Bee." As I looked on, Tit turned his body slightly as he stepped over the canopy railing to scale down the ladder backward, as customary. With Tit no more than three steps down, my eyes bugged out in disbelief as I witnessed the ladder dislodge from the canopy railing. A helpless Tit fell away from our Phantom backward to the concrete ramp with his "tree let-down" rope pack on his back, still draped in his bulky survival vest, arms clutching his helmet and map bag and fingers clinging in a death grip to the ladder. I winced in empathetic pain as his head ricocheted basketball style off the cement ramp. Horrified at the spectacle, all I could come up with was the cliché fighter pilot exclamation, " What the fuck!"

Tit was knocked out from the blow. Still perched high in the air frozen in place, peering down in utter amazement, I wondered for an instant if he was dead, lying motionless flat on his back. The crew chief, realizing he had failed to properly hook the ladder to our airplane railing, became hysterical, "Holy shit! Ooohhh shit."

Scrambling to remove the ladder from the top of Tit's body, the crew chief quickly moved it back to the canopy rail where I reluctantly waited to try my hand at dismounting our treacherous beast.

After a moment, with two of us assisting, Tit groggily pulled himself upright.

"Jesus Christ, you shittin' me?" he said half-dazed in embarrassment. I let out an uncontrolled guffaw, instantly impressing myself with my rudeness and insensitivity, but damn he had a silly grin on his puss. It reminded me of cartoon character Elmer Fudd with his sheepish chuckle. The crew chief was overwhelmed with the thought of his monumental blunder and flooded us with apologies and self-derision for being so stupid not to have secured the ladder. Always the disciplined soldier committed to following procedure, Tit robot-like and bleary-eyed, requested transport to maintenance debrief to write up the jammed refueling door, which, in all the calamity, I had forgotten.

As we departed maintenance, we got the word. News had spread instantaneously along the flight line about the accident. The duty officer intercepted us to take Captain Titmus to see the flight surgeon for a precautionary checkup. My God, I thought, Wes Darrell (another GIB in the 390th) had gotten thrown over a bar during a drunken party at the club and landed on his head. He was unconscious for no more than a few seconds, but the flight surgeon grounded Wes for six weeks. Flight safety was understandably a biggie in the Air Force with pilots. I feared what might be discovered if they examined Tit.

He was whisked away to the base hospital for a physical while I hung out at base operations, waiting for the results. Before he left, he mumbled to me, "Bee, have 'em fill us up for the trip back."

Damn, I thought, *this cat never lets up--ever the forward planner and optimist.*

More than an hour passed before a major finally appeared in the doorway, "Lieutenant Settles, Major Compton, supervisor of flying. I just left the hospital and it appears Captain Titmus is okay, but he does have a nasty bump and minor laceration to his scalp. The flight surgeon wants him to remain at the hospital for twenty-four hours for observation. We've got you set up to stay in the VOQ (visiting officers' quarters) until the doctor clears you fellows to return to Da Nang." Having heard Tit was "bloodied but unbowed," I was beside myself with glee—a free night off in Thailand.

Major Compton dropped me off at the VOQ and briefed me on how to find the officers' club. That was all the help I needed. With a check cashed at the bar, I would be ready for people. I didn't know anyone at Udorn. Since most of my F-4 classmates were at Ubon, I suddenly realized that Bill Walton and John Allen were supposed to be here in the Phantom. They were two cool brothers I had hung out with a few nights while training.

I showered quickly and borrowed some deodorant from another guest in the VOQ. I disliked having to put the same flight suit back on, but it was fresh that morning so it wasn't that funky.

The Udorn officers' club was a thing of beauty, well lit, with exquisite wood grain paneling, glass teardrop chandeliers, and last, but not least, gorgeous Thai waitresses and barmaids glorifying the atmosphere. My goodness, I thought, this could be tough on a horny bastard from Da Nang. There was no question about having a good time.

I was unable to hook up with either Bill or John; one was flying and the other was in Hong Kong on leave. That night my money was no good at the officers' club. The F-4 jocks heard the story about Tit and wouldn't let me buy a drink, rubbing it in by referring to us as these poor shits from Da Nang. That was okay by me; my glass was never empty. Gin and tonic flowed through the afternoon and into early evening. My new buddies bored me with reason after reason why life at Udorn was so great. There was easy, unlimited travel to Bangkok, great fishing in the rivers, shopping for great buys, and many boasted of apartments off base where their tee locks—a man or woman totally available and faithful to one person, a main squeeze— hung out with them. I became ill listening to these tales of life in paradise.

A doll of a barmaid named Cato kept eyeing me in puzzlement, as if she couldn't figure out what I was—not exactly white and not like any brothers she had been around. She had a tight-fitting satiny orange dress that accentuated her athletic build supported by symmetrically shaped muscular calves. During our brief teasing exchanges, I could tell she was an intelligent young woman who was aggressively going forward in creating a good life for herself. In the frequently interrupted chats between her back-and-forth trips to the bar for refills, she shared with me her role taking care of family members, saving money, and hoping someday to go to college.

I shared my hearts and flowers story about being stationed at Da Nang and how pleasant a change it was meeting someone so gorgeous and intelligent. The longer she talked to me between customers, the more drawn to her I was. One could have made the case that anyone would have been refreshing compared to what was available at Da Nang, but Cato was special, like all the other special ones. Her full brown lips spread often into a gleaming white smile that revealed well-cared-for pearly teeth. A coy sophistication made her irresistible. Attempting to pace myself to avoid a premature trip back to the visitors' quarters for a nap, I throttled back on the gin sipping and ordered a sixteen-ounce T-bone cooked rare with a baked Idaho potato on the side. I ate in the bar rather than enter the dining room and sacrifice the spectacular scenery.

As the club activity began to wind down, I lauded Cato for being so special and asked if there was any way we might continue our visit after she got off work. At first she said no, that Thai employees weren't allowed in the officers' quarters except for maids and maintenance; she could lose her job. Besides that, working at the officers' club, she was already admired by and recognizable to many of the officers on base.

Feeling that all hope was lost, and parked at the end of the bar in the way of the other barmaids, I was oblivious that the other bar beauties had discovered a certain lieutenant seemed sweet on Cato. I was ready to throw in the towel and bid her goodnight when she spontaneously nestled up to me and asked if I wanted to accompany her off base. I felt a light-headed confusion at having to make a quick decision with too little data. My stomach fluttered. Incredulous, I immediately began to construct obstacles. "Cato, I only have a flight suit to wear. Where could we go?"

"Oh, don't worry, Lieutenant Bee, I have a nice little place," she assured me overconfidently. My skeptical mind began to race ahead into all kinds of bizarre scenarios. Why was she suddenly so accommodating—it was a setup. How would I get back to the base and when? How would we travel? Did she have a car? I was silently floundering in a deluge of uncertainty. I wondered if I really was mature enough to be out on my own in the world. I felt fear, but I had to get some answers quickly.

"Cato," I inquired, "how are we going to get to the nice place?"

"No sweat, Lieutenant Bee. We walk front gate; take jitney. You okay that?" she said, almost laughing, knowing I was taking her bait—hook, line, hip boots, fishing boat, and pier.

Reluctantly, I responded, not feeling so hip. "Yeah, that's cool."

The club closed at 0100 (1 AM), and I discreetly waited outside on the veranda for her to close out her accounts and give her barmaid cohorts time to leave ahead of us. Soon she came out alone, smelling freshened up.. We walked three short blocks to the front gate; shame surged through me upon getting signed off the base with Cato—in a flight suit. The security guard rendered an I-know-what-you-are-up-to parade ground salute, saying, "Have a great evening, sir." I returned the greeting. There, outside the gate, as if waiting for us, was one lone jitney. I mentioned to Cato that I had American dollars, but no Bhat, the Thai currency.

"No problem, Lieutenant Bee."

At this point, her formality was feeding my paranoia. "Cato," I implored, "stop calling me Lieutenant Bee; just call me Bee."

"Okay, Lieutenant Bee."

We got into the jitney. A vision of a dazed Captain Titmus in a hospital bed flashed into my thoughts; it vanished in five seconds.

After a five-minute ride through a modest neighborhood of humble homes, impoverished abodes of low-wage occupants, it occurred to me I was with a person I didn't know, in no-man's-land where no one in the world knew how to find me. Cato chirped some instructions to the driver in Thai and after a few bouncy twists and turns down the narrow streets, we suddenly veered around a dark corner and screeched to a stop in front of a place looking like a grass hut–made of wood and literally jacked up off the ground on poles that looked like stilts. Hesitating as Cato paid the driver a few Bhat, I perused her beautiful face for any sign of reassurance that this adventure was going to work out. I couldn't help thinking I might have been luckier being the first one down the ladder earlier that day.

We quietly ascended the stairs of the bungalow, not wanting to wake someone inside. Cato led the way. To my amazement, the two-room apartment with its shack-like exterior was cozily appointed with a worn white couch, some velvet-textured wall hangings, an inexpensive television set, and simple bright-colored drapes hung over the small windows. The dozen or so *Playboy* pinups adorning the walls caused neon caution signs to blink within me. It all fit together; I was in some dude's apartment, a playboy or a pimp's pad. What the hell was going on? I thought. I had to ask Cato. "Looks like somebody stays here besides you, Cato."

"You right, Bee. This belong my tee lock."

Terror once again took over as the prevailing mood. "Jesus Christ, Cato, you brought me to your boyfriend's apartment? I need to get out of here quick," I exclaimed.

"No problem, Lieutenant Bee, he go away. He no here for three more day."

Good Lord, I thought, this lady is too fast for me. I arrogantly had assumed I was the player; Cato suddenly had me feeling like an over-his-head chump. To settle me down she offered me a drink and not a minute too soon. The bar cabinet was stocked with every kind of booze one could want. Must be a together dude, I thought, Great setup, foxy Thai babe, off-base bungalow for her to live in. She cooks, cleans, and makes love whenever he wants. Sounded like paradise to me. Dude was probably married with a wife waiting faithfully at some base stateside for him to return. I dismissed that thought rapidly.

Cato invited me to use the wash basin in the corner if I wanted to freshen up. I felt fresh enough, so I passed on the invitation. There was one small lamp in the entry room. It had a dim light that induced a romantic ambience. Cato went into the bedroom and slipped into a sheer satiny gown. She plopped down on the bed, fluffing her pillow for a backrest against the headboard. I got the hint the party had shifted locations and joined her, snuggling next to her legs. She yawned. I expressed how honored I was she would trust me after so little time to come home with her, to her tee lock's place no less. But before I could feel too flattered, she boldly announced she thought I was a very gentle and nice guy, but that all we could do was kiss because she didn't want to get in trouble with her man. Wow! Not exactly what I had in mind. The question often issued by Amos in *Amos and Andy* came to mind: "Awww, Andy, what is I gwanna do?" Layin' up next to a Thai goddess all night and she's savin' herself for the old man. Noble, I thought, but could she pull it off in bed with me till morning? I was a sex-crazed escapee from Da Nang who could not imagine going through the night without making love with Cato.

Sensing that protest was not an appropriate response, I rallied to the side of sincerity, humility, and self-sacrifice and stated, "Well, Cato, lying here next to you until morning and being denied the ecstasy of loving you would be cruel and unusual treatment, but, if that is what you insist upon, I must honor that, no matter the depth of agony I must endure upholding your wish." I was in love with my own rap, whether anyone else was impressed or not. As if sealing my pledge, I leaned over and pressed my lips to hers, and the bodily fireworks shifted into automatic mode.

War and preoccupation with death had caused me to surrender to sensuality and hedonistic predilections. It was definitely not the season for self-denial; whatever brought pleasure was in command. One simply could not squander valuable time bogged down in preoccupation with guilt or the vengeance of consequences. On judgment day, all that would be left to say was mea culpa and then get in the long line of those going straight to hell.

Kissing Cato's full, beckoning lips made me ashamed of my weakness for the flesh. I was enamored with laying and getting laid. The whole romance scene for me was a ritual of divulgence and sharing myself, like going to confessional for spiritual cleansing. It seemed also to be a powerful means for fomenting pity. Cato began breathing in mild gasps. Captain Titmus's face appeared suddenly in my mind again; I squished my eyelids tightly to expel the image as it dawned on me that his misfortune had been my lucky strike. I held Cato in my arms, squeezing her tightly, as if she was the only human left to save me from falling off the edge of the earth. I could feel her become limp under the strength of my arms. She moaned. I joined her. We kissed passionately. I slipped her gown strap down over one shoulder and froze momentarily in time and space absorbing the visage. Cato had been blessed by nature with beautifully shaped breasts; her large brown nipples protruded in full extension. Suddenly, it was as if I were all the depraved infants and lovers of time immemorial about to nurse at the breast of mankind. I wanted to melt inside Cato and disappear forever as I took her steamy nipple gently into my mouth. She pulled back, whispering, "No, Bee."

I cuddled in her arms, nuzzling my head against her chest, comforted by her closeness and searing body heat. We were both wet with perspiration. I fell asleep in her arms with no more words spoken between us. Whatever it was, something had been reassuringly soothed in both of us in that gentle communion in that distant place a world removed from those I loved and was longing for.

The pain of a ballooned bladder awoke me early the next morning. Cato slept peacefully. As I stood up, shaking and rubbing my head to help clear the cobwebs from all the drinking, my consciousness suddenly hit the wall of clarity like an Indy 500 racer plunging off the track into the stands. I was in another man's place, with his woman, sleeping in their bed. *Settles,* I thought, *you must have slipped off the edge somewhere along the way and no one bothered to tell you.* Thoughts of the tee-lock guy bursting through the front door flooded my brain as I enjoyed the relief of a shrinking bladder. I had to place faith in Cato's assurance he wouldn't return for three more days, two now. I crawled back into bed and set the clock for ten, thinking momentarily of Titmus. Looking over at Cato, I admired her sleeping beauty, her full breasts and now relaxed nipples that continued to stick out in unavoidable prominence. I kissed the left one gently, softly touching it with the tip of my tongue, and went back to sleep.

The rude alarm clock shattered the silence of our slumber in what seemed like ten minutes after I returned to bed. It frightened us both. Wanting to get back to base by early afternoon in anticipation that Tit would be released, I knew I had some early-morning leisure time. Cato slipped into the bathroom, pausing to brush her teeth, a positive sign, I thought. I couldn't help feeling the painful ache between my legs that was miserable for attention. As Cato returned to bed, I didn't know what to expect. She snuggled next to me to recapture the heat she had sacrificed in leaving the warm bed. I pulled her body close to me as we both lay on our sides facing each other. She kissed my face. I thought about her tee lock; I kissed her face. I thanked her for letting me spend the night with her. She kissed my lips. I was self-conscious about my breath being foul after all that gin. She didn't seem to care or notice. Cato appeared more at ease and in a giving place. As we hugged our way into petting, I pushed my groin toward her upper thighs. It was warm, magnetic warm, and I sensed the animal rush taking over both of us. I spread her legs with my left thigh and rolled gently and slowly on top of her as her gown hem crept up magically above her waist. She issued a soft whimper as I began to massage the exterior of her private place with my fully agonized readiness. She offered no resistance; it was no time to dissect and analyze the unexpected change of heart. I quickly and discreetly slid my boxer shorts down off one leg with an acceptable level of fumbling. What a difference a few hours and a little sleep had made.

There was a flush of madness in the mating hysteria that made it impossible to even think about disease or pregnancy. She couldn't be dirty, I reasoned. She was shacking with an active-duty Air Force person. Irresponsibly, I didn't go near the subject of possible pregnancy as I had done months earlier with Eva. The Muncie mentality had taken me over: get the leg and ask questions later—a dumb policy. Maybe I was lazy or, more so, inexperienced in rapidly sliding on the rubber glove. In the mania of passion's call for lightning-fast penetration, condom donning could seem as complicated as overhauling an engine.

The heat and wetness of Cato had me holding on for dear life, not to blow the groove prematurely. I thought of fishing on White River back in Muncie, playing ball for the Bearcats, even going back to Da Nang and what chores needed to be done upon my return. It was all in vain. Cato began to take control, thrusting her pelvis against me in an undulating rhythm that usurped prerogative. I could have been skydiving—it wouldn't have mattered. The groove was too sweet. She milked everything I had in me into her, as if she knew she would never see me again, but wanted me to remember her special sacrifice. I collapsed onto her chest, breathless and perspiring. Why had God made such a fundamental part of the human dynamic so irresistible, and, under my circumstances, taboo. Guilt and betrayal swept over me. Ironically, I felt some sick, misplaced empathy for the tee-lock dude, whoever he was. Out of a need for sanity, I blanked out visions of Celeste risking her life on the snow-covered winter roads between Indy and Muncie pursuing her master's degree, a sacrifice we hoped would one day embellish our future together. And I was holed up in Thailand on a lark out in the bush chasing the bunny, with my aircraft commander in the hospital. Was that why combat veterans always said war is hell?

After the cold shock of a wash-off with water from the twenty-gallon ceramic jug, I put my flight suit on while Cato went next door to use the phone to call a jitney. Evidently, the neighbors could be counted on to protect Cato's secrets. Pensively, I surveyed the apartment one last time while awaiting Cato's return. Soon she was back looking wonderful in the morning sun wearing jeans and an Air Force T-shirt as if headed for a church picnic. Finally I popped the question whose answer had held no interest for me up until that instant: "Cato, is your tee lock another Air Force pilot?"

"No, Bee. He master sergeant. Manage NCO club at base."

Wow, I thought. *Wouldn't he be thrilled, an officer doing his sweet thing—a fighter pilot to boot.* Cato hastened to add, "He have wife back in States." In that moment, indifference replaced empathy for the sergeant. I felt sadness for Cato, working on getting ahead to attend school, being put up in this humble little place by a cat paying her to stay with him. When, I wondered, would she get a nice guy to love her and be with her only, free of being used by the desperate lovers like me who came and went? The hug I gave her good-bye was more than just a hug. It was a modest effort to reach into Cato, to connect, to touch her heart and let her know she would never know the depth of my appreciation for what she had shared. Ultimately, the question remained unanswered: was all really fair in love and war? The jitney beeped outside the cottage and I pensively departed Cato's side and descended the stairs. I never saw Cato again, but the memory of her has never left my mind.

Captain Titmus was cleared to return to Da Nang late that afternoon. Meeting me in base ops with a slight gleam in his eye, he asked, "Well, Bee, did you enjoy your one night off from the war?"

"Tit, out of not wanting to see a grown man cry, I will simply say you wouldn't believe it if I told you and leave it right there. I'm glad you're okay, man."

An hour later, we blasted off for Channel 77 with another combat story to tell, if we were lucky enough to get out of the war alive.

CHAPTER 19: SPRINGTIME AT THE EDGE

The alert trailer was my home away from the Q at Da Nang; it had a crude makeshift extension built on to accommodate six bunk beds. The trailer floor had light green military-issue twelve-inch linoleum squares. The newly constructed facility had walls that were a combination of Sheetrock and low-grade wood paneling and three-inch trim. Like a photo gallery, unlimited color and black-and-white pictures of the U. S. Government hierarchy from President Johnson to Secretary of the Air Force on down to the Commander of TAC hung gallery style on the beige walls of what we still referred to as the alert shack. It sat directly across the hundred-foot-wide taxi ramp from the reinforced revetments blanketed by twelve-inch thick concrete roofs where the Phantoms were parked, each in its own private nest.

The only combat missions that really counted for me in Vietnam, that kept me going and enabled me to look myself in the mirror, were the gunfighter sorties launched from alert duty to recover downed crewmembers or rescue American ground troops pinned down in battle against the Cong or NVA forces.

In the 366th TAC Fighter Wing, we had twelve F-4s assigned to alert duty twenty-four hours a day, seven days a week. We never knew the destination of a launch until that instant when the command post called the shack.

I recall that unusually tranquil spring morning of June 19, 1969, one month after I turned twenty-five. I had two months of survival challenge remaining. The sky was nude of clouds and the deepest blue an hour or so after sunup; it was a serenely camouflaged harbinger of the day's ominous events. A wave of calm had descended upon the flight line following the early-morning launch chaos. It seemed one of those spring days too resplendent to belong to Vietnam. Sparrows chirped gleefully and fluttered about on the ground outside the alert shack, taking impromptu bird baths in the vacant tire-track puddles left by construction vehicles.

The morning operations briefing was completed at the command post. My flight gear, map bag, helmet, and knee clipboard were stowed on board our bird, tail number BS 439. Captain Ted Mackle and I were assigned to fly wingman as Gunfighter 8 in a flight of two set up to carry soft ordnance, each of our birds loaded with four 800-pound napalm canisters on the outboard bomb racks and six 500-pound high drag bombs on the center ejector rack, three forward and three aft. It was a weapons load of unbelievable destructive power, designed for close air support, to be dropped on enemy troops and equipment that were engaging American or ARVN forces in combat. Both Snake (high drags) and Nape (napalm) were released at shallow dive angles, 450 knots and low altitude, making the deliverer more vulnerable to small arms and .50-caliber machine-gun fire.

After checking out our war machines, the auxiliary electrical power units were shut down and the crew chiefs took breaks in small groups, smoking cigarettes and kidding around like teenagers gathered on the high school steps waiting for the class bell to sound. That bright June morning, I was struck with the tranquility and beauty of the flight line in the backdrop of concrete ramps cluttered with delivery systems of mind-boggling destruction. The regular early strikes had launched, the power units were silent, and there was just deep blue sky overhead that contrasted magnificently with the brownish-green silhouette of Monkey Mountain along the horizon across the runway on the Marine side of Da Nang Air Base. H43 and Huey helicopters hovered and darted past the mountain's face like bees excitedly buzzing back and forth between their hives and the nectar-filled flowers in the warm early day sun. I could imagine Mama's flower garden in our backyard in Muncie. I reflected on the simple splendor of the new spring grass in Indiana, perennially a lush dark green. The spring Hoosier sky, like Da Nang that day, was often the bluest of blues. My imagination could feel the buzzing bees back home in the morning stillness along with the warble of chirping sparrows, robins, and cardinals that accented the air with their solitary sounds. I marveled as I stood alone staring at the small flocks of sparrows on the flight line, wondering if those peeping and bobbing birds might have been related to the ones that used to bounce on toothpick legs along the ground in our backyard. Seeing the sparrows frolicking beside the alert shack rejuvenated me and made me appreciate simply being alive. Occasionally, spontaneous, pantheistic acknowledgments of the lushness of Southeast Asia and its profound jungle beauty burst through to reaffirm our oneness with nature despite the killing and dying.

Once settled down in the alert shack, I slipped into the letter-writing mode for the morning, lying on the yellow vinyl couch for hours with a borrowed cushion propping up my back, pen in hand and a legal pad on my folded legs while the other crewmembers watched TV and gibbered back and forth. Snug in my G suit and flight boots, I was ready to go fight the war at any instant.

Aside from the feeling of incarceration and long twelve-hour shifts on alert, the duty was a great opportunity to write and read, but always surrounded by the suppressed anxiety wondering when or if the alert phone would sound. I was habituated to the muted tension of prolonged uneasiness in that atmosphere. A creepy exhilaration lurked just under the surface, like waiting on the bench to go back into the lineup to help win a game against a superior opponent who was dominating you.

The morning had been quiet. I finished three letters and was in the final chapters of William Styron's *Confessions of Nat Turner*. I was in a creative groove, calm within myself, at peace and painfully aware of my desperate need to snuggle up to whatever contentment I could find within the madness of war's routine. Without warning, the abrupt sound of the alert phone shattered the silence. Its ring was a muffled staccato rattle, like a woodpecker's beak on an oak tree. All of us leapt to our feet from our positions as if sitting on firecrackers. Major Metcalf was the first to pounce on the green military-style phone, as if it would explode if he let it ring more than two times. Slapping the phone to his ear, all he said was "Alert Pad," paused, then, "Roger that. Scramble Gunfighter 7 and 8!"

In a flash, peace and tranquility disappeared, replaced by controlled panic. We bounced off of one another, sprinting to get out the door first, all arriving simultaneously. We broke toward our revetments as the crew chiefs joined us running alongside, intent on beating us to the birds to get the electrical power and pneumatic air start units fired up.

Within three minutes, both Pratt and Whitney JT-79 engines were cranked and whining with a deafening high-pitched scream. Our helmets were on, but unstrapped. The quick alignment of the inertial navigation system was completed and we waited for Gunfighter 7 to check in on inter-plane frequency to start the show for taxi. We heard him come on frequency, and it all began like a combat-fighter symphony.

"Gunfighter 8, you up?"

"Gunfighter 8," I responded almost instantly.

"Go button three," lead commanded.

"Gunfighter 8," I responded as soon as Gunfighter 7 had released the microphone switch. I got a real rush of delight in the precision tightness of discipline in fighter formation flying, the kind of marrow-deep job satisfaction that the fighter gang referred to as Sierra Hotel.

"Da Nang Ground, Gunfighter 7 and 8, flight of two Fox 4's ready for taxi, alert scramble Runway 35."

"Roger, Gunfighter, cleared to taxi to Runway 35. Switch to tower, your discretion," the ground controller issued back.

" Gunfighter 7, taxiing."

"Gunfighter 8," I acknowledged. Mackle gave the thrust levers a hefty shove forward to get a good start out of the revetment to be at idle thrust when we turned out to prevent our jet exhaust from scattering start carts and ground equipment all over the ramp. The engines whined with a screaming high whistle that would ruin unprotected hearing permanently.

We quickly fell in behind Gunfighter lead to taxi out in trail formation. Taxiing at a rapid clip, we arrived at the ordnance arming area at the runway end, holding position and nestling up on the left side of lead. The armament ground crew did their thing removing the safety pins, giving our weapons the freedom to kill. We got the thumbs-up signal indicating our snake eyes and napalm were armed, hot, and ready. Lead revved up his engines while giving us a nod and taxied from right to left in front of us to shelter us from his direct jet blast. We pulled out immediately after he passed in front of us.

"Gunfighter, go Button Four," he commanded.

"Gunfighter 8."

"Da Nang Tower, Gunfighter flight ready for takeoff."

"Roger Gunfighter. Winds zero one zero at five, cleared for takeoff."

Lead led the way onto Runway 35; we lined up in fingertip with our wingtip almost overlapping theirs. Lead looked over at us and gave thumbs-up as he advanced his throttles to eighty percent of rpm and did an engine instrument scan before releasing brakes and quickly slipped the throttles into afterburner. It was the ultimate power trip to feel that earth-shaking vibration as our bird shuddered in the quake and rumble of lead's takeoff roll. Captain Mackle advanced our throttles and said, "Bee, you ready back there?"

"Before takeoff checklist complete," I responded. Thirty seconds after lead we were rolling in full afterburner, rumbling and spewing exhaust smoke and fire chasing lead into the unknown shadows of the mission. Accelerating to 250 miles per hour, we joined in fingertip formation on lead and headed south of Da Nang toward the highlands north of Pleiku. Cruising at 300 knots, we were on the target area in less than ten minutes. The terrain below us was mostly flat with clusters of small green forests bordered by tiny areas of rice paddies, brush, and elephant grass. Tiny streams snaked their way through the lush jungle from east to west, occasionally widening into rivers and fords. The ground color was a reddish brown that reminded one of the red clay of Georgia. The browns, blues, and greens of the landscape and sky blended into an outrageous visual aesthetic, a beguiling beauty in a distant, dangerous place poised to suck you and your life from the sky into a serene and silent grave.

Lead changed us to the standard radio frequency for rendezvous with our FAC who would conduct the air strike on our target. The FAC's call sign was Covey 23. He described in routine precision our target as a platoon-sized force of Vietcong soldiers who had ARVN soldiers and a handful of American Special Forces rangers pinned down at the base of a rapidly ascending ridgeline.

Covey 23 briefed us on the target area terrain and where exactly the good guys were located. He wanted our high drags at the base of the ridge and the nape on the second pass farther up on the enemy retreating toward the crest of the thick jungle ridgeline. Gunfighter 7 called over the radio, "Okay, 8, pull her back to set up some spacing. I'm accelerating."

We acknowledged, "Gunfighter 8, roger." As lead accelerated to put adequate distance between us for the strike, Mackle and I confirmed our agreement on the target location described by the Covey FAC. We ran the bomb delivery checklist items: inboard station selector—off, center line station—on, nose/tail selector--Nose & Tail, master arm switch—Arm.

It was early afternoon, almost eight hours since commencing our alert shift. The temperature in the 2 Corps highlands was in the high seventies. The sky was a clear blue with only a few clouds forming over the tops of the high country to the west toward Cambodia and the triangle area. We were ready to go to work—to maim and kill.

Lead called turning final to Covey. He responded, "Gunfighter 7, you're cleared in hot."

We watched lead descend in with a very shallow dive angle. The 800-pound napalm threw up huge black billows of smoke above incredible fireballs of holy terror as lead pulled off. For a brief moment, I thought his pull-off looked odd. At that instant he called off, the sound of heavy breathing in his transmission. "Lead's off." Pausing a second or two, he added, "Hey, 8, watch the pull-off. It's a little tricky."

We rogered the communication. Mackle was turning final, "Gunfighter 8, is in. Are we cleared?"

"Roger 8, you're cleared in hot. Put your stuff just a half click to the west of lead's."

"Roger, 8's cleared hot." We started the roll in at seventy-five hundred feet. Mackle was establishing a shallow run-in, and I was issuing my obligatory airspeed and altitude callouts from which he would perform visual corrections. "Four hundred knots, ten degrees of dive, sixty-five hundred feet. Four hundred fifty knots, ten degrees, five thousand feet." From the experience of dozens of low-altitude, low-dive angle missions I knew there were no set delivery altitudes for pickling off (depressing the trigger to release the bombs). The front-seater simply guided the nose of the Phantom on a track toward the target and, when the gun sight pipper was superimposed over the target, he would push over lightly on the nose to keep the pipper focused until depressing the pickle button. "Four hundred fifty knots, fifteen degrees of dive three thousand feet." We were getting low; I knew it was time to hear him say "Pickling."

"Four hundred seventy knots, ten degrees of dive, fifteen hundred feet. You should be pickling," I asserted in a tone of urgency. At that instant, Mackle came over the interphone with a slow, relaxed response, "Rooooggggerrr, Beeee. Piiiiickling nooooooow." Before he had gotten the *now* out of his mouth, my peripheral vision caught the dark shadow of the top of the ridge disappearing above our canopy. In that fraction of a second, I grabbed the stick and pulled back with instant force, placing an immediate six and a half Gs on our bird.

I felt Mackle pulling on the control stick with me. My hand instantly went down to the ejection handle between my legs, poised to punch out as soon as the tree branches on the ridgeline became distinguishable. Just as we cleared the trees at the top of the crest, the updraft turbulence on the far side of the ridge jerked us violently up and down, left and right. Mackle finally regained control, and we continued climbing in a steep left bank with full throttles. Both of us panting and scared shitless, I couldn't speak until we turned to the downwind. Abandoning all protocol, I hollered at Mackle, "Jesus man, didn't you see that fuckin' ridge?"

There was slight pause before he came back in an apologetic tone. "Gee, Bee, I'm sorry. I kinda had one eye on the target and one eye on the ridge."

My blood seemed to freeze in my body; a hot flush came over my face. I knew he was a lyin' sack of shit. He had gotten target fixation, concentrating so heavily on the ground that he had pressed below the safe altitude and forgotten all about the warning lead had issued on

209

his first pull-off. Mackle apologized again, managing a subtle acknowledgment. "It's a good thing you saw it."

What he had trouble saying is that I, in that moment of blue skies and beautiful lush landscape, had taken control of our Phantom making a routine delivery and pulled it out of a dive pass to keep us from buying the farm.

Lead called, turning in for his second pass. Covey 23 cleared him in hot with napalm, directing him where to place it. No one out there in the mission traffic pattern had any inkling of what Mackle and I had narrowly escaped. The lightning pace of the strike action made it too frantic and tense for commentary or complaint.

We completed the delivery checklist for the 500-pound Mark 82 bombs on our outboard pylon stations. We rolled in after lead called off, not really caring where the bombs landed, other than not on our friendlies. We called off and Gunfighter 7 gave us his position for the rejoin and return to Da Nang. In one minute, we caught up to lead. Over the radio came this: "Hey, Gunfighter 8, we have a Special Forces camp at twelve o'clock. Let's give 'em a little air show as we go by."

"Roger that." Mackle accelerated to 380 knots, maintaining our separation from lead of about a quarter of a mile. Above the canopy rail on my right, I could see lead in a steep, almost vertical, climb. Mackle came over the interphone. "Here goes, Bee." My helmet bounced off the left side of my canopy as Mackle snapped us into tight consecutive left aileron rolls and popped the throttles momentarily into burner. The exhilaration was so overwhelming Mackle and I both let out uncontrolled laughter—the kind that bursts from you at Disney World or Great Adventure on a roller-coaster ride like the Matterhorn. It was a wonderful sensation, something magically exciting that placed your spirit somewhere between euphoria and mild panic. It was also a playful flash of the machismo of flying fighters at 400 knots, rolling inverted to look up at the ground, feeling the burst of 60,000 pounds of afterburner thrust that literally pinned you to the seat.

As we spiraled upward giggling, draped in an azure world in tight aileron rolls, I imagined the spirit of belonging in the vicarious thrill the Special Forces troops must have been experiencing down below looking up at us from their jungle home, hooting and howling at our free air show. Ground and air forces in harmony were doing their part for the "free world," maintaining the esprit de corps, three cheers for the nation. The paradox suddenly hit me as we leveled out at twenty-four thousand feet on the rejoin with lead; fifteen minutes earlier I had pulled us out of a dive pass that would have left us buried forever deep in the side of a ridgeline in South Vietnam with our Phantom as a permanent casket. How odd and cunningly deceptive that we were laughing hysterically in our two-and-a-half-million-dollar war machine returning to Da Nang after killing a few Vietcong and saving the lives of a platoon of South Vietnamese soldiers along with a handful of U.S. Army Rangers.

Coincidentally, I had my tape recorder set up in my cockpit that day. I had turned it on after first contact with Covey 23 and it had slipped my mind that I had recorded the strike. By the time we finished maintenance debrief, our alert shift was completed and we were relieved by replacement crews. After securing my survival gear in the personal equipment shack and bidding Mackle a catch you later, I walked the short distance across the open dirt lot with my tape recorder under my arm. It was breezy. The dust swirled perpetually from all the heavy military personnel carriers that roared up and down the road adjacent to the flight line. Blue sky was sharing its space with clusters of white cumulus, and the late afternoon light was surrendering to early evening. Ironically, it was still perceived as a magnificent spring day. I entered the front door of the 390th. The entry hallway was devoid of activity. I exchanged a quick "hey" with the duty officer who was contentedly scribbling in the next day's schedule of sorties on the Plexiglas board with a grease pencil. "Hey, Bee," he responded. Nothing else was said as I entered the squadron game room off to the left. I went to the refrigerator, got myself a can of Pabst Blue Ribbon, and sat down on the dark green vinyl couch and hit the rewind button on my recorder. As the small black box did its silent whirl, I panned the room slowly, admiring the precision and thoughtfulness of the interior decoration. The official tournament dartboard from England was mounted properly beside the refrigerator, the neat rows of coffee cups were assembled on the Peg-Board wall, and the cactus-green creatively hung drapes concealed non-existent windows. The linoleum was a matching dark green embedded with light gray veins, giving off the illusion of marble. As I listened to the replay, I became numb with a sort of posttraumatic horror at the fate we had dodged. My palms became sweaty; I felt queasy and a clamminess on my skin. Suddenly, my throat wouldn't work right to swallow the large gulps of beer I was trying to get down. I could not believe what I was hearing, staring into the slowly rotating tape reel, that it was me, my action, instantaneous, instinctive and desperate, that had saved our lives.

The thought of that five-second act made me shudder and jerk my head in an effort to throw off the vision. The boldness of taking an airplane from a commander's control petrified me. It was one of those seldom visited arenas of aviation when a subordinate crewmember has to make a split-second call on whether a situation has become out of control and potentially lethal. You better be right or it would be your ass, maybe your wings, when you got back on the ground.

I sat balanced on the couch cushion, swirling in the dizzy numbness of delayed shock. I had a microscopic clarity of the awesome call I was forced to make, taking that airplane from Mackle's control. An anxious pride nuzzled into my thoughts that I might have pulled off a legitimate heroic act, unintentionally, in a split-second. What left my flesh cold in prickly goose pimples were the indelible images of fellow squadron buddies Tweety Bird, Vince, and Rothschild, all back-seaters just like me, who had suffered premature cremations in perfectly good F-4s. No chutes. No beepers.

Those of us left behind wrestled in our private disbelief at the enigma of fate, denied the consolation of explanation that unraveled the mystery of how some bright, highly trained combat crewmembers had not been able to recognize the slippery footing at the edge of the abyss in time to save themselves from catastrophe. Their trusted front-seaters, aircraft commanders, had killed them pressing the target down into the weeds, trying too hard to put bombs on a bunker, to release napalm in the front door of a hooch, or strafe water buffalo on a beach. And they met their maker trying. I was gaining life's invisible gifts of wisdom and insight in flashbulb spaces of time. In grim determination, I was left to face two more months of mission-by-mission, day-by-day survival.

CHAPTER 20: THE LAST HURRAH

A simple twelve months on the calendar live differently when the pages are turning over in a war zone. Through unearned divine intervention, I was closing in on my last six weeks at Da Nang. It was July 4. Nothing seemed real any longer. It was as if I were starring in my own private Fellini movie and all the other actors were imaginary characters, but the events surrounding me actually existed. My mind had shown me snapshots of that perception before, as if life was a continuum of imagined circumstances designed specifically to spice up my experiential trek. In that reality, I was the only human who existed.

The time warp repetition of bombing, drinking, and writing home had induced an anesthesia to the dangers around me and numbed my embarrassment over the shaky courage camouflaging my fear of dying. Reality had long ago crossed over into unreality. My only consolation was tied to a desperate conviction that my ordeal was delivering a profound life-altering lesson and the life I would pursue after learning it.

Being a fighter pilot had forced me to robe myself in the habit of the ancient gladiator, who daily entered the ring, fought the fight to death with an opponent, and returned to the warriors' quarters to rest up for the next battle. In the case of Vietnam, the enemy's resolve transcended mere struggle for life and immediate survival. It was about greater issues of communist-structured nationalistic determinism and sustaining the historical collective will of a xenophobic people who had outlasted the French, the Japanese, and then us. I had no loftiness of purpose. I was merely hanging out in a bad place, worse than the street corner, simply hoping to escape alive.

For eleven months, my front-seater--whoever it might have been--and I had always returned to base safely, our bird damaged by flak only twice, a marvel in itself, given the lethal hardware thrown at us on most missions.

My buddy, F-4 FAC Admiral Nelson, stopped by the room on my anniversary to get smashed, finishing off a quart of Gilbey's gin; three days later I was still in recovery. The combination of heavy gin and inadequate grapefruit juice chaser had left me with the raving munchies after his visit, but I was too shitfaced and too far from the chow hall to get something in my stomach to sop up the booze. I had searched the sparsely stocked refrigerator between my room and the guys next door and found some poorly wrapped remnants of tuna fish that was well past its danger, do-not-consume deadline. Unable to count on reason in my famished, inebriated condition, I made a sandwich out of stale bread and aged tuna and mayonnaise and gluttonously washed it down with a Pabst Blue Ribbon.

I paid the price for that dangerous combination of youth and stupidity for several days. I woke up the next morning feeling as if I was on my deathbed; I was in a cold sweat with fever and a gurgling stomach that repeatedly surrendered its acidic contents. My illness was horrendous. I had to go DNIF (Duty Not Including Flying) for three days. I vowed never to do anything so ignorant again and, to publicly declare it, I posted a sign over my headboard: **"I Will Not Drink, July 3, 1969"---- Bee Settles.**

My mind would not erase the images of my bosom classmates, Vince and Grant, meeting their doom a few months earlier, heightening my sense of mortality and the gnawing question, *"Am I next? Will I make it out alive or, worse, blind, crippled, or crazy?"*

That fear grew more intense and took me hostage as the weeks and days edged closer to completing my tour. I had become detached, more isolated and estranged from my routine. Alone in the death silence of my thoughts, my mind raced like a rat in a maze struggling to find the way out. I reflected on my dead buddies, my family back home, the July 1 wedding anniversary that came and went, illusory and remote. I wrestled with self-pity. I was recovering from food poisoning, which added a perfect emotional spice to my woeful countenance. I sensed that Grant's death in particular had triggered an uncontrollable fear I might not make it either. In the days following my recovery, I shifted into another valley of struggle--insomnia.

After mid-July 1969, I was being scheduled for mostly day strike missions with "early gos" and 0500 (5 AM) briefing times. I had to force myself to go to bed early.. Avoiding my buddies and drinking were not the challenge since I was assuming a new discipline. What snuck up on me unexpectedly were insidious nightmares of my demise. I seemed inextricably caught up in a giant whirlpool of thoughts that could not be banished and some invisible diabolical force was testing me to see how much it would take to exceed my breaking point and thrust me into insanity.

For days I got no sleep, only night sweats filled with tossing and turning. I flew my missions zombified with fatigue. I had no roommate during this period; there was no social distraction. I had withdrawn from contact with my social partners. I forced myself to hit the sack early, knowing I had to get my eyes closed to visit sleep. I would lie in my bed surrounded by stillness and a disquieting silence—a silence that had a faint but continuous swooshing sound like wind blowing through a dark forest at midnight.

On each occasion that my head sank into the pillow and my eyelids lowered, my mind automatically clicked on the mental movie projector, and I was taking off on a combat mission. It might be to North Vietnam. We'd be over a railroad bridge, preparing to drop our stuff, and a missile would launch from undetected radar guidance and score a direct hit, blowing us to microscopic bits. As soon as I was killed in the dream, my mind would slip in a new reel and I would be off on another combat mission. The ensuing sortie might be a cluster bomb drop over the infamous Mu Ghia Pass. In that dream, our aircraft would take direct hits from level 7 North Vietnamese Army gunners and we'd have to punch out in Laotian territory. I'd hit the ground after ejecting and immediately be captured by vicious murder-loving Pathet Lao soldiers who would instantly commence their joy by thrashing the shit out me with sticks, fists, combat boots, and rifle butts. When they became bored with beating me, the giggling torturers would strip off my flight suit and boots, tie my hands together and then my feet with hemp rope, and knot me to the tail of a water buffalo. The soldiers would bicker and draw straws to see who got to swat the beast across the ass with a five-foot long stick. The horrified animal would streak off across rice paddies, leaping over dikes with me bouncing and ricocheting off the ground like a Raggedy Ann doll on a rope. The soldiers would laugh hysterically and light their opium-laced cigarettes and drink rice wine, slapping their knees at their crafty innovativeness in meting out my suffering. Finally chasing the panic-stricken buffalo down, they would drag me back to the holding area and string me naked upside down with my legs spread wide apart eight feet above the ground. The Pathet Lao henchmen would then sit around the campfire laughing loudly, getting more stoned, and beaming with palpable pride at their trophy, playing more straw selection games to determine which lucky one would get to deal the next sadistic blow.

After I had been hanging there for hours, one of them would suddenly stand up and approach me carrying a razor-sharp three-foot-long machete in his right hand and wearing a smirk of devilish delight. He would slowly circle me, twitching up and down the long machete clutched behind his back, forcing me to shift my head around in odd angles to keep my eyes on his orbit. After the prolonged, gracefully stepped off paseo, in a flash of arms and elbows he drew up the machete and sliced me like a cantaloupe in the split of my groin, chopping me into two perfect halves. At that instant in the nightmare the mind projectionist would flip in the next horror reel and I'd be up in the Phantom on another mission to an equally macabre demise.

The death preoccupation insomnia was doing me in and mental breakdown seemed imminent. I shut myself off socially, didn't want to be around people, and began to despise who I was for behaving this way. I couldn't drink because of my pledge of sobriety, but the runaway dreams were scaring me to death every night. I needed help badly, but there was no direction to turn. I hadn't been to the base chapel often enough to feel deserving of seeking deliverance from the chaplain.

Fighter pilots must be brave and live by their can-do attitude. Big boys aren't supposed to cry, but I was slowly losing it in my preoccupation with doom. Pilots are often outspoken about their feelings, personal, political, or otherwise, but not many were courageous enough to admit fear of cracking under the pressure--it just wasn't done. I was desperate. I had embarrassing flashes of suicide, which provoked outright laughter from me to think of the irony that I would be saving the North Vietnamese or the Cong the expense of having to pay someone war wages to shoot me down. Self-elimination--a most bizarre form of altruism. But how could I escape these thoughts that haunted my every idle moment? How could I get some sleep? Asking the flight surgeon for sleeping pills would have exposed me to the light of psychiatric evaluation.

Early one evening I was lying on my cot reading my week-old editions of *The Muncie Star* sent to me direct from the newspaper office. I was waiting for Captain Chuck Guthrie, who bunked across the hall, to return from the officers' club. Around 9:30, I heard the slam of the end hallway door as someone wearing boots approached. It was Chuck. Unable to resist looking into my open room as he unlocked his door, he said, "Hey, Bee, What's happenin' kiddo? You didn't go to the club tonight, huh?"

"Naw, man, I been layin' low these days," I responded sheepishly.

"Yeah?" Chuck replied with a degree of puzzlement in his voice. Chuck was genuinely a good dude; he was an F-4 aircraft commander in the 389th, our sister squadron. We had shared the rare professional joy of flying a mission together, although we were assigned to different squadrons. Chuck was brown skinned, had a medium build, and wore his hair freshly barbered with a short-cut Afro that was flat on top. He kept his black mustache neatly trimmed. Like most of the brothers, he was conscientious about staying up with if not ahead of his peer competition. The opportunity to go to the altar and confess my sins had arrived with this encounter, As we say in the business, I was out of airspeed and ideas and needed a helping hand—at the very minimum, a listening ear.

"Hey, brother Chuck, you got a minute so I can rap to you about something?" I asked.

"Sure, Bee, come on over." It was mid-July at Da Nang, hot as holy hell outside, but chilly in our individually air-conditioned rooms.

"What's up, brother?" he inquired after I entered his room.

Hesitating for an instant, and taking a deep breath, as if on the precipice of a grave confession to Father Maloney, the resident Catholic priest, I admitted, "Man, I got insomnia. I got one month to go and I can't sleep. My classmate Grant over at Ubon bought it at Mu Ghia on my birthday and another pilot training classmate Vince Scott ran into the damn ground on a nape pass with his AC down in the Triangle area the month before. We've lost sixteen crewmembers in our squadron since I been here."

Chuck's eyes regarded me with an intensity that bespoke disbelief in the shocking truth of my statistic. All he could say was, "I heard that."

It was not quite the response I needed, so I continued. "Chuck, I'm getting short, man. I got a chance of getting out of this crazy place soon and I'm freaking out that I ain't goin' to make it. I keep having nightmares about buyin' it when I try to go to sleep." Then I hit the question I desperately hoped would make all the difference. "Brother man, do you ever worry about not making it out of here?"

Pausing momentarily, Chuck admitted, "Yeah, man. I think about it. I got a wife and baby girl back at MacDill waitin' on my ass to get out of here. She's only two. I worry about not seeing her again. I try not to, but some time you can't shake it. I just try to block it out."

"Yeah," I said, exhaling in relief he hadn't said, "Naw, man, that shit never crosses my mind."

I told Chuck that nightmares were flooding my consciousness every night and that I had sworn off drinking after getting sick from food poisoning. It was ironic that Chuck ended up being the selected savior for my plight since I had not been particularly close socially with him. Some labeled him boring and a little too stiff, all knotted up in straitlaced discipline—a trait that might have been good for me. He was several months behind me with less than half a year remaining. He had seen me raising hell at the club many times with my partner in crime, Carl Gamble. He probably thought I was curiously wild.

Having had the courage to abandon the macho I-am-a-survivor-hear-me-roar fighter pilot ego thing and be a human being in front of

Chuck opened the door for some rare relatedness between two individuals struggling to survive the same ordeal. My angst had forced me to step outside my comfort zone, to permit myself and my self-esteem to be at risk for the possibility of something that was not available—liberation from the grip of my own self-doubt and fear. Being able to confront my sense of vulnerability and reveal it publicly produced a breakthrough. The commonality born out of sharing our humanity within the bond of being African-American pilots was the crucible that made the difference that summer evening, as I sat beside Chuck's bed. After that, I never lost another night of sleep and, miraculously, the dogged nightmares vanished.

CHAPTER 21: SECURITY BREACH

In the days following the chat with Chuck, my mortality obsession became manageable and my mind began to cooperate once again with the goal of sleeping. I had less than six weeks remaining at Da Nang. The anticipation was mounting but I guarded my cool about it, did not brag to others, not wanting to jinx it. I had made a lifestyle of downplaying great news, I once pulled off a two-month resistance to picking up my state championship letter jacket my sophomore year until the last day of school before summer break.

Ten years later, with only a few weeks left on my Vietnam tour, having survived 185 missions, I was flowing through each day in equanimity, thumbing the rosary in my mind and praying daily to leave alive.

My former roommate, Perry, was engrossed in pulling a going-home party rabbit out of the hat for our F-4 training classmates at Ubon before our return to the United States. I had received my next assignment to KC-135 refueling tankers and permanent change of station to March Air Force Base, Riverside, California. I was quietly ecstatic and anticipated living in Southern California, reunited with Celeste, and going to rock concerts to hear Crosby, Stills, Nash and Young, Jimi Hendrix, and Santana. My dearest friend Butt would still be holed up in Berkeley; I was bursting inside with anticipation.

On July 22, the officers' club had a USO show with sexy-looking female dancers with great legs who did a Tina Turner and the Ikettes kind of dance thing. The club was rocking. The band was above-average wanna-bes and versatile in its musical renderings. Booze flowed heavily that night for a standing-room-only crowd of mostly Air Force, Marine, and Navy officers. I certainly had reason to celebrate, but, consistent with macho policy, my partying that night was simply about the foxy chicks dancing on the makeshift stage. By nine o'clock, the club was packed to the rafters and alive with the buzzing cacophony of isolated conversations competing within the multitude.

The main dining room was specially set up for the big bash. Thirty rectangular tables seating ten each had been laid out symmetrically with adequate aisle space to satisfy Air Force regulations for fire evacuation. Ten gray metal fold-up chairs were placed at each table, four to a side and one at each end. The band stage was set up at one end of the room with a plastic banner hung crescent-like behind the band. It read, "The High Five."

The band was better than most that ventured through on tour. The atmosphere was festive, deafening with cheers, hooting, and hollering from a mostly smashed crowd of depraved officers. The ubiquitous, self-proclaimed cocksmen were gathered close to the stage perimeter to grasp first shot at rapping to the dancers during the inexorable pauses. There were a couple of real cutie-pies with the troupe, but I was too proficient at avoiding manmade lines to talk to any honey who had crowd-drawing appeal, even if it meant forfeiting possibility to the alpha studs.

Pleasantly bombed after an excruciating hour and a half of visual intimacy, I decided to leave before the band started its last set. I was in a rare great place with the quiet comfort of knowing if I could just live for another five weeks, I would be getting the hell out of that killing place. Awkwardly, I swayed out of the club and hitched a ride outside the main compound with a passing bread van. Thanking the driver for the short lift, I stepped off the van, turning up a small cloud of dust with my boots shuffling back at a walking pace as I arrived at the front door of my new squadron. In my solo groove and feeling no pain, I got the inexplicable bright idea to visit my old squadron building next door, the 390th. It was newly constructed shortly after we made the move to the new fiberglass dorms across the street. I had been arbitrarily assigned to the 421st Tactical Fighter Squadron from Eglin Air Force Base in Florida.

The new squadron needed some experienced copilots to keep its green aircraft commanders from killing themselves before they got a couple of missions under their belts. I didn't like being reassigned away from my chums in the 390th but, big deal, I was short. It no longer mattered what color scarf I wore, although I was partial to blue.

Turning the brass handle of the dark blue painted door with a boar's head insignia tacked on it at eye level, I pulled it open. There was no sign of activity down the long hallway and no one behind the duty officer's desk to the right inside the front entry. The overhead track lights revealed the creative interior-decorating job: the walls were coated a light vanilla and contrasted esthetically with all the doorway frames trimmed in dark mahogany stain. Immediately to the left was the beautiful game room lounge. Coffee cups labeled with individual crewmember names hung on a brown Peg-Board. A richly grained maple bar counter made an L shape in front of a five-foot-high white refrigerator. I would never forget that lounge whose refuge I had sought after surviving the near miss with the ridgeline flying with Mackle. The place oozed coziness uncommon to military decor.

I knew there had to be a duty officer on the scene, a twenty-four-hour deal. Maybe he's running a crew out to their birds for a mission, I thought. Then I heard the *clack-clack-clack*ing down the hallway of the irregular strokes of someone unseasoned in typing. I examined the four-by-eight foot clear Plexiglas board mounted behind the DO desk on which the crew assignments for the day's flight schedule were neatly printed in yellow grease pencil. The black background made the yellow letters so bright they seemed to glow like neon. In the right lower corner of the board was a nicely lined box titled Duty Officer. It had the name "Lieutenant Marcus Mullis." I exhaled in amazement that his parents had concluded that this was a great name for a kid. To make it worse, Mullis was tall and gangly with big ears and bulging eyes, somewhat like a young Abraham Lincoln. He was a new guy who had just arrived to the 390th and, wanting his star quality to shine early, had volunteered to put his English minor from college to good use. Being sympathetic to anyone who took the time to read or write, I secretly admired him for starting a squadron newsletter appropriately titled *The Wild Boar*. That explained the typing; Mullis was back in one of the rear admin offices using the first shirt's typewriter feverishly working to get out the next issue of his tabloid by his self-imposed deadline.

In that moment, too blitzed from the USO show, I wasn't able to count on my mind serving me well. For reasons that reside somewhere outside explanation, I got the not-so-bright idea to play a little joke on Lieutenant Mullis, probably out of some jealousy that he gave a shit enough to come up with and implement the literary idea of starting a squadron newsletter.

Retrieving a clean sheet of eight-and-a-half-by-eleven paper from the duty officer's desk, I scrawled, "*Gentlemen, stopped in at 0130 to admire your new building. Front door was unlocked and no one around. Are you confident classified documents are secure?*" I signed it Colonel John Roberts, Wing Commander. Leaving the note on the desk, I slithered out the door in numbed giddiness toward my quarters across the walkway.

Bad news travels on swift wings. I woke up just before noon that morning. I was scheduled to fly later that evening, so my sleep was aligned with my duty shift. I moseyed over to the chow hall for lunch after a long shower and close shave. I was whistling a happy tune; it was a rare time when all was right with my world.

Entering the chow hall, I ran into one of my F-4 classmates and former squadron buddies still assigned to the 390th, Lieutenant Gerry Edmunds. He was wearing a look of anxiety like you'd expect to see on novice dope smugglers at the customs inspection station entering San Diego from Tijuana. Nervously reaching in his flight suit shoulder zipper pocket, he fumbled to get a cigarette lit.

"Hey, Gerr, what's happenin'?" I said, puzzled by his anxious countenance.

"Aw, Bee, you wouldn't fuckin' believe it," he responded, agitated and trembling, taking a deep drag.

In a tone of genuine concern, knowing that shit was always going wrong for many of us with family members back home, I inquired, "What's up, man?"

Gerry exclaimed excitedly, "Lieutenant Colonel Peters is bullshit this morning at the squadron 'cause the wing commander made a no-notice stop by last night and no one was up front at the duty desk

I responded, "So, big-ass deal; why do you give a shit if he came by?"

"'Cause, Bee, I'm the fuckin' squadron security officer and Lieutenant Colonel Peters thinks Colonel Roberts may have tampered with or taken something classified from the squadron last night."

Oh God, I thought, groping for a question with an easy answer that would ease Gerry's mind. "Why would Colonel Roberts take anything?" I questioned.

"'Cause, Bee, goddamit, he left a note saying our security sucked."

"So, what the fuck? You weren't there," I said, trying to bail Gerry out of his panic, realizing that his officer's performance report was in jeopardy if Colonel Peters wanted to make him a scapegoat for the wing commander drawing attention to a security breach. Servicemen were routinely punished merely to render the appearance that the guilty had been properly disciplined and justice served. Gerry had not noticed that beads of sweat were suddenly forming on my brow.

"Shit, Bee," Gerry nervously continued. "Lieutenant Colonel Peters has me and the admin sergeant inventorying all the top-secret files in the squadron, including all the .38s, which we now keep in a locked drawer. It's a real goat-rope pain in the ass."

I was being overwhelmed by empathy, but not sufficiently to dare rescuing Gerry's mind by a confession. He was frantic; I needed time to think. I wished him a guilt-laden good luck as I eased forward into the chow hall to see if I could get my breakfast down.

Seated at the table alone, I could feel my own version of panic as I pondered how to get Gerry off the hook without getting myself beheaded. *Jesus Christ,* I thought, *those poor bastards are jumping through their asses trying to find any confirmation that Colonel Roberts actually took anything classified as a test of their security program.* Lieutenant Colonel Peters thought, due to my forged note, the wing commander was busting his balls and Lieutenant Colonel Peters had Gerry working feverishly to assure Colonel Roberts he was properly responding to an apparent security failure. Poor Marcus

Mullis. I figured the next issue of *The Wild Boar* would include Mullis's suicide note. My conscience, thanks to Mama's many morality lessons, was thoroughly gnawing at me. Bee Settles' juvenile prank had become a ten-headed fire-breathing Hydra. I could feel my eyelashes being singed. Did I dare sacrifice myself to save Gerry? It wasn't quite on the level of what Jesus Christ did to wash away the sins of the world, but it felt similar.

Filled with a natural affinity for guilt and curiosity, thoughts of Gerry sweating over stacks of classified documents looking for the missing needle compelled me to drop by the 390th after breakfast. It was less than twelve hours later and I was once again twisting the knob of the door of my former squadron. I couldn't stop the cliché in the out-of-control turmoil of my mind: "The criminal always returns to the scene of the crime."

I could feel the liquid pools forming in my palms and checked my boots to confirm I didn't have two left feet. There was a blur of activity behind the duty desk as a tech sergeant and Senior Master Sergeant Boykin were verifying that document numerical assignments agreed with a master roster of classified materials. I spied Gerry at the gun cabinet absorbed in checking serial numbers on every .38 revolver assigned to the squadron. He looked up just long enough, as if it was a challenge to waste a fraction of a second speaking.

"Hey, Bee, what a fuckin' mess."

I could hear Lieutenant Colonel Peters on the phone in his office loudly bitching about his embarrassment that the wing commander caught the squadron with its security pants down. I didn't want those people going crazy, spending all day busting their asses over a hoax. The option for Lieutenant Colonel Peters contacting the wing commander was a Catch-22 since Gerry had admitted at the chow hall earlier that the operations officer wasn't sure if the note was legitimate. To call Colonel Roberts for confirmation of the visit would expose the squadron to the very real charge of lax security. Not calling left the dilemma of doing nothing in response to the note and waiting for the boot to drop or going for an atta boy by inventorying all classified material and finding the document or item they assumed the wing commander took. Lieutenant Colonel Peters opted for the latter response.

Witnessing the flurry of activity, I couldn't help thinking this was the revenge of Murphy's Law, "Anything that can go wrong will go wrong." The agony of furtively observing Gerry rifling through the thick stacks of classified shit in the six-foot-high gray metal file cabinets was maddening. I couldn't resist any longer. "Gerr, how long you think it's gonna take to finish?"

"Shit, Bee, we'll be in here at least another day and a half. I took myself off my flight this afternoon to be sure it gets done," he said, squishing out his neglected cigarette butt that had burned down to the filter. His armpits had darkened symmetrical rings of wetness. Suddenly, observing the frantic scene and imagining the growth of a huge ulcer in Gerry's gut, I realized my adolescent behavior had created all this grief. I had to bite the bullet.

"Hey, Gerr," I whispered from the counter.

Exuding impatience and probably wondering why I was hanging around thrashing out a bunch of unhelpful questions, Gerry hurriedly approached. Motioning with my right thumb, I said softly, "Step outside with me for a quick minute." He followed me out, exhaling forcibly to register annoyance. He shut the blue squadron door behind us and we proceeded to the side of the building like we were going to pull out our dongs and take a leak.

Looking him in the eye as if talking to a priest in the confessional, I acknowledged my sin. "Gerr," I said sheepishly, "there's no need to be going through all those changes inside the squadron."

"Why the fuck not? The colonel's in my ass to get this inventory done—now!" Gerry shouted back.

"Gerry, you don't understand. I wrote the damn note," I admitted, hoping for Gerry to grasp some relief.

"What? Bee, you piece-a-shit cocksucker. That was your idea of a fuckin' joke?"

"Yeah, Gerr, it was a fuckin' prank I played on Mullis when I stopped through a little smashed from the club last night. I didn't expect this madness," I said as Gerry shifted his weight to the opposite foot, his hands clasped on his hips. He looked at me like I was a complete idiot.

"Bee," Gerry responded, "you're a sick fuckin' puppy. What the fuck am I supposed to do now?"

Anxious to provide guidance for Gerry that would avert my crucifixion, I replied, "Well, you can continue with a half-assed inventory, confident that nothing is missing."

"Fuck that, man," Gerry barked.

"Or, or, or," I said, "you can tell Peters you have it on reliable information the wing commander did not leave the note."

"Bee, goddamit it, what if he asks how I know that? What if he wants to know who left the fuckin' note? What if he wants to know if I know who signed the wing commander's signature?" Gerry grilled me like a Philadelphia lawyer.

I responded, "Shit, just tell Peters you know for a fact Colonel Roberts didn't leave the note and that it was no longer necessary to check the classified stuff. And that you had to protect the identity of the prankster in exchange for his confession."

Backing away from me, Gerry asked, "Bee, what if he says 'fuck confidentiality? Lieutenant, I want a name.' "

I surrendered. "Gerry, resist divulging my name if you can. I got a good reputation, and I'm short. If the honchos want to fry my ass... Do what you gotta do. I admitted I did it to rescue you and give you some relief," I said, hoping to appeal to Gerry's sense of gratitude that brother Bee had taken the fall for him.

"If you can spare me, cool. If you can't, well, at least you're off the hook."

Moved by witnessing a grown man's pleas for compassion and leniency, Gerry seemed to be feeling sorry for old Bee Settles towering over him. I felt we were reliving a scene from *Of Mice and Men* and I was Lennie, the naïve oaf dreamer who was always being brought back to reality by his friend George, the realist. Gerry stepped toward the entry door and said over his shoulder, "Bee, I'll do what I can, but the colonel's gotta know it was a prank. Where you gonna be? I'll let you know. Thanks, Bee, for telling me the truth."

Stretching for any sense of consolation in Gerry's thank you, an awareness of Mama's success in planting a few seeds of righteousness swept over me. It was that fuzzy feeling again—with thorns at the edges. Like the father of our country, I could not tell a lie and was rolling the dice that honesty would prove to be the best policy.

Back in the steel cage ambience of my room, I paced in overwhelmed distraction, mentally trying on exotic scenarios of the final play-out of my self-imposed drama. After an hour staring at the first page of a letter from Mama, desperately attempting to read her words, there was a soft rap at my door. Not bothering to get up from my makeshift desk, I shouted, "Come in." The door eased open with what appeared to be deliberate slow motion. It was Gerry. He looked relieved, but I needed some good news before I could look the same way. "What happened?" I asked.

Gerry responded evasively, as if delighted over being in charge of my Chinese water torture.

"Bee, the guys in the squadron are relieved the chaos is over." I sighed in relief. "But Lieutenant Colonel Peters is pissed— rrreeeeaalll pissed."

Surrendering to uncertainty, I sputtered, "What the shit can they do? Court-martial me, Article 15, reprimand? What is the appropriate punishment for my crime?"

Appearing to elevate himself to sadistic judge and jury before my eyes, Gerry said with full condemnation, "Bee, you forged the wing commander's signature, you dumb shit."

"Oh God have mercy," was all I could reply.

Gerry glared at me. I asked "Did the colonel say what my punishment would be?"

"No. He just said he would have to deliberate over what action he could take."

Anxious to leave me wallowing in my misery, Gerry coolly excused himself saying, "Bee, I got to get back to the squadron to button up the files. Good luck."

Yeah, right, I thought. you're off the hook thanks to Ol' Bee falling on the sword. Now I'm gonna swing at sunrise.

That night, sleep evaded me. Three gin and tonics seemed to heighten my expectancy of impending demise. Embarrassment oozed from my pores as I imagined the echoing hoots of base-wide laughter erupting from all who got the news Bee Settles had been so stupid as to forge the wing commander's signature. Holed up in my room, I languished in self-imposed house arrest; I was the incredible shrinking man.

The deafening din of silence drowned out the efforts of any taped music to console me. I didn't even have the distraction of a combat mission to take my mind off the anticipated execution.

I crawled out of bed after a night of interminable tossing. As my bare feet planted on the cold linoleum floor, morning hunger surfaced, but it was quickly replaced with a choking sensation in my throat. The silence was shattered by what seemed like an abrupt knock at the door. What the shit? I thought, shouting back to stop the invasive banging.

"Yeah!" I yelled across the room.

"Bee, there's a call on the hall phone for you," the unrecognized voice shouted back.

Jesus Christ, I thought, *it's my court-martial notification.* "Okay!" I replied. Slipping my feet into the thong slippers at the foot of my bed, I dragged myself toward the door wearing a white T-shirt and army-green boxer shorts, aware of the tingling resonance of my metal dog tags strung onto a thin beaded chain necklace. I shuffled down the hallway to the phone.

"Hello, Lieutenant Bee Settles," I said.

The voice at the other end responded, "Hey, Bee, it's Gerry. Lieutenant Colonel Peters knows you're not flying and wants you in his office at 1000 hours (10 AM) on the dot." There was a discernible satisfaction in Gerry's tone.

I deserved his revenge for what I had put him through and I seeped remorse. "Okay," I answered. "Did he give any clue of what he's going to do?"

"I have no idea, Bee, but he's pissed 'cause he feels he was made into a buffoon by a smart-ass lieutenant named Bee Settles," Gerry said.

"Shit, man, I got a good record. I haven't screwed up once in my whole tour over here in this chicken-shit place. Ain't nobody on this base who wouldn't fly in combat with me," I pleaded, as if he had anything to do with my punishment.

"Bee," Gerry proclaimed, "you know what they say—one 'awe shit' erases ten 'atta boys.' "

"Fuckin' great, Gerr. Thanks for the words of inspiration."

"Bee, goddamit, don't bust my balls; you're the one who fucked up," Gerry shot back.

Feeling abandoned and convicted, I rendered an obscure and insincere thank you and told Gerry I would catch him later. His parting words echoed in my ear: "Good luck, Bee."

For a person who didn't give a damn about the war, I was puzzled at the mounting hysteria within me over what punishment I would receive. The hallway back to my room seemed a thousand miles long; the walls along the way appeared to be closing in to crush me. I had to work at breathing normally. I actually laughed out loud when the thought of hanging myself in my room flashed across my mind.

It was 0915 hours (9:15 AM). Luckily, the 390th TAC fighter squadron was less than fifty paces from the end of my quarters. I had plenty of time to get ready for my sentencing. Being acquainted with the trifles that carried weight in the military, the first thing I did when I got back to my room was pull out my shine kit and spiffy up the shine on my boots. I retrieved a fresh flight suit from my closet, laid it across the bed, took a quick shower, and then did a careful shave. By 0945, I was dressed and admiring myself in the bathroom mirror. I thought I looked real good for a public hanging.

The morning sky had a bright blue clarity. Fighter sorties roared down the runway launching into that blue familiarity only to be enveloped by the disguised splendor of an azure deception called the unknown. Leaving the dorm, I felt an unexpected sense of calm and courage sweep over me as I walked, straight and tall, drill-team style, toward the back door of the squadron. Head held high, I stepped proudly, going to the gallows for the heroic nobility of a cause. I even wore my blue piss cutter in lieu of my baseball cap, routinely tilted to the side in cocky defiance of conventionality. It was the ultimate surrender to the gravity and formality of the occasion. The only thing missing was snare drum rolls.

As I strode down the long corridor of the 390th, I was dizzied by the bright contrast from the outside sunlight to the dimness in the hallway. In less than twenty-five steps, I was standing at the entrance to Lieutenant Colonel Peters' office door. It was open. I saw him seated at his desk, leaning back in his gray swivel chair, hands clasped together behind his head, as if pensively waiting in sadistic delight and anticipation of my arrival. His hair was short, thin, and slicked back. He had on one of the old-style gray flight suits that were no longer authorized for combat missions because they weren't fire resistant like the green Nomex. He wore his satiny sky blue squadron scarf around his neck, one that came from the batch I had last ordered from Clark Air Base when I was still squadron fund officer. Stopping at the doorway, I saluted and bellowed loud and clear in exaggerated formality, "Lieutenant Bee Settles, sir, reporting as ordered."

"Come on in, Bee," he responded, returning my salute, filling me with shock that he had chosen to disarm my formality by addressing me by my nickname. He began his speech. "Bee, you sent us through a lot of grief around here over the last thirty-six hours. How the hell could you sign the wing commander's name to that silly note?"

Feeling like an imbecile, I responded in my rehearsed explanation, "Sir, I got a little bombed at the USO show celebrating gettin' short. Out of sentimentality for my old squadron and feeling somewhat funhearted, I stopped through just to absorb the atmosphere. To my surprise, Lieutenant Mullis was not at the front DO's desk but in the back typing feverishly away on the next issue of *The Wild Boar* I presumed. The note was never intended to be taken seriously; it was supposed to be a silly little gotcha between Mullis and me. Loaded and giddy, I went back to my quarters and forgot I had written the note. Next thing I know, all hell has broken loose and Gerry Edmunds is telling me he's jumping through his butt over a security breach. I never expected it to get this far out of hand."

Lieutenant Colonel Peters listened to my explanation with his arms folded judgmentally across his chest. "Lieutenant Settles," he responded, becoming ominously formal, "You could get an Article 15 for what you have done. I could place a formal reprimand in your permanent military record. That would fuck you for promotions the rest of your career."

I could feel individual balls of sweat skiing down my torso from my armpits as I listened to the chastisement. He went on, "But I don't want a brief moment of stupidity to ruin your career, particularly since the news about what happened has stayed in this squadron. As far as I am concerned, the matter ends right here, right now. However, I can't let it go without some kind of response to your immature and thoughtless act. Accordingly, Bee, you are hereby banished from this squadron and are not to step one foot inside these doors for the remainder of your tour. You got it, Lieutenant?"

His words hit me like a load of bricks. I should have been feeling enormous relief, but instead my first thought was indignation. I was there at Da Nang in the 390th, putting my ass on the line before all of them. The 390th was my squadron. How could they dare ban me from my squadron? Snapping myself back to reality, the truth spread quickly over me like a cold shower. I was a lucky to be getting off from the crime so cheaply. Had I not been so well thought of, Lieutenant Colonel Peters could have burned me good. As it was, the banishment was a mild slap on the wrist, intended more to embarrass than punish.

In half-baked humility, I thanked the operations officer for his leniency, sugarcoating it by assuring him of my compliance. I saluted and left his office in an exaggerated, drill-team precise about-face as he dismissed me.

Swiftly striding toward the front exit of the 390th, passing by the duty officer's desk, nodding a departure greeting at the unrecognized lieutenant, I opened the door and walked out. As if God were toying with me, who should be walking down the sidewalk toward me but Marcus Mullis. Fighting back the redness coming over my body, I greeted him with a guilt-coated, "Hey, Marcus."

"Hi, Bee," he said with a sleepy, sheepish demeanor. His eyes were uncontrollably bulging, bespeaking a unique heredity. Overwhelmed by the sight of Marcus's Abe Lincoln countenance, I was overcome with an inspiration to seek atonement and asked, "Marcus, did you get any grief about Colonel Roberts stopping by the squadron the other night and leaving that note?"

"No, not at all. Lieutenant Colonel Peters asked me if I was at the squadron on duty that night and I told him I was, although I was in the back admin office writing articles for *The Wild Boar*," Marcus responded.

Feeling a sense of relief that Marcus had not suffered for my sins, I confessed again, "Marcus, to stop the panic over Lieutenant Colonel Roberts stealing classified documents from the squadron, I admitted to Gerry Edmunds I wrote the stupid note to play a joke on you."

"On me? Why me? We hardly know each other. I'm a FNG [Fucking New Guy] and you're an old head." I surrendered and said, "Marcus, I was an English minor back at Ball State in Indiana, and a Spanish major. I have studied the classics in English and Spanish and enjoy writing and reading. I admire all the spirits in the world brave enough to write. When I heard you had the creative inspiration to start a squadron newspaper, I thought it was a hot idea and was jealous I had not thought of it first." Looking Marcus squarely in his eyes, I said, "In my bombed state the other night, I was envious of what you were doing and wrote the note signing Lieutenant Colonel Robert's name just to rattle your cage. It snowballed totally out of hand and now I've been punished for it."

Staring back at me in blank amusement, he issued a dumb sounding chuckle and said, "That's funny, Bee. Thanks for the compliment, but I told Lieutenant Edmunds that note wasn't serious. I knew it was a joke from the moment I read it, but no one would believe me. That is funny, ain't it?"

CHAPTER 22: CELEBRATING TWO HUNDRED

It was the last steamy week of July 1969 when I awoke to discover a note taped outside my door. It was from Perry, written in purple crayon,

> *Bee,*
>
> *I've arranged a good-bye war get-together at Ubon with our classmates. Squadron CO already said yes. Thought you might be interested. See me for details.*
>
> *— Perry*

As I pulled down the message, I thought, *Another Perry boondoggle,* but his note did hit a soft spot. We were all bigtime ready to get the hell out of Nam. A party on that subject was always in order.

The new CO in the 421st had no problem approving travel orders authorizing us to hop a C-130 from Da Nang to Saigon, a plane change in U-Tapao, and on to Ubon Air Base, home of the Wolf Pack, the famous 8th Tactical Fighter Wing. Whenever Da Nang weather forced us to divert to Ubon, my body tingled with exhilaration simply setting foot on the common ground with these aerial heroes. The place filled me with an undeniable sense of awe; being on that base was like having a front-row seat at the unfolding of history. Yes, no doubt, I wanted to go to a class party at Ubon.

From the beginning of my tour when we were assigned as roommates, I had always admired Perry for the way he got stuff done; he was a can-do kind of guy. He didn't know it, but I respected the unstoppable way he took on his life. Because Mama was a lifelong Christian, I could never hold religious zeal over his head as a flaw. As mischievous and condescending as I had been toward him, I was honored by his devotion to keeping me a friend.

What the hell, I rationalized, Perry and I, by our very survival for eleven months, had moved unwittingly into an elite group of combat veterans. We were still alive. That itself was something to party about. All survivors of life-threatening challenge share a profound bond, a kindred spirit that lives beyond simple human relatedness. Becoming part of that fortunate group was an enviable achievement, but it often carried a high cost in suffering for veterans and the families whose prayers they dragged along with them.

Coincidentally, Perry and I were both approaching two hundred missions. Perhaps we had done little more than be lucky. I couldn't believe with any real conviction I was any better pilot than my buddies who were no longer with us; many of them were among the best and brightest.

Three days passed and we were into August. It was the fighter squadrons' policy to sit crewmembers down from flying combat sorties one week before their return home date. No need to push the issue, they reasoned. If I attended the bash at Ubon, I calculated I would return to Da Nang just in time to fly my two hundredth mission and make the last week sit-down rule. It was perfect. Go get shitfaced with my classmates for a day in Thailand, come back, fly the last mission, and call it a war.

I couldn't wait to catch up with Perry to tell him ol' Bee would be making the good-bye reunion. Having been banished from the 390th, I had to delay confirming my attendance at the bash until I ran into Perry at a neutral location. When I finally saw him sitting at, of all places, the DOOM Club sipping a Coca-Cola with a bunch of drunken rowdies, I realized even Perry had finally lightened up. Being a Baptist teetotaler, he avoided the bar scene and the embarrassment of being reminded of his passive righteousness around fighter jocks who made a lifestyle of getting smashed and living in that bizarre comfort zone beyond the fringes of most men.

Perry's eyes lit up when I swaggered into the dimly lit smoke-filled main bar. "Hey, Bee, how you doin'?" he hollered out ostentatiously and, before I could respond, asked loudly, "You comin' to Ubon for the class reunion, aren't you?"

In that instant I was face-to-face with a sadness—a sense of compassion while witnessing Perry's desperate need to be liked, to be seen as special, to be acknowledged. All of us in our heart of hearts desire what Perry seemed to crave for himself. The crossover into diminishment occurs when neediness overpowers wistfulness, when overindulgence and hyperbole are the main sustenance for our cravings. It is a point at which we arrive at our most basic self: weak, awkward, and dominated by invisible forces we can't or won't understand. It made me ache to forgive him for trying so hard to be liked. I realized the glowing inside me was a sentiment I recognized as love for Perry because he labored so diligently at being a good Christian. I silently envied him, but lacked the courage or will to emulate him. Mama would have been proud of me for the compassion in my heart.

"Yeah, Perry, I'm goin' try to make it," I responded, inspiring him to leap to his size-fourteen feet and render an awkward give me five with his gorilla hand. I gave him five, and in a moment of spontaneous and rare public humility, thanked him for leaving the note on my door.

It was all settled. Perry had arranged for Gerry Edmunds and me to get travel requisitions on the C-130 transport that would take us to Ubon. We would party for one day, return on Monday afternoon, and be back to Da Nang by nightfall. I would brief and fly my last mission at 0800 hours (8 AM) on Tuesday August 12. Great. Eight days before my return to the good ol' US of A.

During the trip over to Ubon, aside from the constant deafening hum and steady vibration of the huge reciprocating engines of the C-130, Perry's nonstop kid-in-a-candy-store chatter drove us up the wall. Gerry cracked first, shouting, "Perry, Jesus Christ, man. We goin' to party. Yeah, it's gonna be fun. Chill, man."

Upon our arrival at Ubon, the motor pool van took us to the visiting officers' quarters to check in. Perry had it all set up, including the time we were to meet at the club for our class dinner in the private reception room he had reserved. Luckily, my old Laredo Air Force Base classmate, JO Johnson, who was also an F-4 copilot, was on leave and had okayed my bunking in his room. It was a relief that Perry was so competent with making arrangements—less for me to worry about. I was purely along for the ride.

Like a mother hen, Perry couldn't help admonishing, "Now, Bee, don't get too drunk. We got that morning departure day after tomorrow to get you back to Da Nang in time for your last mission."

"Yeah, yeah, Perry, I know," I responded, annoyed at Perry's public skepticism about my sense of responsibility when unsupervised.

The Sunday evening dinner resembled a Cossack feast. Our class of twelve navigators and twelve pilots had endured an extraordinary year of personal sacrifice. Incredibly, the entire class had made it through the tour alive. My heart was numbed in heaviness that I could not say the same for my Laredo pilot training buddies. Vince and Grant had both been killed with less than four months to go on our year. I held a profound reverence for their ultimate sacrifice. There was rarely any control over watery eyes at the thought of them somewhere out in the jungles of Laos and South Vietnam, no funeral, no burial, no hymnals, no eulogy—only man and metal decaying into dust.

Of course, most of us, except Perry, got bombed. But, in his spiritual way, I'm sure Perry was also high. The dinner party ended and spilled over into the Ubon officers' club bar where the booze continued to flow. The fighter jocks and hospital nurses in the bar found out what we were celebrating and our money was suddenly no good. We all had drinks three deep stacked up in front of us. It was the ultimate smash-o-rama.

As the evening wore on and good judgment became fleeting, there was a growing momentum for one last mass excursion down to the bathhouse just off base, the Scrub and Rubb, a Thai massage parlor that was always open for business. None of us was aware that it was Sunday, but in Nam every day was the same. In typical mob mentality, a dozen of us were up and out the door to get our tubes flushed one last time before the big trip back to our loved ones in the States.

A quick stagger to the front gate, guffawing and slapping one another on the back all the way, we arrived at the entry checkpoint where jitney drivers awaited the predictable procession of midnight ramblers from the base. We boarded four each in three waiting bhat buses and headed for the Scrub and Rubb. Our skin glistened with sweat in the warm humid Thai air as we bounced along the bumps and ruts of the primitive streets. Moments later, we were piling out in front of a massage parlor on Thu Bang Avenue, its bright neon sign alternately flashing blue letters—"Scrub"—and red letters—"Rubb."

The thrill of overseas exotica filled us with childlike euphoria, as if we were kids just entering the front gates of the state fair in Indianapolis in August excitedly eyeing the Ferris wheel and Tilt-a-Whirl rides. A freedom of anonymity unharnessed the freak show side of us. We entered the parlor door. An elderly Thai hostess wearing her hair in a neat bun, too elegantly dressed to greet our lusty entourage, was flanked by a muscular Chinese-looking bouncer dude who reminded me of the bodyguard in the James Bond movie *Goldfinger*. She greeted us at the reception stand by the door. What a weird scene, I thought.

The hostess graciously showed those of us slow on the draw to the viewing windows on the opposite side of the room behind which sat a dozen splendidly dressed Thai maidens. A one-way mirror protected the young girls behind the window from self-consciousness over the selection process that culled them out to perform acts of pleasure for the revolving door of clientele. The room glowed bright white from two six-foot-long fluorescent light tubes in the ceiling.

The young girls all wore lanyard necklaces that displayed a number hanging down just above their chest. My Ubon classmates who were frequenters of the parlor quickly selected their favorite numbers and vanished behind the solid wooden door. After paying the indulgence fee to the senior greeting hostess who welcomed us, they were buzzed through the entry door like pentagon brass entering a classified military briefing room.

In country boy amazement at this phenomenon, I froze in place at the viewing window, staring at the girls inside—some gorgeous, some not so fine, some homely. As usual, I was bogged down in deliberation and analysis. After much hesitation and slight squeamishness, I selected, for reasons not fully clear to me, one of the homelier hostesses. Who knows, perhaps I inwardly felt sorry for those who probably didn't get chosen often and wanted to make them feel better about themselves. I shyly uttered to the matron in charge, "Numba thirteen."

As if in disbelief, she loudly repeated, "You say numba thirteen, GI?"

Awkwardly, I affirmed, "Yes, ma'am."

She collected the equivalent of five dollars and buzzed me through the security door. Someone behind a counter in the corner called the girlie pit by interphone to notify number thirteen of her selection.

Number thirteen met me in a hallway that had the look of a long hospital corridor with a dozen closed doors. My mind played tricks; I thought I smelled burning meat. Politely, I greeted her. "Hi. I'm Bee."

She responded in a puzzled voice, "You, Bee?"

Confused at the snarl in introductions, I asked in that mock poor English people tend to use on foreigners, "What you name?"

Grinning widely, number thirteen smiled and said, "Sabria."

With the greetings out of the way, Sabria led me down the hallway to the last room that had an open door and beckoned me in with a wave of her open palm. She shut the door and invited me in broken English to "put you clowe on chair, Mr. Bee. You like Coca-Cora?"

"No thanks, Sabria. You have 7-Up?" I answered, seeking a suitable chaser to go with the fifth of Smirnoff the gang had entrusted me to carry. "Only got Coke, Mr. Bee," Sabria replied.

"That's cool, Sabria. Coke's fine." She placed my clothes on the chair with seasoned care. I stood before her naked like a pilot preparing for a physical.

Sabria wrestled for a moment with the bottle opener before the swish of success and handed it to me. I took a healthy hit from the vodka bottle, chasing it with a gulp of Coke. I crawled onto the table and lay upon my back. I was nicely numb, feeling no pain, and had forgotten in the automatic behavior of too much freedom that I was inside my PCOD (pussy cutoff date), the term used by short-timers who had to get disciplined about sexual contact to avoid returning home with exotic cargo.

Unable to control my desire to touch Sabria as she applied warm oils to my body, I extended my left arm around her waist and began to squeeze her arms and buttocks with my free hand. In the consistent swirl of nature's magic, arousal took control and I motioned for Sabria to get on the gurney-like bed with me. I was being overwhelmed by the affliction again; I wanted to have her, not get an Acme hand job. She politely resisted and I resorted to man's back-up strategy when skill and cunning failed—begging and pleading.

"No, Mr. Bee, you nice man, but I get in trouble I make love you. Get fire."

Understanding in that moment that giving hand massages only was her job, I relented. I took a time-out for a moment to wet my whistle and once again laid back in the groove of studying Sabria's face as she pulled and stroked me, occasionally cupping and gently squeezing my scrotum in her silky soft hands. Gazing on her light cinnamon face, even though she would probably not have been a finalist in a Thai beauty pageant, I felt the sensation of world-class physical pleasure. In that moment of magnified titillation, I had the epiphany of understanding why guys inexperienced in intimacy could marry the first woman who gave them sexual pleasure, no matter how homely she might be. There was something about sexual mania that nullified the prerequisite for beauty. But when a lover was gorgeous and muscular and could love you fully self-expressed like there was no tomorrow, that was the ultimate station for such a simple satisfaction.

Fully mellowed out by the adept victory of Sabria's magic fingers, it was time for either a nap or to catch up with the rest of my drunken classmates. The time spent attempting to rap my way onto Sabria's bones before she did a job on mine delayed my release from the massage room. Graciously thanking Sabria for her soulful handling, I greeted her with a goodnight hug and placed a few extra bhat in her moist palm. Walking down the corridor and out to the front vestibule, I inquired of the elderly hostess waiting on fresh customers, "Where buddies go?"

She replied, "They go, long time."

"Shit," I exclaimed in a low breath. "Now what?"

Politely bowing and saying good night, I left as the elderly hostess hollered, "You come back, see us."

I didn't know what to say other than "Thank you."

Outside in the sticky night air there was no sign of the gang. It was a Sunday night—alive and abuzz with activity. The flurry of people made it seem like a Friday night before midnight. There were couples on mopeds. Jitneys darted by on the two-lane streets spewing blue smoke exhaust clouds into the air. Clusters of missionless people strolled up and down the streets as if browsing but not really looking. I thought of Ernest Hemingway and how he had made a lifestyle of absorbing his spirit in the mix of foreign exotica. Like a Bowery bum, I toted the Smirnoff in the brown paper bag as if it were a security blanket.

With tubes cleared and head still buzzing, I strolled into the human current of diminutive Thai people moving down the sidewalk. The scene was surreal. I felt as if I was in an Asian wonderland or maybe once again starring in another Fellini movie, not understanding what was being said in any of the conversations that swirled around me. In the open street, barbecued chicken and goat parts smoking on flat grills were being sold along with Thai beer and soda. Most of the strangers I passed didn't resist staring. They knew I was American from my dress and height. I was different looking— not Black or white, but different. It seemed they had never seen a yellow-skinned American. Strangely, throughout my life in America, there was not all that much difference from the curious glances being intercepted that night in Ubon Ratchathani, Thailand. Enthralled in the menagerie of smells, language, and Thai culture, I glimpsed small enclaves of meandering beautiful young women with every turn of my head. In this trance of visual hypnosis, I was overcome with inspiration to meet a representative of these gorgeous, cinnamon-skinned Thai beauties—once again ignoring my commitment to the PCOD.

Walking away from the open-air moviegoers toward the street curb, I spotted a bicycle rickshaw powered by a brown-complexioned driver whose feet were strapped to sandals. He wore pants cut off at the knees and a white dress shirt. His hair was jet black, shiny, and slicked straight back. In standard foreign bad English, feeling emboldened by the vodka, I asked, "You take me find pretty girl?"

Nodding and grinning, he responded in a tone I heard as sinister, "Yes, Mr. GI, you come go me. Get much pretty girl." As he gestured for me to board the rickshaw, a sudden foreboding swept over me. I felt like the Ugly American. I was twice the size of my diminutive chauffer and he was peddling his rickshaw dragging my big ass down the street to find a Thai woman of the dawn, one of his fellow citizens. I had always prided myself on operating at a more tolerant level than most of my white Air Force counterparts in how I treated the people I met in foreign lands, but at that moment I was someone I didn't want to be.

The driver peddled down four or five blocks. The concentration of people began to thin, and, suddenly, the streets became dim and vacant. The only sound in the night air was the exhalation of the driver pacing his respiration. My imagination began to trip, canvassing for frightening thoughts. Was this driver armed with a knife? Was he a black-belt mugger transporting me to my doom? How would they explain my death to Celeste? His body was found in a dimly lit neighborhood where streetlights were spaced one block apart. What was he doing there? Looking for a good bridge game? I couldn't help focusing on the scary scene that would have been unacceptably creepy to anyone in their right mind. Each block was flushed in darkness. The shadowy silhouettes of large-trunked trees lined the street and hovered like gangly ghosts in front of small bungalows that made up the neighborhood.

After whisking past the second dark stretch of houses, the chauffer slowed his peddling and made the carriage stop. He turned his glistening face toward me and panted, "You wait here. I go get nice girl, pretty red dress." Horror swept over me as he proceeded across the street and into the black shadows between the trees. Why did the neighborhood seem so far off the beaten path? Staring at him as he disappeared into the obscurity of the night, I suddenly caught consciousness of another sound—a vehicle advancing toward me rapidly. It was a jeep, an Air Force military police jeep that switched on its red rotating light as it arrived alongside the rickshaw.

Oh shit, I thought, *can I get busted for this?* I was mildly intoxicated, but that wasn't against military rules. In habituated paranoia whenever police showed up, I inventoried myself. Yes, I had an open jug of Smirnoff, but, thank God, no reefer. What could they want? I was too mellow to be intimidated. Seeing they were enlisted MPs, I prepared to shock them with the announcement that I was an officer. The MP not driving shined a five-cell flashlight in my face, eliciting an instant reaction, "Hey, hey, no need to shine that thing in my face!"

Without removing the light away he shouted, " Are you U.S. military personnel?"

"That's affirmative," I shouted back. "What's the problem?"

The driver of the jeep commanded, "We need to see your military ID, Airman." I guess he assumed I had to be an enlisted person roaming around in the middle of the night in a rickshaw.

I responded, "Roger that!" and began patting my pockets, desperately hoping I had it on me. Finding it tucked into my back pocket, I exhaled in a swoosh of relief as I rendered my Air Force picture ID card.

He instantly spotted the paper sack on the seat beside me, but, without responding, took my ID. After a moment studying it, he asked, "Sir, are you assigned to the Ubon airbase?"

I quickly responded, "Negative. I'm a pilot with the 390th TAC fighter squadron out of Da Nang."

"Da Nang, sir? You're a long way from home."

"That's right, sergeant. I'm here at Ubon for a class reunion before we head back to the States after finishing our combat tours," I boasted, hoping to soften his formality with me.

"Sir, you not being assigned to the 8th Tactical Fighter Wing you obviously don't know that this area is off limits to all military personnel due to the stabbings that have occurred in this neighborhood over the past month involving U.S. servicemen."

A chill came over me, closely followed by hot flashes of terror. "Jesus Christ, you shittin' me?"

"No, sir, we're serious," the MP driver assured me.

Overwhelmed with a sense of proximity to having my throat slit and a greater sense of my stupidity, I prevailed upon the MPs, "Gentlemen, I don't even know where the hell I am. Can I get a lift back to the base with you?"

"Yes, sir, but you'll have to ditch the jug."

"Not a problem. Gladly," I proclaimed, stumbling out of the rickshaw to make my way around to the backseat of the jeep. At that moment, the rickshaw driver emerged from the darkness across the street, seemingly oblivious to the MPs, and gestured rearward with his arm toward the female figure wearing a tight red dress standing in the shadow of a large ginkgo tree. I delayed entering the jeep and approached him apologetically stating, "Sorry, no can stay. Take bhat. I go police." I handed him an ample payment for his trouble.

He accepted it with a look of puzzlement and perhaps disappointment that I was walking away from the night goddess he had arranged for me. Fumbling as I piled into the jeep, I peered into the shadowy light and caught a quick glimpse of the face of the lady in red and mumbled, "Damn, she's a stone fox too."

As we drove off, I listened to reassurances from the airmen of how lucky I was they happened by. Pondering the authenticity of my rescue and the deeply buried motivations that had gotten me lost in space once again, I was left to soak in my thoughts. I massaged the question of why I couldn't be like the others— nice guys who had their fun and returned to the safety of the base. But not Bee Settles. I wondered what had instilled this spirit to always take chances, to be at risk, exploring alone, outside the unknown, outside the normal human comfort zone and simple common sense. Was the answer buried in my abandoned childhood dreams of family after Daddy left home? Did it lie in some self-destructive reaction to a sense of alienation and detachment from not feeling acceptable back there as a biracial adopted orphan? Would I ever know the answers?

CHAPTER 23: THE LAST MISSION

Hungover and sleepless, I struggled to find my way out of the head fog that had settled in after my escapade through the streets of Ubon Ratchathani following the going-home party. The memory boards of my alcohol-soaked brain had apparently shut down after the military police let me out at the front gate of the air base since it was a complete mystery how I had gotten back to my room and into bed. In an inexplicable return to consciousness, I rolled over and took a bleary-eyed glance at the clock. A bolt of panic hit me as I deciphered it was already half past noon. Damn, I was not going to be at operations to catch the one o'clock C-130 back to Da Nang.

Anxiety-stricken that I had missed my flight to Da Nang, I leapt out of bed and shuffled through the base information guide desk until I found the Base Operations listings. I spotted the telephone number quickly but it became an Olympian effort to perform the simplest act- - standing up without staggering and bringing printed materials into focus--and, as I discovered when I got through to the tech sergeant on duty, babbling in clear sentences. I was a mess. Still bombed, I fumbled through three attempts to dial accurately before getting it right.

"Good morning, this is Lieutenant B. Settles desperately trying to catch the flight to U-Tapao. Is it still here?"

Frantic to be told by the duty sergeant that the one o'clock to U-Tapao was late departing, I was informed instead they were cranking engines on time.

Oh my God, I thought. No way I can shower and shave, get my things together, and clear the cobwebs out of my head sufficiently to make it to that passenger terminal in twenty minutes, not to mention filling out the travel authorization papers, which that morning would have been equivalent to taking an SAT exam. I had blown it. Suddenly I had another embarrassing insight: I was still shitfaced from the night before. My skin crawled and my head pounded like a small bass drum. I was convinced I could actually feel the hypoxic blood forging its way in surges through the capillary plumbing in my brain.

"Well, sergeant, is there another flight that could get me back to Da Nang today?" I pleaded.

"Stand-by, sir, I'll check the transient aircraft manifest," he responded. After what seemed like a day-and-a-half pause, he came back on the line. "Yes, sir, lieutenant, there is another C-130 departing for U-Tapao at 1700."

"Beautiful, sergeant, can I get on that one, and how about continuing on to Da Nang?"

Again, "Just a minute, Lieutenant, while I check on that for you."

Jesus Christ, I thought, *I'll be insane by the time this guy finishes checking for me.* The earlier flight would have connected me with a nonstop out of U-Tapao to Da Nang, getting me on the base by eight o'clock that night in plenty of time to rest and prepare for my last mission. It was the hallmark event I had been waiting for and dreaming about for an entire year.

The sergeant came back on the line. "Yes, sir, there is a connection to Da Nang but with a plane change in U-Tapao that then proceeds on nonstop to Da Nang."

A thing of beauty, I thought; I don't have to go through Saigon. What did it matter? I had no choice. "What time does that get me into Da Nang, Sarge?"

There was another pause; inappropriately, I exhaled impatience. The sergeant after all, was being helpful in a timely manner; the time warp of my befuddled mind simply could not grasp it. I felt like a jerk for my unwarranted exasperation.

"Midnight, sir," he answered.

"Jesus H. Christ," that perfect guy inside me exclaimed. "You sure know how to do things the hard way." Okay, no sweat. Midnight was all right. I could still get some sleep and be ready at seven in the morning for the brief for the two hundredth mission.

"Beautiful, Sarge, nice work. I really appreciate your help on this thing. I'm supposed to fly my two hundredth combat mission tomorrow out of Da Nang and I'm starting to sweat bullets about getting back. Would you please list me on the 1700 flight?"

"Yes, sir. Lieutenant D. Fettles was it?"

"No. It's Lieutenant B. Settles, like the airplane *settles* to the runway."

With that bit of clarification, I heard the sergeant snicker briefly on the other end.

"Got it, sir. You're listed. Just be here thirty minutes before departure."

"No sweat. And thanks again, Sarge," I added in humble appreciation.

"You're welcome, Lieutenant, Good luck on your last mission."

Oh Lord, I thought, why'd he have to say that? His parting wish gave me a funny feeling like a black cat crossing in front of my path. I wasn't prone to superstition but always seemed aware of black cats, ladders, and Friday the thirteenth. I figured shit was going to happen one way or another and all any of us could do was the best we could. But the Sarge's good luck wish still reverberated. I collapsed back on the bed for a couple more hours of shut-eye.

A quick three hours later I woke with another jolt of panic and realized I had not set the alarm. Still struggling with the blurred vision that regularly comes with the deep slumber of post carousing, I once again focused on the clock sitting on the nightstand. Quarter 'til four, time to go.

An itch of aggravation pricked at me as I hurriedly showered and shaved. It was as if my body at times realized I was a pain in the rump to myself. Leaping into a fresh flight suit, I tidied up JO's room, made the bed, and left a thank you note. With my lightly packed B-4 bag in hand, I scanned over my shoulder to check for anything I might have left behind. Good move, there was my wristwatch on the nightstand.

Stepping outside, I hitched a quick ride on a passing jeep to base ops. The cloudless afternoon sky was a deep blue, and the sun was still shining brightly at four-thirty. Weather shouldn't be a factor, I thought. The loud roar of an F-4 two ship take-off shattered the otherwise tranquil ambience. Quickly jumping out of the jeep, I thanked the airman for the ride and bid him a great day. He saluted and I returned the protocol.

Good news and bad greeted me upon checking in at the transient travel window. The C-130 was late arriving, but was on its way. With that information I backed up the departure and arrival times for the remaining trips and put myself at Da Nang by one o'clock in the morning, still plenty of time for a few hours of shut-eye. I walked out on the tarmac outside base ops to light a Salem and bask in the notion that it was all coming to a close. It was a magnificent, clear day in Thailand. I had gotten nicely buttered with my classmates at the party, enjoyed a happy ending at the Scrub and Rubb, and now I was waiting on the bird that would take me back for the mission I had been living for—the last one.

My stomach suddenly growled its notification of neglect. Damn, I thought, extinguishing the half-smoked Salem on the sole of my flight boot, I hadn't eaten. There was time for a quick cheeseburger and fries, and maybe a beer to chase off the hangover fuzzies we called the hanks. What I really wanted was a big pile of scrambled eggs and bacon, biscuits, and a beer, but my bad hours had blown it for breakfast.

A comforting redundancy of Air Force life was the cookie-cutter character of every base—same shops, same BXs, same chow halls, officers' clubs, and base ops with snack bar close by. The time passed quickly with excitement and appreciation stirring within me. My spirit was at a rare, but cautiously wonderful high. If I could just survive the next week, I was going to make it out of there, escape the war, and head home to freedom and resumption of my long-anticipated life with my bride.

The camouflaged C-130 Hercules roared into the ramp area with the deafening metallic scream of high-pitched squealing of the four turbo-propellers that fanned up mini dust storms behind it. I peered into the cockpit area as they taxied by, thinking, fingers stuck in my ears to protect my hearing from further damage, that these were Air Force pilots flying around Southeast Asia just like me, doing their job hauling people and cargo for their paycheck. I was helping to drop bombs on Vietcong and NVA troops and getting shot at daily for my paycheck. As much as I had agonized over the decision to participate in combat, I felt a strange superiority complex—an arrogant condescension for these so-called many motor drivers who flew the powder-puff aircraft on daily trash-hauling flights, boring along straight and level beneath the tropopause, safe from the madness of combat missions and triple A antiaircraft fire. These drivers were just as lonely and isolated from their families as fighter pilots. They perceived their missions as amply laden with challenge and uncertainty also, but we all knew as military pilots that the fighter-pilot lifestyle was on a whole different level.

Once they had off-loaded passengers, refueled, and cleared the return passengers to board, I quickly scaled the entry ladder, popped my head into the flight deck, and greeted the fellas flying the bird, attempting to confirm everything was in the green for the short trip down to U-Tapao. I was embarrassed by my inability to suppress my excitement about getting back to Da Nang for my two hundredth mission; I oozed giddy euphoria. The crew issued a sincere congratulations and good luck on making it toward the last mission. Yeah, I was in a great place. Comforted by knowledge of being on time to the stopover, I fell sound asleep before we took off from Ubon.

I regained consciousness during descent into U-Tapao. The loadmaster announced over the PA system that an en route message had come in from U-Tapao Operations informing us that there would be an aircraft swap for the next leg and, instead of flying direct to Da Nang as scheduled, the carriage of a honcho from Seventh Air Force headquarters necessitated a stop in Saigon before proceeding to Da Nang.

Oh, shit, I thought, this thing is getting a little pucker to it. "How much of a delay would there be in dropping the bird colonel off at Tan Son Nhut Air Base?" I asked the loadmaster.

"Not that much," he responded, "maybe forty-five minutes with the plane change. We're going to try to fuel through to Da Nang out of here."

It was reassuring they were planning ahead, but I fought back a sickening feeling that this return might be starting to unravel right before my eyes. A new wave of anxiety overcame me. I labored with the mental gymnastics of recalculating an arrival time based on the loads info. Damn, I would now be arriving close to 0200 hours (2 AM)—leaving me five hours to sleep before my brief. I could sense Murphy's Law starting to peek at me. But, we were making progress toward the destination; it was premature to begin wrestling off panic attacks.

"Mellow out, Bee," I whispered to myself, "it's goin' be all right."

After another bag drag, we boarded the replacement Hercules and settled in with our gear. Again, I poked my head into the cockpit and reminded the guys I was counting on them to get me in for that last mission. "We'll get you there, man. We'll get you there," the aircraft commander reassured. The VIP colonel, gaunt and arrogant, appeared sporting a close-cropped haircut that was well inside neatly groomed guidelines, boarded, and went to the rear of the bird. Recalling that the C-130 aircraft commander had invited me to ride up front, I decided to take him up on his offer. Despite having to trust other pilots to get you to your destination, it always rendered a greater sense of being in control or knowing the pulse of what's happening when you're on the flight deck.

We blasted off, vibrating like we were straddling a small jackhammer. Night had set in before we left the ramp at U-Tapao. Soon leveling off at cruise altitude and heading east toward the next stop, I noted how dimly lit the cockpit was. Not as dim as we kept the lights on night Phantom missions, but there wasn't the same type of scary stuff outside the windows of a transport cruising at twenty-six thousand feet across Laos to South Vietnam. On the flight deck, besides the dull glow of white instrument lights, there was the wonderful, almost surreal reddish hue of map reading lights that had red lens covers, which gave the dark atmosphere a red glow. Suddenly the muse of pretty lights was shattered by an exclamation from the copilot, "Shit, Skipper, that number two tach is getting squirrelly. I been watchin' it for a few minutes now."

"Yeah," the AC responded, "I didn't want to say anything just yet."

"Roger that," the copilot answered.

Fuck me again, I thought. Is this going to go to hell all of a sudden? In a matter of minutes I had my answer. The number two tachometer needle began to fluctuate more widely. We could all hear the huge eight-foot propeller on the number two engine surging intermittently. It looked like Murphy had advanced from peeking to creeping upon the scene.

Naively and wishfully, I asked, "You think the tach will be okay to get to Tan Son Nhut, guys?"

Being so close to U-Tapao, the AC expressed doubt about being able to proceed with a malfunctioning tach. The copilot suggested disconnecting the cannon plug from the back of the gauge to see if resetting it might return it to normal readings. "Good idea," the AC said. "Try it. See what we get."

The copilot initially fumbled, attempting to get the screwdriver to loosen the screws holding the gauge in place. He removed his fire-resistant Nomex gloves and quickly got it out of its slot. The other engine tachometer needles were steady and in place, accurately reading the cruise power settings on the three other props. After a cursory examination of the cannon plug, the copilot attached the gauge to its fitting and put it back in its socket. All our eyes were glued to the face of that gauge. "Shit," the AC exclaimed, "still fucked up."

I couldn't help myself and blurted out, "Now what, Captain?"

Unnecessarily apologetic, he explained they would have to contact their operations people since we were still in range of U-Tapao to see if there was adequate maintenance at Thon Son Nut or if they would have to RTB (return to base) U-Tapao to replace the failed gauge.

The copilot changed the spare radio back to the ops frequency and notified them of the bad tachometer, asking if the flight was approved to proceed to Saigon. If it could get bad, it would get worse. After a short pause the answer came over the radio. "Yeah, Blindbat, maintenance wants you to return here for the fix. We have the parts in supply."

Damn! Damn! Damn! Both the AC and the copilot turned to me as if to notify me there was a death in my family. The look on their faces told the whole story: Arriving for my two hundredth mission was now up for grabs. How long would the repairs take? Then add that to the time to fly to where we were and back to U-Tapao. I stared at the hands of my watch, unable to make any sense of what they were telling me, feeling my mind beginning to snap shut on simple math calculations to determine new estimated times of arrival. I was flushed with annoyance over being so irresponsible as to put myself in this position. I could possibly arrive at Da Nang Air Base by 0400 (4 AM). Not much time to work in a nap, but still there for the pre-mission command post briefing.

The engines issued a loud swishing sound as the throttles were retarded for descent back into U-Tapao. The aircraft shuddered and vibrated noticeably. Even experienced fliers could have easily concluded that the plane was in trouble from all the rattling and rumbling in the fuselage, but it was a normal flight for the old workhorse Hercules.

Once we were on the runway at U-Tapao, the tower cleared us to taxi to the maintenance ramp close to the parts depot. The VIP colonel had also been apprised of our mechanical problem; he seemed in no particular hurry to reach his destination, unlike me. By the time the engines rumbled to a stop, I had developed an unshakable case of nerves.

The maintenance personnel met the aircraft and boarded quickly to remove and install the new tachometer. The tech sergeant maintenance chief grunted, twisted, and grunted some more, busting his knuckles to get the cannon plug of the new gauge to match up and screw into place. There was a flurry of head scratching, swearing, and puzzlement. Finally, eureka! Parts supply had sent a tachometer gauge for a different model C-130 engine--that's why it was a no fit. I was pacing on the ramp away from the aircraft, chain-smoking Salems and appearing like an expectant father waiting outside the delivery room for triplets. We waited for what seemed like weeks for the maintenance sergeant to return. His van lights finally showed as he sped across the ramp toward us like the pony express in black-and-white cowboy movies. We had been there for an hour.

Soon there was a loud muffled bullhorn announcement so obscured by scratchy static it might as well have been shouted in Chinese. It was time to reboard. Thank God, I thought, but the time window was narrowing. The pilots again apologized and quickly got all four engines going, once again performing a quick static run-up of the number two engine to be sure the replacement tachometer had fixed our indicating problem. Everything looked good. Maintenance finished the logbook sign-off, saluted the crew, and hastily departed.

Again, I sat up on the jump seat in the cockpit. Even though the bad gauge had been replaced, I couldn't keep my eyes off the number two tach. I busied myself with repetitive glances at my watch, alternating with equal distractive stares at the tachometer and gaining nothing from either activity. It was 03:45 (3:45 AM) by the time we reached cruise altitude. An hour flight time to Saigon, a quick turn on the ground, and off to Da Nang. With a crackly voice, I inquired, breaking the silence on the flight deck, "What do you figure for a Da Nang ETA now?"

The captain, Butch, looked at his watch, then at me, and shouted, "Looks like shortly after 0600 (6 AM) now, Lieutenant Settles."

My Lord, there goes my night's sleep, but still doable, I thought. Knowing that I'd be flying my last mission on adrenaline laced with caffeine, I told the two pilots I was going to slip out for a little shut-eye. They rogered me, and I went to the back. Despite the stress-loaded uncertainty, I managed to escape into slumber almost instantly and I wasn't even conscious for the landing or takeoff at Tan Son Nhut. I felt the airplane lurch and bounce, descending through some cumulus buildups. I awakened in a panic, as my eyes snapped open to greet the hysterics that I had again overslept. My mouth felt like sawdust had been soaking in it and I could smell my foul breath. I was a mess. Hurriedly, half stumbling forward, I staggered up the four or five steps leading to the flight deck. Daylight was breaking through the cockpit window. I checked my watch. Shit! It was 0645 (6:45 AM).

"We starting down fellows?" I asked.

"Yep," Butch answered nonchalantly. "You gonna make it?"

"How much longer to the ramp?" I came back.

"Thirty-five, maybe forty minutes," he replied.

Okay, I thought, little sleep and I miss the mission briefing at the command post. No sweat! I was the most experienced F-4 copilot on the base. I had been through 199 intelligence briefings and I could do my job blindfolded and backward. Trying to think ahead, I asked the copilot if he minded switching to the F-4 command post frequency to let them know Lieutenant B. Settles was landing in a matter of minutes and would be there in time to fly his mission. The duty officer rogered the copilot's communication. A silence fell over the radio. Uneasy with no response, I asked the copilot to please inform them I would meet my aircraft commander at the personal equipment shop. I knew the crew would stop there on the way to retrieve survival gear, helmets, guns, and letdown rope backpacks. Again, another short "roger that" from the duty officer. Beautiful, I mused, I'm gonna pull this thing off after all. My mind was fully revved up.

"Butch, I appreciate you guys bustin' ass to get me back." Pushing my luck, I inquired, "Do you think your ground people can meet me with a van to shoot me over to the PE shop?"

"Sure, Lieutenant. We'll shake somebody loose for you. Hope you make it," he responded. Wow! These guys are great, I thought. The C-130 landed and fast taxied to the ramp and cut off the engines. The loadmaster opened the huge hydraulic ramp door; I grabbed my B-4, shook the guys' hands, and hit the doorsteps. Just like I was a VIP, the van was right there. I checked my watch for the umpteenth time. It was 0725, thirty-five minutes to engine start. I was going to make it. Within minutes, I was thanking the young airmen first class from the C-130 detachment at Da Nang for the lift. I rushed inside the PE shop, blurry-eyed and sensing that my body was still vibrating from the hours of riding on the C-130. Tech Sergeant Bronson had early duty in the shop that morning; I greeted him with a bounce in my step.

My other crewmembers hadn't arrived yet from the pre-mission briefing. As I was slapping my survival vest over my shoulder and just starting to slip my arms through the cut-off sleeves, I heard the phone ring. Sergeant Bronson was slow to respond, as if he were shocked that anyone would be calling that early. By the third ring, he quickly picked up.

" Personal Equipment, Sergeant Bronson."

There was a brief pause as he listened to the voice on the other end, turning his head in my direction. "I believe so. Stand-by, sir," he added. Watching me stride up the aisle with my helmet, he held his hand over the mouth portion of the phone as if giving me a chance to say I wasn't there without the party at the other end hearing my response. "Lieutenant Settles, right?"

I nodded, wondering who was on the phone. Sergeant Bronson whispered in a soft tone, "A Colonel Peterson."

Oh, hell, I thought, remembering the former operations officer of the 390th TAC fighter squadron who had banned me from the squadron due to my Colonel Roberts prank. He had recently been reassigned as squadron commander of my new squadron, the 421st. As I reached for the phone, I wondered what the colonel wanted with me. What is he doing up this early?

The moment I raised the phone to my ear, the front door of the PE shop swung open and four crewmembers preparing to go out on Tropic flight—my flight—walked in. "Lieutenant Settles," I snapped into the receiver.

"Good morning, Bee. The command post duty officer called me to inform me you were arriving late for your flight briefing and told me of your intention to go straight to PE. But, in all good conscience, I had you replaced on Tropic flight."

The colonel's words hit me like a two-by-four; I suddenly couldn't detect my heartbeat, and my mouth gaped open. There was an awkward silence. "Did you read me, Bee?" Colonel Peterson asked.

"Yes, sir, Colonel, I'm here. I'm the most experienced GIB on the base; why wouldn't you think I can fly this mission?" I queried with dismay.

"Bee, it's not that I don't think you have the knowledge and experience to do the mission. For me, as your commander, you didn't make it back here in time for your intelligence briefing. Do you know how I would feel if you got shot down on your last mission before going home? Maybe getting captured by the North Vietnamese because of some escape and evasion information you didn't get because you missed the mission briefing?"

More silence on my end. The colonel's logic, as much as I wanted to resist it, was coldly on the money. Being honest with myself, were I in the commander's boots, I wouldn't have wanted that specter over my head either. He could never have defended his position to his superiors were we to get shot down. I was devastated. I wanted to continue arguing the case for going on the mission but I listened carefully to Colonel Peterson's mulling over his position. I dismissed any notion that it might be further payback for the security breach prank. It occurred to me the entire previous twenty-four-hour ordeal to get back to Da Nang was a warning that the flight was not meant to be. I wasn't superstitious, but in that microscopic moment I was overcome by an inexplicable haunting about omens.

Major Henry Larson, Bullet Hank, who had made arrangements to fly with me on my last mission, brushed by, sympathetically patting me on the back as he passed, issuing a sincere "Sorry, Bee," knowing I had been replaced at the last minute. "I was looking forward to flying your last one together." Tears formed in my eyes, blurring my vision as the crew of Tropic flight walked out the PE shop door and headed across the street. The echo of Colonel Peterson's voice on the phone repeatedly calling my nickname snapped me back from my trance. I finally responded in a cracked voice, "Okay, sir. I got it. I'm off the flight."

Slowly, I replaced the phone back on its hook as I stared at the nothingness in the room. The smell was that of a football team locker room. I went back down the third long aisle lined with rack after rack of G suits, helmets, and survival vests and hung my equipment back on the peg labeled "Lieutenant B. Settles." Sergeant Bronson kept his eyes glued to me, knowing without knowing what had transpired. He understood why I was unable to say good morning as I left the shop.

It was a short walk across the open lot from the PE shack to my quarters. It was 0800 (8 AM) on August 12, 1969. I had made it back in time for the mission. The halls of the dorm were silent as if the world were suddenly vacant. I glided slowly toward my room. I

257

could not feel my feet touching the linoleum and was deaf to their sound. I jerked with a start at the ring of the phone down the hallway breaking the silence. My first impulse was to ignore it. Inexplicably, given my state of mind, I opted to walk down and answer it, wondering why I was bothering. Acting annoyed that anyone would be calling to disturb the dorm at that time of the morning, I grabbed the phone, "Yeah. Lieutenant Settles." It was Colonel Peterson again. "Hi, Bee, glad I caught you. I got you on the schedule for the same flight—Tropic flight—tomorrow for your two hundred, okay?"

In a flash of clarity it suddenly it hit me that tomorrow would be Wednesday, the thirteenth. I responded instantly without thinking, "Naw, fuck it, Colonel. I appreciate your spirit of support, but, as far as I'm concerned, my two hundredth mission was a C-130 ride from Saigon to Da Nang."

Incredulous at my arrogant, borderline disrespectful response, Colonel Peterson responded, "Are you sure about that, Bee, that you're not just upset and will regret this later?"

"Yep, colonel, you can sign me off; I've flown my last mission. The war's over for me."

CHAPTER 24: FREE AT LAST

The interminable months of isolation's agony were slipping into history. I was perched on the threshold of surviving a combat tour in Vietnam. The last week before departure was a mellow lounging in the zone of disbelief—like the state of the lottery winner whose real treasure is the brief basking in the light of good fortune's broad smile. In characteristic fashion, I was grappling with denial that I could actually be on the precipice of escape from the war. I would not grant myself permission to fully embrace the liberating euphoria of leaving this dangerous place.

The miracle of joining the ranks of combat survivors begets new challenges. It would seem that some of us are perpetually in search of something about which to be neurotic or preoccupied. I welcomed substituting my reality challenges in Vietnam for the new frontier conjugal challenges of being safe at home with Celeste, creating a future together over which I had logged a year fantasizing.

There is a kindred spirit among warriors (and perhaps prisoners) that makes them eternal brothers because they have visited the edge and returned. Family, friends, and well-wishers, while supportive out of a profound desire to empathize, cannot know the place from which we have emerged. It is the great irony for combat survivors: you can never adequately share the impact of your experience with those around you who have not been to that place. In most cases, the returning veteran may not have a workable strategy that would be effective in smoothing out the emotional ride back into society. The combat training manuals don't have a chapter titled "On-the-Job Training for Posttraumatic Stress Disorder" during combat recovery, leaving us to rely on music, stimulants, family love, and more idle pensiveness in our new solitary confinement. Those who had faith in God were the blessed ones.

During the last days at Da Nang, these thoughts sprang in and out of my consciousness like fleas on an alley cat in summer. I was a front-row witness to my absurdity as a voluntary, expendable pawn of the U. S. Air Force war machine. Yes, I had dropped my dime in the slot to pull the handle on living through being a fighter pilot. At the point of realizing I had pulled off the gamble hiding behind my hypocrisy, I was still left searching for consolation or value in having prevailed. I didn't want my return from war to be anticlimactic. I wanted my sacrificial suffering to mean something beyond simply rendering one mind-blower of a lifetime adventure for drunken storytelling on the back porches of the future with family and friends.

Pondering how to make my tour matter in my life or, better yet, perhaps the lives of others, I had imagined my going-home party being the perfect occasion to start delivering the message.

Several weeks before I finished my last combat mission, just after the tuna fish poisoning in early July, I awoke early from a restless slumber to discover uncontrolled words in thought patterns running across my mind. The words, the points I needed to make in my going-home speech, were like neon ducks promenading in an arcade shooting gallery. I crawled out of the bed and wrote my speech weeks before the final party.

The day before the party I thanked Colonel Peterson once again for offering to get me on the schedule for my two hundredth mission and apologized for my insolence. Three days remained before my flight on the Freedom Bird back home. Wrestling to overthrow any departure anxieties, I hung out in seclusion, privately high-fiving myself that it was over. There was still a latent contradictory aching in my pilot heart—a sense of longing and loss confronting the realization I would never fly the F-4 Phantom again. I had passed on signing the volunteer statement guaranteeing an upgrade slot to aircraft commander if I agreed to come back for a second tour. No way.

With completion of the tour, my fighter pilot days were over, but I had locked away within my being a memory treasure that would influence my psyche for the remainder of my life. I was a Vietnam combat veteran who had been kissed by God's good grace to come back relatively whole to talk about it.

Those last days on the base were pure nirvana when I allowed myself the luxury of ecstasy. At times, I was beside myself with a goose-pimpled joy in my heart that I would be reunited with my mother, sister, and Celeste, and, yes, Major my cat. I was vicariously jubilant they no longer had to fret and thumb the rosary; I would be home safe back in their arms.

My imagination projected forward to potentially awkward conversations with Celeste about my faithlessness. A small distraction was my not knowing of her fidelity to me. Would the old cliché "What you don't know won't hurt you" ring true? I had insisted on a high standard of honesty and self-expression with Celeste from the beginning of our relationship, but my mind deliberated long and deep on the spiritual diminution that honesty about all my unfaithfulness could unearth: Hong Kong whores, chasing schoolteachers at Clark, wanting to fall in love with the magnificent blonde Qantas Airlines rep, the green scene with Eva Burg, and the lovely cinnamon-skinned Ubon barmaid, Cato. Good Lord, I thought, confessions to this truckload of perpetrations would destroy a homecoming, lead to immediate divorce, or, worse yet, poison the trust in our union that would set in motion a slow, insidious decay from the inside out of our marriage that would inexorably lead to its demise. Guilt management would have to suffice until more profound strategies showed up.

My mind regularly sought to avoid thoughts of adjustment challenges for a soldier boy returning home from spoiling my last days. I was, in flashes of cognizance, beside myself with excitement and anticipation. I dropped out, didn't want to be around the few partners that were left, lost the desire to drink a lot, found repose in mellowness, became philosophical, and actually stopped writing letters. I was so short I would now be able to beat the letters home. It was like finishing a PhD, passing the bar exam, maybe having your first son. There seemed to be no higher high than making it through alive.

My going home bash was special. In the luck of the draw and to save the expense of renting a private reception room at the DOOM Club, I was having a joint end-of-tour party with Colonel Frisby, the squadron commander of the 480th Tactical Fighter Squadron, who had just finished his tour, as well as Major Ernst and Captain Titmus, who got knocked out falling off the ladder that day we diverted into Udorn.

The arrangements were final. The squadrons had pooled their monies to pay for chicken wings, finger sandwiches, and potato salad. They also paid for a one-hour open bar. With a squadron commander ending a tour, all the base honchos would be in attendance, even the wing commander, General Roberts, whose signature I forged in the security breech prank that backfired on me. Fighter pilots from all three fighter squadrons would be there as well as my buddies. I had a speech written over a month earlier that was composed with the expectation that only a handful of well-wishers would listen to it at a small celebration. Now everyone was coming and my enthusiasm was battling against the trepidation of delivering my message to a great throng. I wondered if what I had to say would end my career. Privately, I wrestled with issues of being a man and having the courage to stand up for my beliefs as rendered in the profound inspirational examples of Gandhi and Reverend Martin Luther King Jr. I would never have been able to face a mirror again if I waffled.

The day of the special event came, and I was less than forty-eight hours from escaping the Da Nang purgatory. It was August 22, 1969. I was two days short of one year and the tearful good-bye to my friends in San Francisco. The weather at Da Nang Airbase on party day was hot, dusty, and windy. I pulsed with excitement; I was Mr. Amicability, merrily greeting everyone I encountered. I joked with the admin fellows about getting my pay records in order, my permanent change of station orders, my final per diem check, and, yes, my travel orders authorizing me to get on that freedom bird. All was right with the world, except that the war still raged, soldiers on both sides were dying in the hundreds every day, the Paris Peace talks were bogged down in protocol and posturing, but Brian Settles was goin' home.

Despite the joyous hysteria bursting within that the war really was over for me, there was an uneasiness that kept me from the total intoxication of ecstasy. There was melancholy, a lamentation for the people of Vietnam, North and South. They would be left behind in a country defaced by the depredations of war. The streets leading to China Beach on the South China Sea were still lined with potbellied babies whose deformed bodies advertised the squalor of their existence. Bone-thin women in black pajamas still could be seen squatting, their buttocks resting on their heels, chewing betel nut and smoking unfiltered hand-rolled cigarettes. The dry ever-present wind whistled; the dirt and dust danced in a cyclonic swirl. The scene was a suspended animation, a continuum of meaninglessness, and my presence and our sacrifices hadn't changed one whit of reality for anyone over there. It had simply bestowed upon me indelible memories of disillusionment and loss, which I could not replace.

The only thing worse than living in vain was dying in vain. It appeared I had escaped the latter fate, but, ultimately, it was my dignity and self-respect that were on the line. I had to be unstoppable in embracing the rare opportunity to render my pep talk, a lashing indictment to provoke thought, and perhaps, just perhaps, alter the perceptions of one or two of my fellow fighter pilots that might prevent them from joining and remaining in the ranks of the ugly Americans.

A pensive mood dominated the day of the party. It seemed a betrayal of the Zen groove of my mission to stop by the DOOM Club for a pre-game warm-up drink. I deliberated and fought off the appeal of the potion. My mind jousted with itself in uncontrollable anxiety about my speech. I wanted to drink that afternoon, but I didn't want to be buzzing for the awards speeches segment of the party since I felt I would undermine or detract from the credibility of my message if I was not completely sober. And I was uneasy that I was having panel discussions with myself about drinking or not drinking--had the war made me a lush?

It was 1530 hours (3:30 PM); I walked back to the officers' quarters from the compound, denying myself a libation, not only because I needed a reassuring macho act of resistance, but also to grasp more fully the last vestiges of the hypnotic traffic noise, soldiers, and dust. When I arrived at my room, my old roommate,

Tim Bannon, who was just coming out, greeted me. "Hey, Bee, you lucky shit. You all ready for your party tonight?" he exclaimed.

"Yeah, I guess," I responded sullenly.

"You shittin' me, Bee? I'd be doin' handstands."

I couldn't respond. Tim left shaking his head in puzzlement, assuring me he would be there at the party. I pulled off my boots, laid down on the bed in the reassurance of the fetal position, and took a nap. The only thing missing was my thumb in my mouth. I fell into deep slumber to the sounds of Phantom flights roaring off into the blue destined for the uncertainty of their combat missions.

Dao, my favorite maid, ironed my shiny blue squadron scarf. Despite not being a GQ sort of guy, I couldn't fight off the pride swelling inside over how cool I looked in my fighter-pilot party ensemble with the contrasting hues of green, brown, and black of my flight suit, accented by the three colorful unit patches sewn onto my breast pockets and sidearm. My final act of rebellion was to resist getting a going-home haircut. I combed it neatly with a part and gooped it heavy on the sides so the natural curls of my birthright didn't stand out too much. Indulging my narcissism, I silently acknowledged my satisfaction with the image in the four-foot-long mirror attached to the closet door. The collar on my flight suit was turned up, a la James Dean, except I was more like the rebel without a clue. My three-foot-long scarf was draped around the outside of my collar and tucked into the flight suit opening just high enough to offer a peek at my red unauthorized T-shirt. Rich satiny blue scarf, green camouflage, red, and yellow. I was a knockout. I even dowsed myself in English Leather cologne--why, I don't know.

I patted the thigh pocket of my flight suit to confirm my neatly handwritten speech was onboard. Fifteen minutes later, I swaggered into the DOOM Club feeling like the MVP of the NCAA basketball championship playoffs. Peeking into the dark lounge where the usual happy hour crowd gathered and noticing that the place seemed sedated, I strolled on down the dimly lit hallway to the opening from which muffled laughter and chatter emanated. Good Lord, the place was packed—standing room only. I had deliberately arrived just before the official ceremony to avoid having to interact and make small talk. As I entered the room, I observed a sea of red, blue, and green scarves; all three F-4 squadrons were well accounted for. Heads swiveled toward me as I made myself a part of the crowd; eyebrows rose followed by a repetition of pats on the back and "Congratulations, Bee" from pilot after pilot.

Everyone in the room was there to honor the distinct sanctity of the occasion. For one year I had repetitively prayed for the gift of surviving long enough to reach that night. I was ecstatic to behold the fighter pilot chorus assembled there to envy our lucky foursome for having finished the tour, a feat a quarter of them in that room would never experience.

I slowly approached the makeshift bar and requested a Schlitz to wash down the dust and take the edge off my nerves. Soon there was a *ting ting ting* on a water glass and Colonel Frisby's operations officer called the room to order; it was already beginning to get loose. The four of us finishing our tours were introduced over hooting and howling from the room full of fighter pilots, admin, and maintenance personnel. To my surprise, given that I was the junior officer on the agenda, they switched my award order to first rather than last. I guess they wanted the presentations to crescendo upward, concluding with the squadron commander. I was smacked with a sudden bolt of fear that I would be the first to receive a plaque.

The ops officer began, "Gentleman, I present two plaques this evening to Lieutenant Brian 'Bee' Settles. Bee flew one hundred fifty-four missions as a 390th Wild Boar and was transferred over to the newly arrived 421st toward the conclusion of his tour." Cheering and shrill whistling erupted. "And we have a plaque with an inscription for forty-five missions flown as a 421st Black Spider." More hoots and howls. The colonel continued, "And Lieutenant Settles, since you didn't get a two hundred missions parade, I now present your bottle of victory champagne. Do you have any parting words for us?"

Amid the applause and catcalling, I couldn't help sensing, despite my borderline eccentricity, that there were some buddies in the room that night who really did admire, maybe even respect me. I approached the bare-bones podium, a solitary floor stand microphone with a friction knob halfway up for adjusting its height. The colonel presented me with a bottle of champagne and two oak plaques that had shiny gold plates engraved with my name and the number of combat missions flown for the two squadrons. I reached down to unzip my pocket, withdrew the folded handwritten speech, and delivered my Da Nang swan song.

General Roberts, squadron commanders, and gentlemen, this indeed is an incredible place in time for me. I feel very, very fortunate to be standing here before you.

I've been waiting one long year for this blessing. I hope you all have the good fortune to also stand here on your tour completion day. Since I survived to make it here, and it is partly my party, too, I beg your indulgence while I share with you some reflections and sentiments on my year at Da Nang as a copilot in the F-4 for the United States Air Force.

While the experience flying the Phantom in combat has been the thrill of my lifetime, honestly speaking, a sense of dignity with the mission has rarely been available to me. I read the daily headlines of the Stars and Stripes and witness the delayed news accounts of the cities burning due to racial strife back in the States, and I am saddened and ashamed. As I recall the two Davis-Monthan F-4 instructor pilots in the locker room talking the day after Dr. Martin Luther King Jr. was assassinated, I can never remove from the listening of my mind the stinging words, 'Well, he was asking for it.'

With the racial strife at home and knowing there are neighborhoods all over America where my family and I are not welcomed to live because of the color of our skin, it leaves me feeling I sold out on remaining at home to fight for racial justice and equality. It would have made dying over here on Vietnamese soil the most bitter and tragic of outcomes. When the words gook, slope-heads, slant eyes are spoken, I hear nigger. I have wondered many times if it is easier for us to kill innocent peasants out in the rice paddies simply because their skin is yellow, their nostrils rounded, eyes slanted, and their customary peasant dress is black pajamas. Yes, the Vietcong and North Vietnamese nationalists are fighting for a united Vietnam under a communist government and society. Thwarting that objective is the overriding rationalization for our war, but I wonder if our concealed racism toward these people of color will follow us back home to the smoldering cities of our homeland?

We are guests in this country, ostensibly fighting to preserve democracy for the South Vietnamese against communist aggression, but what about our aggression and arrogance, our condescension toward even our allies? Do we have a franchise to come here and call these people dumb zips or stupid gooks because they drive on their streets the way they do? Do we have the right in their country to scoff at their customs and culture uniqueness simply because they are different from what we know living in America? Like classic ugly Americans, are we justified staring down our noses at these people who were cultivating their civilization a thousand years before America was born? Each of us needs to ask the question if we are individually advancing the best face of America in our treatment of these people—the chow hall help, the maids, and the Republic of Vietnam soldiers. Where is our moral and humanitarian leadership? What does it reveal about the fiber of our character, drunk or not, to flip the bottom half of an unfinished gin and tonic out the van door at a Vietnamese soldier passing on his motor scooter? Are we really winning the hearts and minds of the Vietnamese people with our indifference and cruelty? Or are we, through our behavior and attitudes, creating more Vietcong than we are eradicating?

If America is to realize and retain its position of moral leadership in the world, we, the front line ambassadors who carry the baton of good or ill will, ultimately shall determine whether we are truly the universal standard for humanitarian and democratic principles. We will render that status. Each of you must ask in your private self if your behavior is contributing anything positive that will be left behind when your turn comes to return home. Will anything you have learned here contribute positively to better understanding of people in the life that awaits you back home with your families and friends?

Carrying the burden of these observations around with me for a year has not made it easy for me to be here. But, in concluding, I hope you will re-examine yourselves and seek to cultivate new attitudes that will allow you to be the best that you can be, accepting others and their cultures as worthy of dignity and respect just as you expect it. Finally, in standard farewell, I wish you a safe tour. Keep your airspeed up and watch your Six. Thank you.

I stepped to the side of the mike in a room filled with a stunned audience and echoing silence, thinking, *Damn, they didn't even clap.* I then realized the accused throng was paralyzed with the uncertainty of how to respond. After a few seconds in the interminable limbo of nothingness, a singular clapping arose from the side of the room along the wall. It was General Roberts. After receiving the green light of the general's approval, the room exploded into applause and whistles. Many who were seated stood to express their acknowledgment, not so much perhaps with what I had said, but that I had the balls to say it to that group in that room on that occasion.

Sitting back down in the front row, cross-legged on the floor, I popped the cork on my jug of last mission champagne and took a gagging gulp that left me embarrassed as the tickling bubbles foamed and effervesced out of my nose. I authorized a rare self-pride for myself that night. I had stood for what I believed in the face of a room packed with the guilty. The atmosphere following the speech continued to be festive, but shifted into an obscure strangeness as the other honorees filed up to receive their plaques and deliver their comments. My words had altered the ceremony and rendered all that followed anticlimactic.

At the conclusion of Colonel Frisby's words, General Roberts came forward to the microphone and publicly lauded me for not only an eloquent message, but also for having the courage to deliver it. Having the highest-ranking fighter pilot at Da Nang Airbase say that in a room full of fighter jocks was awesome consolation for a yearlong act that would leave me a little weirded out for the rest of my life.

After the general finished his words, most of the room proceeded to get smashed. The crowd seemed to expand and standing room was at a premium. The honchos had a few drinks and left. The hard-core partiers took over to have their way with the evening. In typical rebel-without-a-clue style, I drank my champagne from the bottle. Buddies lined up to buy me drinks, but all I wanted to do was nurse the evening away with one jug of Piper Heidsieck followed by another.

Within an hour, Major Tommy Rearden was riding his electric moped around the club. Leaning my head back too far to finish the dregs of a second champagne bottle someone had passed along to me, I narrowly avoided knocking out two front teeth when I dumped myself over backward onto the floor. I was going home.

THE MORNING AFTER

I must have been beamed back to my room after the shindig since I certainly didn't recall the return trip when I awoke the next day around noon. Woozy and bleary-eyed, I knew I faced only two tasks: (1) turn in my personal equipment at the PE supply and (2) pick up my administrative records at out-processing. No brain cells would be required to accomplish those missions.

I showered for a long time and then felt mischievous. Wrapping a towel around my naked dripping body, I put on my sunglasses and shower thongs and stepped out into the hallway to have some fun with the maids. As I approached where they were clustered in the center of the long hallway, they leapt upright, shrieking in high-pitched horror as I roared an imitation grizzly bear growl. My fun and games were suddenly interrupted by the blinding sunlight coming from a door that had swung open at the end of the hall.

The bright light silhouetted the ominous figure moving toward me. I couldn't identify the intruder until he arrived directly in front of me. A voice spoke, "Lieutenant Settles, Colonel Banks, the new base commander." I was still too numb to be horrified at his presence in the dorm.

"Yes, sir," I said, feeling rather geekish standing there in the hallway wearing nothing but a towel and shades. The colonel, holding back a snicker, went on, "Lieutenant Settles, I attended the party at the club last night and, over coffee this morning with General Roberts, we decided your speech was special. I came by to ask you for a copy to have my office submit it to the *Air Force Times Magazine* for publication."

Wow, I thought, instead of a court-martial they want to make me a hero. I felt like a rake now that Colonel Banks was attempting to elevate me into some kind of honoree who had to be interrupted while chasing maids up and down the hall half-naked.

"Wow, sir, that sounds great. I'll see if I can put my hands on it and let you know." I started experiencing a sickening feeling that I couldn't recall what I had done with the three sheets of yellow legal paper. I had a vision of tucking it into my lower calf flight-suit pocket, but then I also had a vision of laying it down on the table beside the chicken wings when I had fallen backward. I simply couldn't remember what I had done with it. Here was the greatest of ironies: the inspired speech I had written to chastise my fellow fighter pilots for being ugly Americans was to be published in the national magazine of the Air Force to be read by personnel from the Joint Chiefs of Staff on down to anonymous airmen suffering through their tours. But I had gotten smashed and lost it in the jubilation of liberation from their war.

Later that afternoon I called the base commander's office to tell him of my unsuccessful search. I promised I would rewrite the speech when I got back to the States. After a brief pause, he responded, "Thanks, Lieutenant Settles. It was a great speech and its message should be shared with Air Force personnel worldwide who are supporting the U.S. military mission in Vietnam."

Listening to his words, my euphoria was supplanted by disappointment that I had so many ideas and so little discipline to deliver them to reality. I had blown it--a once-in-a-lifetime chance to be heard, maybe contribute, and I got bombed and fumbled the ball of opportunity.

The going-home fiesta the night before had been all I could have expected. I had two plaques to take home, a standing-room-only audience for my speech, and the Air Force wanted to publish it. The only challenge left was to safely board the freedom bird at midnight and get back to my future. It was the best moment of my life, yet still some invisible force was trying to bind me up, to prevent me from embracing it. I recalled in my the media accounts of departure atrocities of military personnel waiting to board freedom flights home. Too many bon voyages from Nam had been shattered by eleventh-hour attacks on military passenger terminals that left dozens of returning veterans maimed or killed. It was the ultimate horror to die on one's last day in Vietnam.

I worked to control my runaway thoughts. The creepy anxiety of making the local evening news back in Muncie kept me very low-key. I had learned being cool on the streets at home, struggling for an identity and acceptance, not showing emotion. It would have been a violation of machismo rules to ever let anyone know you felt anything or could be moved by something so simple and mundane as the glory of just being alive, loving and laughing at something beyond the pain of other people.

In those last hours, I wanted to be alone and revel in the achievement of having survived. It saddened my heart to bear witness to the unending procession of expressionless GIs trudging single file in a death march along the dusty streets of Da Nang headed for unknown destinations, to encounter ordeals that would forever alter their hopes of being normal human beings again. I pitied them for being the replacement pawns—virgins to the horrors of combat and killing.

CHAPTER 25: THE BIG TRIP HOME

I can't remember who took me to the passenger terminal that last night. It was the same loud, funky place with the same dim low-wattage lights in the overhead ceiling, the open French-style shutters, the crowds of GIs, American, and Republic of Vietnam Army (ARVN), and, yes, the repulsion of sweaty bodies, stale urine, and cigarettes. The scene would not go away, as if it were locked in suspended animation from the night of my arrival one year earlier. Strangely, one year's imprisonment had given me no greater hold on comfort with the compacted crunch of bustling humanity—each individual, each life on a uniquely separate mission warping forward in isolated capsules of the continuum flow. We silently boarded our flight, filing to our assigned seats on the Pan American 707 Clipper carrying us out. The flight attendants, sporting cute light blue flight caps, greeted us with mechanical stewardess smiles.

Once settled into my seat, I could not blank out the thought of how dramatically the Vietnam war had altered people's lives, even the protesters' lives back home, and was continuing to do so moment by moment, day by day, with an unending stream of war supplies and fresh bodies to feed the ongoing war games.

We blasted off on schedule and I finally relaxed into my seat during climb-out, relieved that the landing gear was snuggled safely in the gear-well and we hadn't exploded. I drifted off.

Hours later, we descended toward the rolling waves of the deep blue Pacific waters surrounding the main island of Hawaii. Emotion overwhelmed me. I was unaware of any activity in the cabin during the entire flight from Da Nang. With the distance of the year's trauma now four thousand miles behind me, why did I feel no safer, no relief, no peace? All the sacrifice, all the danger, and all the risk; what had I accomplished that really mattered? Thousands of Americans and millions of Vietnamese warriors were dead or wounded. I was alive and looking good, but enveloped in a new void. As in the revelation that pursed the lips of Peter Fonda at the end of the movie, *Easy Rider,* I realized, "We had, I had blown it." The lesson came into focus that nothing external to us can fill the lonely spaces of longing deep inside our being, created by the burden of our own awful truths. Something happened to all of us, wounding us in a distant psychic place, somewhere submerged in the vague obscurity of our pasts. Being human, we have created great drama and a story around it, living our lives trapped in the hyperbole.

The entire aircraft cabin of GIs was mostly quiet and subdued, as if all of us returning survivors were caught in reflection's trance. As the landing gear extended with its usual metallic thump, I realized nothing in my past had gone away. I was still a "half-breed," an adopted son who had grown up on the streets of Muncie. I was still an ex-Bearcat whose athletic career died young due to knee injuries and a devastating senior year expulsion. I still carried the perpetually fresh, unhealing wounds of childhood teasing from my playmates. I would carry forever the indelible memory of the invasion of the sadistic fourteen-year-old "neighbor" daring to attempt raping my ten-year-old body, trying to force his dark pole into my being. The conclusion that life could be an unsafe, unhappy place was still there. Vietnam had simply added the loss of my adult innocence to the loss of my childhood innocence. What I faced was a future fueled by the wisdom of conquering vicissitude.

As we touched down, the rubber tires issued their usual *skeet, skeet* cry as the concrete runway nibbled off another minute layer of wheel tread. I reflected over and over why I survived and others had not. Maybe it was to write this story. I wondered how many lives would have been altered if my white mother, Betty, had aborted me rather than left me to the fate of that orphanage in Lincoln. Would those whose lives I had touched have missed me or would they have been more blessed without my existence? I promised myself in that moment of contemplation that, if I were granted the amazing grace of living through the nightmare of combat, I would write about my metamorphosis and what happened to me in Vietnam.

The Clipper captain set the brakes at the gate. I kept my head facing the window, hiding the automatic stream of tears skiing down my cheeks from the two soldiers who sat beside me the entire seven-hour flight. Through our mutual tacit agreement to honor the privacy of contemplation, they didn't know a thing about me or what was in my mind, nor I theirs. What I got in that moment of philosophical clarity was the epiphany that none of us can ever flee our Rosebuds, like the fictional character in Orson Wells's *Citizen Kane* whose life had been forged in the pursuit of filling the emotional void of childhood loss.

We departed Hickam Air Base after a brief refueling and catering stop. Four hours later, the Clipper touched down and taxied into the 130-degree heat of the Norton Air Force Base ramp in San Bernadino, California. It was over. Following a short taxi, the pilot set his brakes on our voyage for the last time. The seatbelt sign flashed off and an orderly deplaning of solemn Vietnam veterans began. I deliberately fumbled around, inexplicably loitering as I gathered my briefcase and shaving kit. I made myself the last one off. There was no rush; I had yet another leg to the trip from Los Angeles International to Indianapolis where Celeste awaited. I looked forward to the left front door for my exit. Slowly and carefully, my feet led me as I descended the portable stairs toward the boiling tarmac that shimmered in the afternoon heat. Vietnam at that moment had joined the other Rosebuds of my life. As I eased away from the Clipper, I returned the good-bye waves of the stewardesses still neatly clad in their white blouses, light blue skirts, and matching flight caps. I stepped deliberately, almost cautiously, delaying until I achieved a far enough distance to feel safely outside the fragmentation pattern, should the airplane explode from a delayed Vietcong satchel charge. In awkward optimism, I knelt down on both knees and gently kissed the hot steamy asphalt ramp. At that point, and not until that point, was I confident to finally exhale and proclaim: "I made it." Vietnam was finally in my rearview mirror.

CHAPTER 26: EPILOGUE

Summer 2014
United States of America

It has been said that Vietnam is the war that won't go away. The government of the United States of America has since added Desert Storm, Kosovo, and after the tragedies of September 11, 2001, Afghanistan and Iraqi Freedom to our combat campaigns. The latter conflict has become a tar baby of unending casualties and suffering and is frequently touted as being another Vietnam. The political and popular pressure to bring about withdrawal of our troops could leave Iraq bogged down in the chaos of civil war issuing from the power struggle among rival Muslim factions for the foreseeable future. The loss of lives of our children, husbands, fathers, and now daughters and wives has been added to the horror of war. I have written my story to share the awful truth of war, the classic longing and deprivation, and what it took for some of us to survive it. The stage setting today has replaced jungle with sand, but dying and killing have a universality that remains unaltered. This story is written for wives, widows, mothers, men, and boys—boys whom I hope will never have to know combat. It is understood that freedom is not free. But, as responsible patriots, we must always be vigilant about the military causes draped in the American flag on which our country's political leadership wishes to expend this nation's military, financial, and human resources. The question must be asked: What are we willing to die for? Our property, our mother, our children, our country, our President? Many of us go to war out of patriotism. In Vietnam, servicemen were drafted. Some go merely for the financial and educational benefits. Some go because they cannot believe our political leaders would lie about something as serious as war. None of us expects to die.

More than forty-five years have passed since I scribbled the stacks of agony-filled letters home to my new bride and family. The life seasoning of adult adversity and adjustment to disappointment have ushered me into a clearing where reflection might dominate consciousness. I was eased into a state of courage and freedom to finally issue my confession and tell the awful truth.

No, my story is not of the combat horror genre like the daylong sieges endured by the Marine rifle companies who fought the battles in Ia Drang in the fall of 1965 or the more recent battles in Fallujah, Baghdad, Kabul, or Tikrit. The combat heroes of the 7th Cavalry, Americal, and the 101st Airborne Divisions, who we of the 366th Gunfighters supported on many missions, could never pay for a drink in my presence. Those brave GIs paid the ultimate price; those who lived through it can never escape the unalterable memory that 58,000 fellow American soldiers died and hundreds of thousands more were crippled physically and mentally for life. Today, forty-five years later, 5,281 Americans have been sacrificed in Iraq and Afghanistan while thousands more have returned brain damaged, paraplegics and laden with PTSD issues from a war a majority of Americans now feel was unnecessary, despite the reality that the world has a major challenge finding a solution to the mounting terrorist threat emanating from the radical fundamentalist Muslim element.

Yes, as a combat pilot in the Phantom, it was my life's most extraordinary ride. I knew at the time of my struggle to get through it that, if I survived, I had to write about it. I had to write about how good we looked and what we experienced flying our fighters, wearing our G suits, returning sweat-soaked from the combat arena, taking in the daily luxury of a hot shower

in air-conditioned billets, listening to stereos bought in Hong Kong, and ziggying over to the DOOM Club for fat T-bones, baked potatoes, and bottles of Chianti. And then we did it all over again, day in and day out, until the year was finished or the farm was bought. Our troops today in Iraq are equally brave and dedicated in the déjà vu of another unpopular war promulgated by trumped-up machinations of political leadership.

The great tragedy of Vietnam, which vindicated the antiwar movement, is that this country went to war on another country's soil to prevent a communist domino theory from becoming reality in Southeast Asia. If Ho Chi Minh was successful in unifying North and South Vietnam under the communist flag, the leadership fear was that all of the countries in the area would fall under communist rule. History has rendered clear proof that the domino effect, upon which so much U.S. foreign policy was based during the Cold War years of the fifties and sixties, did not come to pass as McNamara, Rusk, Bundy, President Johnson, and the rest had assured us in justifying our foreign policy in Southeast Asia. Arriving thirty years too late, Defense Secretary Robert S. McNamara rendered his detailed mea culpa for the disaster of Vietnam titled *In Retrospect: The Tragedy and Lessons of Vietnam.* With his usual brilliance and flare for detail, McNamara guides the reader through the labyrinth of uncertainty and confusion the military and civilian advisors experienced as they led President Johnson and the nation down the primrose path to defeat in Vietnam. Sadly, someday in the future, another defense department or military insider will write a confession of leadership failures in America, that cost us so many lives of our sons and daughters, when the real justification for our decision to invade Iraq, and then Afghanistan, becomes more clear, if there is one.

I have asked myself questions many times since the physical war of Vietnam ended for me. Some days my answers vary from those on other days. The questions linger in a philosophical stream. Why did I survive? How valuable to my growth and evolution as a human being was my tour in Vietnam? What did I learn about our political and military leadership? What difference did my participation make in anyone's life? Was my life (or anyone else's) worth this sacrifice? What can I share with others about what war is like, who I was, and how I got there? Why are some Americans (even African-Americans) more patriotic than others? Is there such a thing as blind patriotism and is it bad? Today I examine my grandchildren's toys and see that they are made in China; the label in my Nike tennis shoes and basketball shorts reads *Made in Vietnam.* The question remains unclear: What were we dying for? Every military person, who serves in combat, needs to be clear on the answer to that question.

The epiphanies fueling this book arrived through three experiences that enabled the words I have written to flow onto these pages. In the winter of 1980 I viewed, on a layover in Boston, the rock music cult classic movie *The Wall,* directed and produced by Alan Parker and former Pink Floyd bassist Roger Waters. Magically, the film seemed to be autobiographically mirroring the perceptions and sensitivities of my life experience, which included Vietnam. The message was simply that our most powerful life experiences which at times create great suffering, pain, or regret, mostly generated during our youth, are analogous to bricks in a wall that build up over time and, ultimately, close us up or wall us into our lives.

Second, one morning in 1980 I awoke to witness an author interview between then Today Show host Jane Pauley and my Laredo pilot training classmate Clyde Edgerton. Clyde had been an F-4 copilot out of Laredo Air Force Base just like me but, unlike me, he became a successful novelist. He had just finished *Float Plane Notebooks.* I believed I had some talent in me to be a writer like Clyde but I just had to get started.

Lastly, in mid-1987, after moving to Atlanta, while channel surfing one night, I came upon the American Movie Classics station just as Orson Welles's *Citizen Kane* was being introduced. After watching it, I saw my life. I glimpsed the profound significance of the Rosebuds in all our lives. Here is where reflection and the examined life come into play. I endured the childhood abuses and teasing I experienced in Muncie and arrived at the question of *what is the payoff for man's cruelty to man*? I saw how my sense of sexual inadequacy used me and drove me to use women. I craved hero status and looking good for acceptance and had volunteered to scare the shit out of myself in Vietnam to feed it.

In telling my story, I realized the goal was to unashamedly reveal myself in my isolation, not just as Brian Settles ex-Bearcat from Muncie, Indiana, but also as a personification of American writer Nathaniel Hawthorne's Young Goodman Brown, everyman—

everywoman. What I have essayed in confessing my story of Vietnam, which is a tale of every war with killing and dying, was to share with others the agony of longing that is any war experience and to reveal beyond the horror of being shot at in combat, the practical, mundane cost of war to relationships with others and ourselves. I have chosen to explore, not for cleansing or catharsis, the motivations from earlier experiences in life that influenced my willingness to make choices that were not who I am or, more accurately, who I wished to be. My inner embarrassment and guilt over failure in marital fidelity forced the question of why men are so afraid of and haunted by infidelity of their women, yet themselves practice it so freely. What does machismo really look like? Can we forgive ourselves for practicing flawed love? Be forgiven?

I have not exposed the sanctity of my being for the sheer pleasure of exhibitionism. I hope the rudeness of my example will inspire reflection in readers to examine their own lives—to look at why lives turn out the way they do, to explore why people struggle with issues of overeating and obesity, drug and alcohol addictions, and the predation stemming from sexual cravings. In writing this book, I have taken on a ruthless commitment to be fully self-expressed in the re-creation of the Vietnam War experience as I lived, tasted, and breathed it.

My life in the days immediately following the return from Vietnam was like a long-wished-for dream come true, what a death row inmate must feel after being released from prison at the eleventh hour when last-minute DNA evidence is introduced. It was a living ecstasy being reunited with Celeste and my family. But, in life, so often the solutions to problems beget new problems. Regrettably, my sense of selfishness for having left Celeste behind to suffer while I indulged my F-4 Phantom lark led me to acquiesce to the plan for her to remain in Indiana to complete her master's degree at Ball State while I went through two months of KC-135 training at Castle Air Force Base in Merced, California. I underestimated how much I needed to have her with me. Alone, again, unsupervised in tanker training in California, my neediness for a romantic female presence in my life relaunched itself. It was not fair to place the weight for letting me go to California alone on her, but subconsciously I probably did. My fighter pilot rationalized excuse for unfaithfulness in Vietnam was replaced by a rationalized predisposition for hedonism as consolation for the posttraumatic stress state in which I existed after Vietnam. I metamorphosed into an unromantic romanticist who was in love with the notion of being in love. I surrendered to a lifestyle of unfaithfulness in my marriage, However, my fifteen-year union begot the unparalleled joy of being a father to two amazing sons. Celeste remained an elementary school teacher and retired after thirty-five years.

My life since Vietnam has been colored with highs and lows. Some experiences have not been what I had in mind, such as flying for three different airlines during a thirty-three year commercial flying career and having a two-and-a-half-year odyssey as a cab driver in Atlanta after the failure of Eastern Airlines. My fighter-pilot mentor from Muncie, JJ Winters, survived two tours in Vietnam as both Aircraft Commander and back-seater in the F-4, completed a thirty-plus-year career in the Air Force, and achieved the rank of Brigadier General. My lifelong childhood friend, Dr. Gregory Williams, distinguished himself as a law professor, law school dean, and finally president of the University of Cincinnati. His memoir about growing up in Muncie, *Life on the Color Line,* was a best seller. My sister Margerie became an elementary school teacher, a union representative who fought for teachers' rights, and a member of the National Education Association. Her most courageous act as a union negotiator was enduring an eight-day jail sentence when contract negotiations broke down. She retired in 2013 after thirty-nine years as an elementary school teacher. Mama Settles, God rest her soul, retired after twenty-three years as a librarian at the Muncie Public Library in 1974 and traveled on to glory in 1987. I have had phone and e-mail communication with my biological mother, Betty, since 1990, but we have yet to meet.

At age seventy, I have been blessed to find peace in my third marriage and untold joy witnessing the miracle of my six grandchildren taking on life.